Springer Series: FOCUS ON WOMEN

Violet Franks, Ph.D., Series Editor

Confronting the major psychological, medical, and social issues of today and tomorrow. *Focus on Women* provides a wide range of books on the changing concerns of women.

VOLUME 1
THE SAFETY OF FERTILITY CONTROL
Editor-in-Chief: Louis G. Keith, M.D.; Associate Editors: Deryck R. Kent, M.D.; Gary S. Berger, M.D., and Janelle R. Brittain, M.B.A.

VOLUME 2
THERAPY WITH WOMEN: A Feminist Philosophy of Treatment
Susan Sturdivant, Ph.D.

VOLUME 3
SHELTERING BATTERED WOMEN
A National Study and Service Guide
Albert R. Roberts, D.S.W.

VOLUME 4
WOMEN OVER FORTY: Visions and Realities
Marilyn R. Block, Ph.D., Janice I. Davidson, M.S., and Jean D. Grambs, Ed.D.

VOLUME 5
THE STEREOTYPING OF WOMEN: Its Effects on Mental Health
Violet Franks, Ph.D. and Esther D. Rothblum, Ph.D.

VOLUME 6
THE BATTERED WOMAN SYNDROME
Lenore E. Walker, Ed.D.

VOLUME 7
WOMEN THERAPISTS WORKING WITH WOMEN
New Theory and Process of Feminist Therapy
Claire M. Brody, Ph.D., Editor

VOLUME 8
CAREER GUIDE FOR WOMEN SCHOLARS
Suzanna Rose, Ph.D.

VOLUME 9
A MOTE IN FREUD'S EYE: From Psychoanalysis to the Psychology of Women
Hannah Lerman, Ph.D.

VOLUME 10
WOMEN'S THERAPY GROUPS: Paradigms of Feminist Treatment
Claire M. Brody, Ph.D., Editor

VOLUME 11
WOMEN AND DEPRESSION: A Lifespan Perspective
Ruth Formanek, Ph.D., and Anita Gurian, Ph.D., Editors

VOLUME 12
TRANSITIONS IN A WOMAN'S LIFE: Major Life Events in Developmental Context
Ramona T. Mercer, Ph.D., F.A.A.N., Elizabeth G. Nichols, D.N.S., F.A.A.N., Glen C. Doyle, Ed.D., R.N.

Ramona T. Mercer, R.N., Ph.D., F.A.A.N., received her doctorate from the University of Pittsburgh in 1973. She is Professor Emeritus, Department of Family Health Care Nursing, University of California, San Francisco. She has studied the transition to the maternal role in a variety of differing circumstances—when the infants had a birth defect, maternal age differences, and antepartal hospitalization and other stress. The study of three age groups of first-time mothers, *First-Time Motherhood: Experiences from Teens to Forties* (Springer, 1986), detected developmental differences by maternal age. The all-consuming role of motherhood during the first year raised the question about the long-term impact of that role in later years, and whether women who were not mothers differed in their developmental trajectory over the life course. Dr. Mercer has lectured and published extensively in the areas of the adolescent pregnancy, transition to the maternal role, the impact of stress on parenting, and transitions over the life cycle of women. In 1987, she received the ASPO/Lamaze Research Award, and in 1988, she received the Distinguished Alumnus Award from the School of Nursing, University of Pittsburgh, and the Western Society for Nursing Research Distinguished Research Lectureship Award.

Elizabeth G. Nichols, R.N., D.N.S., F.A.A.N., graduated from the University of California, San Francisco. Her doctoral work focused on health care of the geriatric client, and subsequent research has been directed towards health care for the aged, and preparation of nurses for gerontological nursing. Dr. Nichols, a mother of two teenagers, became involved in this study when she moved to Pocatello, Idaho and became interested in the differential impact of rural and urban settings upon women. Her work with older people, her observations of her own family and family in-law in addition to her experiences as a mother and a professional suggested to her that motherhood took on a different perspective in the lives of women once they were past the intense period of those first years of being a mother, and that the political and social setting in which one lived was also a factor in the importance of a particular role to one's identity. Motherhood was not necessarily the driving factor. For some, yes, it continues to be the central aspect of life, for some, not so. Dr. Nichols is currently the Associate Dean of the College of Health Sciences for the School of Nursing at the University of Wyoming, in Laramie, Wyoming, and is a masters degree candidate in political science at Idaho State University. She is also past chair of the Clinical Medicine Section of the Gerontological Society of America, and on the Board of Governors for the Western Institute of Nursing.

Glen Caspers Doyle, Ed.D., R.N., is the Director of the Interdisciplinary Gerontology Program and an Associate Professor in the Department of Nursing at California State University, Fresno. She oversees the Gerontology Academic Programs, Elderfest, Elderhostel, the Summer Institute on Aging, and the coordination of student placement in a Friendly Visitor program that has over 100 students who make 14 weekly visits to older adults each year. Dr. Doyle's research interests include the effect of caregiving on the family members of individuals with Alzheimer's disease, psychomotor skills of nursing assistants in long-term care facilities, the effect of dialysis on older patients, and the use of assessment tools to measure functional ability of older persons in long-term care facilities. Dr. Doyle has conducted numerous workshops on aging, Alzheimer's disease, and caregiving. She has produced video tapes on aging and Alzheimer's disease.

TRANSITIONS IN A WOMAN'S LIFE:
Major Life Events in Developmental Context

Ramona T. Mercer
Elizabeth G. Nichols
Glen Caspers Doyle

Springer Publishing Company
New York

Springer Publishing Company, Inc.
536 Broadway
New York, NY 10012

89 90 91 92 93 / 5 4 3 2 1

Library of Congress Cataloging-in-Publication Data

Mercer, Ramona Thieme.
    Transitions in a woman's life : major life events in developmental context / Ramona T. Mercer, Elizabeth G. Nichols, Glen Caspers Doyle.
        p.   cm. — (Springer series, focus on women)
    Bibliography: p.
    Includes index.
    ISBN 0-8261-6560-5
    1. Women—United States—Psychology—Case studies.   2. Life cycle, Human—Psychological aspects—Case studies.   3. Maturation (Psychology)—Case studies.   4. Life change events—United States —Case studies.   5. Motherhood—United States—Psychological aspects —Case studies.   I. Nichols, Elizabeth G.   II. Doyle, Glen Caspers. III. Title.   IV. Series.
    [DNLM: 1. Human Development.   2. Life Change Events.   3. Women —psychology.   W1 SP685KD / HQ 1206 M554t]
HQ1206.M399   1988
305.4—dc19
DNLM/DLC
for Library of Congress

Printed in the United States of America

Contents

Contributor

Sally H. Rankin, R.N., Ph.D., is an Assistant Clinical Professor, Department of Family Health Care Nursing, University of California, San Francisco. Her research has focused on individual and family adaptation to cardiac surgery and chronic illness. Dr. Rankin used a life-span developmental framework to study caregiving in her most recent research. She is also interested in gender differences as they affect adaptation to illness by patients and adaptation to caregiving by spouses. Dr. Rankin is Associate Director of the University of California, San Francisco Diabetes Center, and teaches a course in family theory.

Acknowledgments

The study of transitions in the life cycle of women was supported in part by the Faculty Research Funds, Idaho State University, and the Department of Family Health Care Nursing Research Funds at the University of California, San Francisco. We are deeply grateful to these sources of support.

To the 80 women who shared the intimate details of their life course, some of which brought back pain and tears as well as joy and happiness, we owe the most. We feel extremely privileged to have had the opportunity to study the rich data that constituted the fabric of these women's lives, and we thank these anonymous women for their time and caring enough about learning more about women to share their lives with researchers who were strangers to them.

As the study progressed, each of us moved in different directions in our own career trajectories; thus, we worked over holiday weekends and whenever we could get together. Three faithful doctoral students at the University of California, San Francisco, participated in many of our work sessions, contributing their time and creative thinking processes. Our appreciation goes to Victoria Leonard, Sally H. Rankin (who is also author of Chapter 9, The Emergence of Creativity in Later Life), and Connie Smith. Their insights stimulated our thinking and are merged within the final product.

Importantly, our editor, Ruth Chasek, at Springer was extremely helpful. We thank her for her contributions to the clarity of our expressions.

Preface

Despite economic, political, and other disadvantages of power, women have throughout history made numerous contributions to society, science, and the arts. Women outlive men, indicating some physical or physiological advantage. Yet, until the last decade, the study of adult development has focused on men, leaving a void in the knowledge of major transitions in women's lives and the factors that contribute to women's development, as well as knowledge of development beyond the seventh decade of life. Psychoanalytic theorists proposed, and society in general has accepted, that the mothering role represents a developmental stage for women. Women have historically assumed the major responsibility for childrearing, and as a result other roles in their lives have taken a back seat to this responsibility. Women have equated the assumption of the responsibility of motherhood with transition to adulthood despite age differences in becoming a mother (Mercer, 1986a).

The impetus for this study came from several sources: the societal emphasis on motherhood, the general acceptance of motherhood as a stage in adult development, and the overwhelming prominence of motherhood for those experiencing the early years in the role. Obviously, nonmothers also have a wide range of accomplishments that speak to high levels of development. We were concerned with how development proceeded over the life trajectory for women who for various reasons did not become mothers as compared to those who did.

We discovered, however, that historical events, family constellation, and unexpected transitions contributed to very different life trajectories. Our study became much broader than a comparison of mothers and nonmothers. We learned that there was a third group of women whose achievements and developmental trajectory differed, those who had never married. We saw how losses and other such events as geographical moves contributed to women's development over their life course.

When motherhood was placed in context of a long-life trajectory over 60 to 95 years, the challenges of other life transitions such as a chronic or severe illness, and death of a husband or close family member, assumed greater importance. It became evident that the women's own mothers played a central role in their life course. Women talked about mothering they received more than mothering that they did.

Age-normative expected events such as graduation from high-school, college, and marriage varied by birth order, family situations (death or severe illness of the mother, financial problems), and historical influences. Some women had to leave high school to assume family responsibilities. The death of a fiancé during World War II led to marriage at a later age or not at all. Mothers had a very erratic educational trajectory that was interrupted by caring for children, husband's transfers, and other responsibilities.

Non-normative or unexpected life events had enormous impact. The woman's placement in boarding school during early school years concomitant with loss of either a father or mother through divorce or death left life-long feelings of rejection, loss, and resentment. Consequently, their relationships with others, their mothers, and their own children were affected negatively. Severe illness or handicaps from illness or accidents of loved ones often placed the women in caretaker positions that preempted any opportunity for their own development and/or recreational or creative outlet. Many never-married nonmothers had had to assume responsibility for parents and/or siblings during the launching into adulthood period. This contributed to their foregoing opportunities for marriage and the establishment of their own nuclear families. Following the husband's or parent's death, often after years of caretaking, several older women pursued painting, writing, or community project activities for the first time.

Development proceeded in a similar trajectory for mothers and nonmothers. While similar transitional events occurred in each group, the timing of events and the women's view of and approach to the events differed. Mothers reported a greater number of transitions over their life course that were largely child-related.

In Chapter 1 the theoretical background for the study and our approach are described. The women who participated in the study are introduced in Chapter 2, and Chapter 3 follows with an exploration of the political and historical influences on their lives. Common transitions over the women's life course, along with differences between mothers and nonmothers, married and never-married nonmothers, and the women's view of life (family view, worldview, and amorphous view) are discussed in Chapter 4. Chapter 5 focuses on the important mother-daughter relationship from the women's perspective, and indicates something about the intergenerational impact of unresolved conflicted mother-daughter relationships. Chapter 6 continues with the discussion of women's important relationships, including family members and friends. The impact of geographic moves or relocation are dealt with in Chapter 7, and the effects of husband's transfer moves are revealed. Chapter 8 focuses on loss as a transition leading to identity change in both positive and negative ways. The losses include both loss of health and loss of loved ones. The emergence of creativity in later life is highlighted in Chapter 9 and holds promise and excitement for all. In Chapter 10 women's development during adulthood is summarized within the context of other developmental research.

This book presents the interaction of all of the transitions or life events as related to the women's overall development during the life cycle. We feel privileged to have had an opportunity to share the life history of the women, and to catch a glimpse of those factors influencing women's development.

■ 1
Transitions and the Psychosocial Development of Women: An Introduction

Transitions as experienced by women over the life course are the central theme of this book. We interviewed 80 primarily Caucasian women over the age of 60 largely from the United States and asked them to tell us all that they could recall about their life history. We were interested to know how they perceived their life from a retrospective point of view and what events led them to experience a feeling of change or transition. This book is about those women and transitions they experienced that influenced the unfolding of their life course.

Transitions are viewed as a major vehicle for adult development. Initially we focused on women's adult development from the perspectives of those who had experienced one particular transition, motherhood, and those who had not. This particular focus was taken because of society's identification of motherhood as an adult developmental task, even though it is obvious that numerous women achieve adulthood though they do not experience the mothering role. In order to affirm or discount stereotypical beliefs and because of the social view of the centrality of motherhood to womanhood, it is critical to have empirical evidence regarding women's development in relationship to and apart from that particular role experience. As the study progressed we learned that the impact of the wife role was as great or greater than the mother role, and our focus expanded to study the group of never-married women.

√ Transitions are defined as turning points, a point of reference from which a person's life course takes a new direction requiring adaptation or change in restructuring behaviors and roles appropriate to the new direction. In addition to a change in behavioral response and new roles, this new direction in the life course also requires change in responsibilities, goals, identity, and feelings about one's self in general.

Transitions are an important area for study from two perspectives. First, since transitions involve individual change or adaptation over the life span, they contribute to psychosocial development or have developmental potential. Psychosocial development is viewed as progressive change in an individual's adaptive functioning (Waechter, 1974). Psychosocial development is a lifelong process; thus, because of this time frame, development occurs within an ever changing social and historical environment (Baltes, Reese, & Lipsitt, 1980). Developmental processes may occur through multiple forms, by many individual variations, and may be discontinuous as well as continuous (Werner, 1967). Discontinuity occurs when earlier learned behavior no longer meets the role requirements in later life, and a different behavior must be learned for that role requirement; this is in contrast to continuity in which a more complex or higher form of the same behavior evolves as a result of change. An example of discontinuity in development is the transition from childhood to adolescence when individuals must learn new behavior, language, and dress, and adjust to junior high school. Piaget's (1963) theory of cognitive development is an example of continuity. There is greater continuity in psychological or mental development; however, transitions involve much discontinuity in the social role change required, for example, a widow or divorcée must unlearn wife roles and learn widow or divorcée roles.

Psychosocial development is an interactive process between self and the environment in which a more complex, highly differentiated system of beliefs and expectations emerge to be assimilated and integrated by the individual; this higher level of development is irreversible, maintained with some consistency, and is universal (Harris, 1967). As persons move toward greater ability to appreciate others' needs and opinions and the larger group's or societal goals, they are able to contribute to society with greater flexibility and objectivity (Werner, 1967). Development is a fluid, dynamic process that may reinforce, modify, or change individual psychological patterns at any age period (Thomas & Chess, 1980). Development is viewed as ongoing over the life course through transitional change.

Second, transitions are important because they represent a period of disequilibrium or flux for the individual who must adapt to a new situation, new roles, or responsibilities. Feelings of inadequacy and lack of self-confidence are predominant during transitions because of the changes that are occurring (Waechter, 1974) and may contribute to feelings of impatience, frustration, irritability, intolerance, and disorganization (Crummette, 1975). Thus, persons in transition are more accessible to help from others, including health professionals. Persons in transition need to learn from others who have experienced a similar transition and to be linked with information and resources from those who are knowledgeable about their new experience in their particular situation (Silverman, 1982). Importantly, even minimal counseling or health care that facilitates development during a transitional period has potential to have long-lasting effects.

CHARACTERISTICS OF TRANSITIONS

Transitions and development are socially as well as biologically regulated (Neugarten & Datan, 1973; Oerter, 1986). Biological maturation sets the boundaries for the occurrence of normative social transitions, such as readiness for leaving the parental home, marriage, and having children. The social regulation of many transitions leads to the observation that women's developmental trajectories may differ considerably from those described for men because of different societal expectations or social circumstances. Differential treatment as a daughter, sister, woman, wife, or mother all blend to result in different life experiences in what may seem to be parallel circumstances, but that result in different developmental outcomes because of social values and restrictions. Thus, the person's development occurs through an interaction of biological heritage with the social environment and is influenced by normative age-graded, normative history-graded, and non-normative transitions (Baltes et al., 1980).

Age-Normative Transitions

Normative age-graded transitions relate to chronological age and include both biological and environmental determinants that are reliably associated with a particular age (Baltes et al., 1980). Menstruation and menopause are biological maturational events associated with age that represent transitions in many cultures.

All societies and specific cultures within larger societies have age-related expectations for their members over a lifetime so that individuals grow up expecting to experience specific events at specific times of life. As a consequence, one's environment or society in general usually interacts with the individual according to these societal norms or expectations.

Age-graded events that are age-normative transitions include entering first grade at age 6, graduating from high school at 18, preparing for career following graduation from high school, marrying during the 20s, having a first child during the 20s, and retiring from work or career at age 62 or 65. These socially defined events are turning points that lead to a change in self-concept, identity, and the incorporation of new social roles (Neugarten, 1970). However, the social and family milieu are highly variable from family to family, and this variation along with historical events contribute to a multidimensional effect on individual development.

Normative History-Graded Influences

Normative history-graded influences on development are biological and environmental determinants that are related to a historical period. A certain time in history that is experienced in similar ways by the majority of the persons of the same generation becomes a normative history-graded influence (Baltes et al., 1980). Life-course development becomes more historically dependent as the individual ages (Baltes & Schaie, 1973). Two examples of research tying the historical influence of the Depression to development were a study focused on adaptation 40 years after the 1929 depression (Elder & Liker, 1982), and a study of how the changing social and economic climate of the 1929 depression influenced parent–child behavior and subsequent development (Elder, Liker, & Cross, 1984).

Historical events occurring at a specific period often shape or influence societal norms while affecting individuals of different ages quite differently. For example, blacks born after enforcement of the 1954 Supreme Court decision that separate educational facilities could not be considered equal had quite a different social milieu in which to develop their self-concept and social identity than their parents who had faced the bitter struggles leading to that decision. Each generation of blacks or whites that went through that struggle experienced it differently.

Historic events also change societal beliefs. World War II is an example of this. In 1939, two years before United States entry into World War II, a public opinion poll found that 80% of persons polled disapproved of wives working, yet five years later in 1943, 60% of persons polled approved of wives working (McLaughlin, Billy, Johnson, Melber, Winges, & Zimmerle, 1985). This great shift in public opinion was influenced by the national defense effort in which women had to replace men workers who were drafted and sent to the battlefronts.

Non-normative Life Events and Transitions

Some events are non-normative because they are unexpected and occur out of the expected chronological age sequence. Catastrophic events such as accidents, acute or chronic illness, and untimely deaths are crisis events that also offer potential for development. For example, an automobile accident that leads to loss of limbs of an adolescent requires extensive adaptation, thereby influencing that individual's development. Adult development is at times pushed along by these externally precipitated and undesirable or unplanned events that are beyond the individual's control.

Internally Versus Externally Motivated Transitions

Transitions may be internally motivated (intrapersonal) or externally motivated (interpersonal or situational). An example of an internally motivated transition would be one related to personal desire for upward mobility in a position or job. An externally motivated transition could be related to a wife relinquishing her job and moving because of her husband's transfer to a new location.

When the transition is internally motivated and controlled there is greater mental and physical preparation for it. For example, a woman deciding to return to work after several years as a homemaker may opt to take a refresher course at the community college first. This creates an anticipatory period in which intentionality, freedom of choice, and control in preparing for the transition contribute to the ease with which a life change may be made.

Externally motivated transitions are often precipitous, undesired, and provide little time for the anticipatory work to be accomplished in preparing for and adapting to new roles. For example, a 30-year-old husband's sudden death leaves a widow ill-prepared and temporarily in a state of shock. This is a non-normative transition with ensuing developmental change externally motivated. Neugarten (1979) observed that it was the timing of a life event rather than its occurrence that was problematic.

Process and Time Frame of Transitions

There is a process involved in transitions or turning points that results in a person taking on new roles and entering into new relationships, which in turn leads to a new self-conception: this may occur through a single event or experience or occur gradually over time (Mandelbaum, 1973). Transitions are embedded in trajectories (paths, progressions, or lines of development) that give them meaning, such as career or marriage (Elder, 1985). Anticipated events such as departure of grown children and change in work status may have little effect on the life course; an illness, however, comes as a surprise and forces reorganization of the life view (Bourque & Back, 1977).

Parkes (1971) noted that even though psychosocial transitions occur over a relatively short period of time they affect large parts of a person's assumptive world, which is everything the person knows or thinks she or he knows. The processes involved may be difficult because a person is tied to his or her assumptive world by affectional bonds, for example, "my home town," "my job," or "my husband." Persons tend to resist change in general; affectional bonds especially resist severance. Often, fear of possible failure in new adaptations also impedes the process of relinquishing the old form of life (Parkes, 1971).

Transitional periods have been identified in studies of both men and women. In a study of 40 men, Levinson, Darrow, Klein, Levinson, and McKee (1978) saw transitional periods as lasting 4 to 5 years; these periods were times in which the men reappraised their life structures, explored new possibilities, and worked toward their choices. Transitions into major developmental eras were observed as occurring within a 2-year chronological age range. In a study of 124 women aged 30 to 60, Harris (1985) described major transitions as including several, often related psychosocial changes clustered within an average span of 3.5 years.

THEORETICAL BACKGROUND FOR THE STUDY

Prior to the review of women's adult development research, we will present some general principles about human development. This is followed by a brief overview of the adolescent's transition to adulthood to provide a base for understanding later development. The discussion of research focused on women's development contrasts these findings with those for men.

Principles of Human Development

Two major developmental principles underly current developmental thought: the epigenetic and the orthogenetic principles. The epigenetic principle of development is generalized from the growth of life in utero. This principle maintains that a ground plan exists for anything that grows, and from this ground plan parts arise at a prescribed time until all parts have developed to form a functioning whole (Erikson, 1959). Erikson argues that although a child's development may vary from culture to culture it remains within the proper rate and sequence that govern the growth of a personality and an organism, obeying the inner laws of development. Erikson's stages of personality development are based on the epigenetic principle, as were Freud's psychosexual stages of development. Erikson (1959) emphasized continuity from birth in his classic developmental stages, noting that parts of each progressive stage exist in some form before the phase-specific crisis is precipitated by a person's readiness and society's pressure. He identified the major task for each stage and its antithesis: trust versus mistrust, autonomy versus shame and doubt, initiative versus guilt, industry versus inferiority, identity versus identity diffusion, intimacy versus isolation, generativity versus self-absorption, and integrity versus disgust and despair.

The orthogenetic principle of development states that "wherever development occurs it proceeds from a state of relative globality and lack of differentiation to a state of increasing differentiation, articulation, and heirarchic integration" (Werner, 1967, p. 126). Increasing differentiation from the environment along with the integration within self of these developmental changes lead to increased individuation of the person (formation of a clearer boundary between self and environment) (Kegan, 1982; Levinson et al., 1978). As persons become more highly individuated, they are more independent, less egocentric, and more empathic, self-confident, and creative (Werner, 1967). Mahler (1968) described the first individuation process for humans as the separation-individuation process in which the toddler realizes she or he is a separate person from her or his mother. Blos (1962) maintained that a second individuation process occurs during adolescence as close ties to the family are severed and is accompanied by feelings of isolation, loneliness, and confusion.

Psychosocial development progresses as a spiraling or widening in the scope of adaptive capacities in interaction with others in the environment; plateaus are reached before movement proceeds to a higher level of development (Deutsch, 1945; Kegan, 1982; Rubin, 1984). At each developmental transition, elements of each earlier stage are regrouped to

accommodate new experiences of that transition, resulting in articulation, transformation, and consolidation of the novel experience into the
personality structure (Rubin, 1984).

Adolescent Transition to Adulthood

Achieving a secure sense of identity is a major task of adolescence
(Erikson, 1968). Identity achievement is a process of consolidating earlier lifetime experiences and integrating these experiences such that the
individual is able to expand relationships with the world as increasing
differentiation of self occurs (Erikson, 1968). From the parts of historical self and the realities of the world, an inner sameness and continuity
of personality is achieved that is also recognized by the person's social
network with identity achievement (Erikson, 1959). Achievement of
identity cannot be viewed as an end point, however, but as a comple-
ment of a stable view of self along with the flexibility to adapt to new
experiences (Bourne, 1978).

Four identity statuses have been developed for testing Erikson's theory of identity development (Marcia, 1980): (1) Identity achievement is
represented by those who have experienced a decision-making period
prior to pursuing their life's goals. High identity achievers have high
self-esteem, a high level of moral reasoning, and are internally directed
toward independence (Marcia, 1980). (2) Foreclosures are those who
are committed to goals that are usually chosen by others without their
experiencing a decision-making period or crisis. Foreclosures are the
least anxious individuals and the most accepting of authoritarian values,
and tend to be low on autonomy (Marcia, 1980). Josselson (1987) observed foreclosures as women who lived out an unquestioned dream
formed in childhood that was never modified. (3) Diffusions are those
who have no set goals or directions in life, regardless of whether they
experience an identity crisis. (4) Moratoriums are those persons struggling with decisions regarding their life's dreams and goals; they are in
an identity crisis, and are the most anxious, have a high level of moral
reasoning, take personal responsibility for their lives, and have high
self-esteem (Marcia, 1980).

Empirical evidence for the process of identity achievement beginning
and progressing during adolescence is found in Archer's (1982) work.
Archer reported an increase in identity achievement status from sixth to
eighth to tenth to twelfth grades.

Three interesting points were made in a life-span study reported by
Haan and Day (1974). From early adolescence to later adulthood there

was substantial continuity in self-presentation and socialization, a moderate amount of continuity in information processing and interpersonal reactions, and emergent discontinuity in cognitively articulated, affective responses. In another study, adolescents performed less well on emotional tasks than young and middle-aged adults (Blanchard-Fields, 1986). Life experiences or transitional events, such as entry into military service, were also seen to contribute to discontinuities in development (Elder, 1986).

Newman (1979) also suggested that continuity from adolescence into young adulthood was the more typical pattern of psychological development. This notion is in contrast to the view of adolescence as a period characterized solely by upheaval, followed by a somewhat discontinuous more quiescent adulthood. In early adulthood, there is a carryover of major developmental psychological work of adolescence: The consolidation of a coping style occurs; competencies, aspirations, and life choices developed during adolescence foreshadow the articulation of an early adulthood lifestyle; and the individual's ability to experiment and encounter conflict in adolescence may reflect the extent to which maturation continues through adulthood (Newman, 1979). Valliant (1977) identified a group of men in their 50s, who as adolescents appeared mature with few visible conflicts; they had remained "perpetual boys" and had failed to grow in their use of mature defenses as adults or to show the ability to maintain warm, loving relationships. A person's coping style and adaptive devices that seem to be consolidated during adolescence are as important in determining the life course as heredity, upbringing, or social position (Valliant, 1977).

Erikson (1968) suggested different patterns of identity development for males and females, with females working on intimacy issues earlier than males. Others reported that identity formation among women was more related to issues of sexuality and religion contrasted to men's concern with occupation and politics (Schenkel & Marcia, 1972). Douvan and Adelson (1966) also reported that adolescent boys structure their identity primarily around occupational choice, whereas adolescent girls focus their attention on success with interpersonal relationships as a primary source of self-regard. Using an inventory that tapped Erikson's stages of psychosocial development, Rosenthal, Gurney, and Moore (1981) found that males were higher on autonomy and initiative, whereas females scored higher on intimacy. There is evidence that patterns of interaction in family relationships affect identity exploration during adolescence differently by gender (Bosma & Gerrits, 1985; Grotevant & Cooper, 1985).

Josselson's (1987) research on 60 women who were seniors in college is the most extensive research involving women using Marcia's four identity statuses. She was able to follow up on 34 of these women 12 years later to see whether they continued in the same status and how the women's identity status at age 20 to 22 years had interacted with the course of the women's lives up to age 32 to 34 years. Similar to the researchers cited above, Josselson observed continuity in identity status; she also concluded that psychological research that has stressed independence and autonomy as hallmarks of adulthood have overlooked the factors most appropriate to identity development in women—communion, connection, relational embeddedness, spirituality, and affiliation. A major difference between women and men lies in the separation-individuation process: Women never completely individuate from their mothers, and when they initiate the process, they often utilize a boyfriend to transfer dependence to, and, importantly, their dream or vision of a future self is pictured and defined in relational terms (Josselson, 1987). Josselson found that women with foreclosure identity statuses (13% of her sample) were all foreclosures 12 years later; they all were very family-centered women dominated by the need to feel loved and cared for. Foreclosures, called "purveyors of heritage," found security in relationships, and the only foreclosure woman who had indicated internal growth was one who had been divorced during the 12-year interim. Foreclosures had bypassed the adolescent task of individuation; their growth had been through identification, as opposed to individuation.

Josselson (1987) identified 13% of her sample as identity achievement status and called these women "pavers of the way." All but one of the eight women were still identity achievement status 12 years later; the one had reverted to moratorium status. Josselson emphasized that it was the psychological structure of the identity achievements that differed from foreclosures, not the content of their lives: "they are women who choose lives after sifting through options, amalgamating aspects of who they were with whom they wish to become, and, in so doing, have a sense of following a life plan they can claim as their own" (p. 72).

Ten (17%) of Josselson's sample were moratorium status; 12 years later, three had reached identity achievement, one was still struggling, and six were along the foreclosure–identity achievement continuum. The latter had returned to old values and life patterns by choice. Moratorium women, called "daughters of crisis," focused extensively on feelings and emotion. As this group rejects their mothers, they tend to idealize their fathers; they frequently find a boyfriend to support a new view who is more controlling than their mothers had been and experience much guilt. Of interest was that although this group of women were the most critical of their mother during their early 20s, they were closer to their mothers during their early 30s than any of the four status groups.

Sixteen women (27% of her sample) were in the identity diffusion status. Eight of these had severe psychological trauma early in their lives that plagued them into late adolescence; during their early 20s, they could not come to terms with their pasts in which they had lost a parent or suffered emotional neglect and experienced their lives as a succession of unrelated events. This group of eight women were passive, feeling as if they had no control over their lives and that it was futile to plan because of this. Diffusions as a group had moved more frequently and had held more jobs than women in other identity status groups. Of nine women who were contacted during their early 30s, three remained diffuse, one was attempting to make a commitment, three had made identity commitments, and two were dead, one because of suicide following a deep depression.

In addition to identity achievement, two other tasks of adolescence and early adulthood are particularly overlapping, as opposed to being discrete tasks of either period: intimacy and independence. The four major tasks identified during a novice phase of early adulthood by Levinson and associates (1978) are overlapping with the adolescent task of identity formation: formulation of a life's dream; forming mentor relationships; establishing an occupation; and establishing love and family relationships. Formulating a life's dream is central to establishing one's identity. Establishing mentor relationships with experienced adults and establishing an occupation furthers identity achievement and facilitates independence. Achievement of intimacy is central to the task of establishing love relationships and a family.

Early Adult Development

Historically, the family has been the central arena in which most life transitions occurred; for example, marriage was timed in accordance with the need of each person's family of origin (Hareven, 1986). However, other factors also influenced the timing of marriage. Spanier, Roos, and Shockey (1985) studied marital trajectories of women in the United States born during the first half of the 20th century from population survey data. Higher education was associated with a delayed first marriage, as well as older ages at first and last births and smaller completed family size.

Levinson et al.'s (1978) theory of men's developmental change used to study women found that timing of developmental periods and developmental tasks were similar to those identified for men (Roberts & Newton, 1987). Stewart (1977) reported that women showed greater variability in achieving early adult developmental tasks than men, however. This variability reflected different choices: forming a marriage and family life in the twenties, or remaining single and/or pursuing a career during this decade. Stewart observed that women appeared to face greater difficulty in forming early adult life structures than men did because of the cultural devaluation of traditional female roles along with severe sanctions for not succeeding in them. Although parenthood affects both parents, the social disparity of its impact on women as opposed to men has been well documented (McBride, 1973; Roland & Harris, 1979).

Hancock's (1985) findings from 20 women aged 30 to 75 supported that achieving adulthood is a very complex process for women. Women viewed adulthood as making choices and affirming commitments to others. Developmental shifts or transitions usually began with a serious threat to an important relational bond that exposed and challenged the woman's assumptions about her world. The woman who responded best to the disintegration of her old assumptions could draw strength from happy, positive girlhood memories of success.

The type of mentor a person has during the early adult transition is thought to affect negotiation of transitions as well as the outcome. Reinke (1985) observed that women reported older women relatives, friends, and neighbors as role models, rarely reporting the type of mentor described by men, such as professors or senior business associates. Women rarely have mentors in their work or career trajectories (Josselson, 1987). Levinson et al. (1978) placed great importance on the role of the mentor in early adulthood, arguing that poor mentoring in early adulthood had similar repercussions for this transition as poor parenting had during childhood. These findings offer one explanation for Stewart's (1977) and Hancock's (1985) observations that women had difficulty negotiating early adulthood.

Women's biographies indicated that their life dreams were more complex than men's dreams; women had vague images of self in a particular kind of setting as opposed to men who had images of self in a particular occupational role (Roberts & Newton, 1987). The women's dreams that focused on relational emphasis of finding a special partner and maintaining a relationship heavily shaped their adult life structures. Gilligan (1982 a, b) found that males were more oriented to justice and rights and females more to care and response. These two modes of moral reasoning lead to different forms of self-definition and different views of relationships. Women were observed to make life choices according to relational terms, that is, what they thought would be more emotionally gratifying to them (Josselson, 1987). Josselson described a process of anchoring that took place in either the family of origin, partner/children, career, or friends that was critical to their identity formation; relationships within one or more of these four realms provided the anchor for growth, change, or new directions in life.

In a study of women over their first year of motherhood, differences in personality integration and flexibility indicated that women's development proceeds in statistically significant increments by decades from teenage years to the 20s, and to the 30s (Mercer, 1986b). Women in their 20s had significantly greater empathy than women in their teens, but women in their 30s scored between those two groups and did not differ significantly from either. Both women in their 20s and 30s scored higher than teenagers on the temperament trait of adaptability.

Striking among the research findings to date is the consistency of an age-30 transitional period for both men and women (Roberts & Newton, 1987). Levinson et al. (1987) described an age-30 transition period among men that provided a second opportunity for establishing a life structure more congruent with the life's dream. Reinke, Holmes, and Harris (1985) reported that 78% of 60 women aged 30 to 45 reported a major transition that began between the ages of 27 to 30. Reinke (1985) observed a peak in life events during the late 20s and early 30s such as moves, deaths, and illnesses, improvement in relationships with parents, increased time spent on hobbies, deterioration of marital relationships, and interest in work and career development increased.

In a test of Erikson's theory of intimacy and generativity among a group of 50 women aged 18 to 30 and 50 women aged 40 to 55, intimacy was more important to young adult women than to those in middle age (Ryff & Migdall, 1984). Measured attributes of generativity were more important during middle age than during young adulthood only among the middle-aged group. Women did not see their attitudes of control or dominance changing from young adulthood to middle age.

Middle Adult Development

A mid-life transition was observed among men at age 40 to 45 that bridged early and middle adulthood and had three major tasks (Levinson et al., 1978). These tasks were reappraising and terminating early adulthood, beginning to modify negative parts of early adulthood while testing new choices, and dealing with four specific polarities (young/old, destruction/creation, masculine/feminine, and attachment/separateness). These tasks are similar to those Sherman (1987) summarized from Peck's (1968) tasks of middle-age: valuing wisdom versus valuing physical powers; socializing versus sexualizing in relationships; and emotional flexibility in relationships versus impoverishment. The developmental process of individuation (establishing a clearer boundary between self and world) is important at this mid-life transition in forming a more independent and self-generating stance for resolving the polarities (Levinson et al., 1978).

Lowenthal, Thurnher, and Chiriboga (1975) compared men and women facing four transitions: high school seniors (mean age, 17), newlyweds (mean age, 24), middle-aged parents (mean age, 50), and preretirees (mean age 60). High school females were more simplistic and diffuse than male counterparts, but the situation reversed at the newlywed stage when women pursued more complex life-styles. In the preretirement group, fewer women than men had simplistic life-styles. Marital dissatisfaction was greatest among middle-aged women, who also described their mothers rather negatively, and middle-aged women were as conflicted in their self-images as were the high-school seniors. The unrest among these middle-aged women suggest a mid-life transition occurring. Preretired women showed less evidence of conflict and described themselves as more assertive. Women in all four groups reported more stressful experiences than men and provided more complex descriptions of friends, being more concerned with affect and reciprocity than men.

During their early 40s, women evidenced increased interiority and reflection about personal and life's finiteness (Levinson's destruction/ creation polarity of experiencing one's mortality and the impending death of others), increased depth of friendships, improved relationships with parents, increased acceptance of and resignation to realities, and increased mellowness (Reinke, 1985). Matthews (1986) also found that friendships stood out during transitions of moves, changes in jobs, and changes in marital status. During the women's 50s, continued inner stability and life satisfaction were observed; menopause occurring from ages 48 to 53 was uneventful (Reinke, 1985).

Livson (1976) from a study of women from adolescence to age 50 was able to categorize them as either independents or traditionals. The independent group were more autonomous, ambitious, intellectual, and in touch with their inner lives; however, they experienced depression at age 40 that resolved by age 50. The traditional group of women fit the conventional definitions of feminity; they were gregarious, nurturant, feminine, and exhibited much protective behavior. Livson concluded that the less conventional independent women pay a serious price when they internalize traditional role expectations, as evidenced by their depression at age 40. Another argument could be made: the independent group perhaps experienced the transitional bipolar conflicts at age 40 described by Levinson et al. (1978), and their resolution of these conflicts contributed to that group being more highly individuated and having a greater adaptive capacity to deal with the world.

Black and Hill (1984) studied women aged 46 to 61 and concluded that well-educated married women in their 50s were happy regardless of their employment status, age, socioeconomic status, educational level, husband's attitude, life stressors, or menopausal symptoms. The empty nest (departure of grown children from the home) was not problematic for them. The failure of the empty nest to be problematic agrees with Livson's (1976), Neugarten's (1970), and Reinke's (1985) findings. Neugarten (1970) reported that the postparental stage was associated with a higher level of satisfaction than that of any other age group. These findings of greater satisfaction among women during their 50s parallels Levinson et al.'s (1978) trajectory of middle adulthood when successful transition leads to becoming one's own person.

Late Adulthood

Elder and Liker (1982) reported evidence of historical influence on women's lives over a period of 40 years. The hardships experienced during the 1929 Depression when the women were young, married adults seemed to provide an opportunity for learning to cope with losses during old age. Among middle-class women, economic deprivation appeared to foster greater assertiveness, which could contribute to reduced feelings of helplessness in later life. However, Elder and Liker's and Livson's data are from the same source, and the question may be raised whether it was Livson's "independent" group of women who were also more assertive and that their resolution of the depressive conflict at age 40 contributed to their adaptive potential.

Thurnher (1983) observed an increase in assertion among older women and a decrease among older men, supporting the notion that men become less agentic (controlling) and more nurturant in later life while women decline in nurturance. Reinke (1985) also observed that women in their 60s were aware of personality changes through which they became more assertive, expressive of opinions, patient, and mellow. In contrast, Ryff (1982) compared men and women aged 40 to 55 and a group who were 60 and older; women gave instrumental values higher priority during middle age than during older age. Men and women showed differential patterns on subjective personality change but along different dimensions rather than in opposite directions.

Ryff and Heincke (1983) compared 270 young, middle-aged and old-aged men and women to test Erikson's theory of generativity and integrity. All age groups saw themselves as scoring higher on generativity in middle age; no gender differences were observed except that men scored higher on defendence.

Evers (1985) observed two groups of frail elderly women who she categorized as "passive responders" and "active initiators." Active initiators either began new interests and activities in later life or had maintained lifelong interests and activities; they reported a sense of purpose and positive involvement, work outside the home, and hobbies. Passive responders lacked control over their lives, a definite purpose in life, and had usually engaged in unpaid care work for large periods of their life to the extent that they had little time to develop other activities or interests.

Development and Family Life Cycle

Ellicott (1985) examined development in relation to the phase of the family life cycle. Transitions were clustered in the family preschool, launching (first child leaving home), and postparental phases. Women who experienced transitions during the preschool phase had more self-perceived change, more divorce and/or separation, and were older when their last child was born; they were off-time or out of synchrony with the larger society. Those reporting transitions during the launching phase of the family cycle experienced greater personal disruption in the form of marital dissatisfaction, change in self, decreased personal development, increased introspection, and increased assertiveness. Those who had transitions during the postparental phase had experienced internal change with increased satisfaction; they had more children and were younger when the last child left home.

Motherhood and Development

Motherhood contributes to adult development because of both the inner and outer life change that occurs in the transition from nonparent to parent. New mothers have reported that motherhood represented a transition to adulthood (Breen, 1975; Leifer, 1977; Mercer, 1986a; Shereshefsky, Liebenberg, & Lockman, 1973). Benedek (1959) suggested that parenthood contributes to personality development, utilizing the same primary process that is operative from infancy in mental development. As the child matures she or he is the object of parental drives for the parent's own self realization; parents may resolve old conflicts that occurred at these earlier stages, but at a higher level. Benedek (1970) postulated that parenthood as a psychobiologic process ends only with the death of the parent. Adolescents experience a second individuation from parents (Blos, 1979), but Levinson et al. (1978) postulated that the process of separation from parents continues over the life course, never being completed, supporting Josselson's (1987) argument for her observation of women.

Lebe (1982), however, reported that women complete their separation-individuation from their mothers some time between the ages of 30 to 40; during that period a woman achieves the ability to identify with her mother positively and finally detaches from her to become a completely autonomous woman. Lebe's described process is paralleled by the individuation process that Levinson et al. (1978) saw as so critical at men's mid-life transition.

MAJOR QUESTIONS ASKED

Although it has been proposed that there are gender differences in several areas of development, data to date indicate some support for the applicability of developmental theories established with male populations to women regarding developmental eras and transitions. Findings also suggest that the family of origin as a source of role models and socialization for coping style has potential for a powerful long-range effect on women's development. The proposed influences of motherhood on women's development, women's differential socialization and mentoring, and developmental research focused on women provided the theoretical background from which to study and answer the following questions:

1. Are there developmental eras in women's life cycles with comparatively uniform (by chronological age) transitional periods parallel to those described for men?
2. Does motherhood affect women's development over the life span? If so, how is the developmental trajectory affected?

3. What factors and events seem to occur with or precede transitional periods over a woman's life cycle?

METHOD

The life history was selected as the preferred methodological approach. Baltes et al. (1980) emphasized the life history, or naturalistic memory research, as the method of choice in studying adult development because it enables emphasis on the interrelatedness of the person with the social and cultural environment across the life span. Others have also endorsed the life history as a rich source for formulating substantive theory about adult development (Bertaux & Kohli, 1984; Ryff, 1985).

Watson (1976) defined the life history as the person's view and conceptualization of the flow of lifetime experience from the perspective of the demands and expectations imposed by self and others. Jackson (1984) found that life-historical conflict and meaning were recapitulated at every period of respondents' lives; therefore, any conflict from either early parental or family relationships could be expected to arise during an oral account of the life history. Indeed, this was the case among women we interviewed. In one extreme case, a woman who had experienced extensive conflict with her mother from early childhood exhibited the beginning of an asthmatic attack following the review of her life; however, she thanked the interviewer profusely for the interview and stated that she felt "so relieved." This woman was not a mother.

The three dimensions—cultural, social, and psychosocial—proposed by Mandelbaum (1973) for consideration in the collection and analysis of the life history were kept in mind during data collection and analysis. The cultural dimension includes awareness and concern for the subject's cultural life plan in which some expectations are broad and vaguely indicated, whereas others are clearly outlined by the cultural context. The social dimension includes the person's social relations, choices, and decisions as they are portrayed in her behavior. The psychosocial dimension considers the person's subjective views that maintain some constancy, yet at each developmental stage allow for acquisition of new capacities or limitations and reintegration of earlier resources (Mandelbaum, 1973). Cohler (1982) suggests that the sense of stability and consistency over time is the result of a person's continual reconstructive activity rather than constancy in development; individuals construct and maintain a personal narrative of their life-course.

Westbrook's (1976) advice that positive and negative feelings should be considered independently to understand a person's experience of life events was considered. Some women focused almost exclusively on negative life events such as illness, loss, and death and tended to see their lives as "hard," whereas others had a more optimistic view of life and were able to consider all turning points, whether negative or positive, in a favorable light.

Procedure

All of the women were interviewed in their home or office settings, except for one who was interviewed at a hotel. Interviews were done by the authors and graduate nursing students. Summary forms for demographic data, employment history, and transitions were used. Almost all of the interviews were tape-recorded and later typed for analysis. Two women did not want their interviews to be tape-recorded. Handwritten notes were taken during all interviews so that events identified as transitions or turning points could be summarized at the end of the interview and validated with the woman. Questions were open-ended, and usually little prompting was needed as the woman told her life story. The life history usually flowed rather freely, much as a narrative, described by Cohler (1982), with a beginning, a middle, and an alluded to end. Women in their late seventies and older, particularly, tended to mention readiness for death.

Women frequently assumed a hostess role and served refreshments. Many of the women shared photographs of loved ones and other memorabilia. Some women expressed great pride in their rich histories. A few women apologetically stated that their lives were not all that interesting or eventful. The importance of each history was emphasized by the interviewer as providing a more realistic picture of how women's lives unfold.

Taking the life history began with the woman's earliest recollection of events, then moved to school-age and teenage years, and proceeded through each decade of life to the present. Women were asked to describe what they remembered about each period of life, the events in their communities and the world at the time, people who were important to them at the time, their role models or mentors, and transitions or turning points in their lives. Each woman was queried about the specific transition from childhood to adulthood.

Analysis

The typewritten protocols were identified only by code numbers; all identifying names were removed from the transcripts. The protocols were studied for themes, transition periods, environmental contexts, and important persons in the women's lives. Initially, transitions were coded on index cards as either internal (originated by the individual), external (originated by outside events such as death or illness), or both internal and external; also recorded were age of woman at the time of the transition, year of the transition, and the type of transitional event. Cards were sorted into various categories of transitions during phases of the analysis.

To study the historical impact, women were grouped according to their age in 1929, the beginning of the Depression (preadolescent, adolescent, and postadolescent). Constant checking and rechecking of impressions was done. For example, initially it seemed that mothers who were of school age during the Depression faced more long-term effects; however, with further analysis, this group was also aged 17 to 24 at the outbreak of World War II, a more recent event that perhaps had a stronger impact on turning points, for example, a fiancé or boyfriend being killed in the war.

The researcher's awareness of any of her own preconceptions and the necessity of changing these as the life history unfolds to allow a continual dialectical relationship between the researcher and the respondent is essential in this type of research (Watson, 1976). This required moving back and forth from the life history to the current context for understanding. Two initial assumptions were discarded early. We had assumed that the women's mothering role would be central to their life cycles; however, the women talked more about their own mothers and the mothering that they had received than the mothering they initiated (see Chapter 5). Occasionally, such little mention was made of children during histories that specific questions had to be asked. It was soon apparent that for the majority of mothers, when events over the entire life cycle were viewed in perspective, motherhood was but one of many roles. Accordingly, as the women reconstructed their lives, motherhood had less or little impact when compared to other life events such as acute life-threatening chronic illnesses, such as multiple sclerosis or tuberculosis, or death of a spouse or other loved one. One important point to make here, however, is that motherhood was a normative, expected event for many women; therefore, it did not have the salience of the non-normative, unexpected, and undesired events.

A second assumption was that everyone would identify specific life events as turning points, when in fact a couple of the women maintained that they had no turning points: "Life just went on." This finding agrees with that of Mandelbaum (1973), who pointed out that a person's turning point could be a gradual shift. Apparently for the few women whose "life just went on," developmental changes were so gradual—"I always lived a steady life," or "Nothing dramatic; I always planned to get my master's and doctorate"—that they left little perceptible memory of adapting or changing to new directions. Thurnher (1983) reported that 6% of the respondents in her study did not feel as if they had experienced any turning points over the previous 8 years.

The enthusiasm with which the women shared their life's experiences and the richness of their data made each interview a pleasurable experience for interviewers. The recall of early unpleasant experiences, however, also brought back the emotional impact of that event and was, in part, a catharsis. Although many women cried during the interviews, at the end they were in good spirits though fatigued.

Because we promised to protect the anonymity of the women who so generously shared their histories, no single history will be presented in its entirety. Excerpts from histories are shared throughout to illustrate the conclusions drawn or postulated. Fictitious names are used, and identifying characteristics are changed in these excerpts without changing the thrust of the quote.

■ 2
Profile of the Women Studied

Criteria for participation in the study were simple. We required only that the participants be 60 years of age or older at the time of interview, that they be able to converse in English, that they were maintaining activities of daily living without assistance, and that they were mentally alert. A total of 80 women consented to be interviewed. Of these women, 50 classified themselves as mothers, and 30 as nonmothers. All but one of the mothers were biological mothers; one woman had adopted a child.

SOCIAL SETTINGS AND GEOGRAPHIC REPRESENTATION

In order to understand the lives of women, we wanted women from as broad a range of backgrounds and experiences as we could manage to obtain. This desire had to be tempered by practicality since our funding was modest for this research project. We had, therefore, to be creative and enterprising in expanding our own contacts with potential participants.

Early in the course of the study, one of the authors moved to Pocatello, Idaho, a small city in a rural farming area of the intermountain west. Additionally, one of the doctoral students who was helping with interviewing returned to her home in Indiana. Another author had family in the upper midwest and often visited, thus making it possible to obtain interviews from acquaintances in that area, also. At first we started by interviewing personal acquaintances, neighbors, and relatives who fit the criteria for inclusion in the sample. This was quickly expanded to include a broad range of volunteer subjects recruited from a variety of settings, such as senior centers, retirement homes, community organizations, church groups, referrals from previous interviewees, and referrals generated through media coverage (as was the case in Idaho). Even though women were recruited primarily from rural and urban areas in Idaho, Indiana, and California, most of the women had lived mobile lives, as will be discussed in Chapter 7. Thus, we obtained a group of women with wide geographic and experiential representation; one mother and two nonmothers were born in England, one mother and one nonmother were born in Canada, and one mother was born in Norway. The remaining subjects were all born in the United States.

We wanted an equal number of mothers and nonmothers; however when we had recruited a sample of 50 mothers, we found that we had only 16 nonmothers. This was, in part, a reflection of family life-cycle typology for women of the age we were studying. For every 1,000 females at age 15 and born between 1890 and 1894, 80 did not marry and 185 who married had no children; for every 1,000 alive at age 15 and born between 1910 and 1914, 60 were single and 145 who married had no children (Uhlenberg, 1974). Through a concerted effort, we were able to find and interview an additional 14 nonmothers. The consistency of the data we were obtaining from nonmothers, the qualitative nature of the study, and the difficulty in locating nonmothers all provided a basis for ceasing additional data collection.

Two particularly important and sensitive aspects of female development were not addressed by our data. None of the women discussed having had sexual experiences with other women; nor was lesbianism disclosed. One must keep in mind that the social stigma of lesbianism was much stronger during the era in which the women grew up. Additionally, no admission of sexual abuse was made; however, allusions were made by two women. One woman reported fighting off a rape attempt successfully. Thus, the impact of sexual orientation and sexual abuse on female development cannot be determined.

The characteristics of women who participated are grouped into sets of variables that reflect early adulthood developmental tasks and factors that might be expected to influence the outcome of those tasks: personal characteristics, social context, family of origin constellation, and marital family constellation. The chapter is concluded with profiles of each of the three groups of women we identified: mothers, married nonmothers and never-married nonmothers.

PERSONAL CHARACTERISTICS

Age, Marital Status, and Living Arrangements

The women we interviewed ranged in age from 60 to 95 years of age, the average age being 73.5 for the total sample. Nonmothers were slightly older than were the mothers, their average age was 75.6 years of age, standard deviation (SD) 7.4; they ranged in age from 62 to 91 (born between 1891 and 1923). The average age of the mothers was 72 years of age, SD 9.1; their age range was from 60 to 95 (born between 1888 and 1925).

As a rule, mothers married earlier; average age at marriage was 32.8 years of age for nonmothers, compared to an average age of 23.3 for mothers. One-fifth of the mothers were married by the age of 19. All but one of the mothers who married by the age of 19 were from large families with 3 to 15 children; the one was from a family with two children. There was less variability in the age at which mothers married: SD 4.9, with a range of 15 to 36 years. The range was broader for nonmothers who reported first marriages at ages 18 to 50: SD 8.1.

All of the mothers had been married; at the time of the interview, 54% had been widowed at some point in their lives, but three had remarried so that 48% were widows at the time of the interview. One mother had lost three husbands. Sixteen percent of the mothers had been divorced at some time during their lives, and 8% were divorced at the time of the interview. One mother had been divorced three times. Two of the mothers had been both divorced and widowed.

Just over one-half (53%) of the nonmothers had ever married. Among those who had ever married, nine had been widowed, but one had remarried and her latest husband was still living. Five of the ever-married nonmothers had been divorced, of these five, two had been both divorced and widowed and one had been divorced twice and widowed once.

At the time of the interview, 73% of the nonmothers and 42% of the mothers were living alone. Living alone meant that the woman lived by herself in a self-contained unit; a mother-in-law apartment connected to a child's home was not considered living alone.

Menses and Menopause

The onset of menses and menopause are often cited as significant transitions for women as they herald the beginning and end of the reproductive phase of life. Generally, the span of reproductive fertility, as estimated by menstrual history, did not differ between the mothers and the non-mothers. The average age of the onset of menstruation for mothers was 13 years of age, for nonmothers it was 13.9 years of age; the average age of menopause was 46 years of age for the mothers and 46.7 for the non-mothers.

Neither mothers or nonmothers attached any particular significance to either of these events; however, the majority of subjects could recall the onset of menstruation, even though that event occurred as much as 75 years prior to the interviews! The women characterized the onset of menstruation as "no big deal," although one mother stated, "It was a shock to find out it happened every month. I thought it only happened to you once in a lifetime." Generally the women had been prepared for the onset of menses by mothers, gym teachers, or sisters (Rankin, Mercer, Leonard, & Nichols, 1987). These findings agree with others that puberty does not lead to psychological turmoil (Petersen, 1988).

The age at menopause was somewhat more difficult for the women to recall. It was not characterized as a particularly eventful time, although some of the sample had surgically induced menopause, and some had been maintained on hormones postmenopause. Common remarks about menopause were, "I just stopped one day, and that was it," or "It just dribbled on for 10 years." The women who experienced difficulties with menopause had concurrent personal life crises, findings consistent with Lock (1985) and McKinlay and Jeffreys (1974).

Education

Educational achievement of the mothers and nonmothers differed in that more of the nonmothers had baccalaureate and graduate degrees and more of the mothers had post-high-school vocational training. Only 17% (n = 5) of the nonmothers and 12% (n = 6) of the mothers had less than a high school education (compared to the 1940 women's national average of less than 50% non-completion rate [McLaughlin et al., 1985]). Close to one-fifth of both groups of women had completed high school: 18% of mothers and 20% of nonmothers. Among mothers, 32% had short business or other vocational training such as teaching certificates (often obtained in one or two summers post-high-school) or nursing diplomas, as compared to 13% of nonmothers. For 25% of the mothers, a baccalaureate degree was their highest educational achievement compared to 10% of the nonmothers; however, significantly more of the nonmothers had graduate degrees (40% compared to 14%).

The group of mothers, who less often had graduate degrees, tended to come from families headed by a parent with higher socioeconomic status positions as classified by Hollingshead (1975) (owners of farms or businesses were classified higher than skilled laborers regardless of their educational level). It was evident that education past the baccalaureate degree was much more likely if the woman did not have children; mothers, with a few exceptions, completed their education before marriage and motherhood. Nonmothers more often continued their education throughout their careers, not necessarily completing their education before committing themselves to a career.

Employment

The women held occupational roles typical of those that women held at that time. Occupational roles are classified by the type of employment that the women pursued during their adult life; for example, women who had worked during their teens or early 20s but later married and assumed homemaker roles were classified as homemakers.

Among mothers 20% (n = 10) were homemakers during their adult years, 14% (n = 7) were teachers, 14% (n = 7) held secretarial or clerical positions, 12% (n = 6) held nursing positions, 6% (n = 3) were college or university professors (included music and nursing), 6% (n = 3) were technicians assistants or practical nurses; 6% (n = 3) were bookkeepers, 4% (n = 2) were executive directors of a business or corporation, 4% (n = 2) were social workers, 4% (n = 2) were waitresses or laundresses, 4% (n = 2) were sales clerks or cashiers, 2% (n = 1) were housekeepers, 2% (n = 1) were librarians, and 2% (n = 1) were medical technicians.

Only 3% (n = 1) of the nonmothers were homemakers, 20% (n = 6) were college or university professors, 17% (n = 5) were teachers, 17% (n = 5) held secretarial or clerical positions, 17% (n = 5) were executive directors of a business or corporation, 10% (n = 3) were housekeepers, 7% (n = 2) were technicians assistants or practical nurses, 3% (n = 1) were cosmetologists, 3% (n = 1) were laundresses, and 3% (n = 1) were journalists. One of the nonmothers who was a high-school teacher in later years was also a lawyer; however, when her lawyer husband died, and she remarried a high-school principal, she became a high-school teacher and was coded as such.

Almost three-fourths (73%) of nonmothers held positions in the top three occupational levels as classified by Hollingshead (1975), contrasted to 38% of the mothers. One-third of the mothers held one of the three middle occupational levels contrasted to 20% of the nonmothers; 13% of nonmothers held one of the lower-level positions contrasted to 6% of mothers. The homemaker position held by 20% of the mothers was not classified by Hollingshead. Mothers' employment patterns were shorter term and erratic, whereas nonmothers' patterns were more stable and long term.

SOCIAL CONTEXT

Ethnic Background

All of the nonmothers were Caucasian, as were 94% of the mothers. One mother came from each of black, Hispanic, and Native American groups. Women who were not Caucasian experienced ethnic and racial discrimination. During World War I, one nonmother whose family was identified by the local community as a German family was not permitted to play with the other children in the neighborhood because of her ethnic affiliation. When one participant and her family moved to San Francisco in the mid-1940s, her husband, who had been the principal of a school in Texas, was unable to obtain a teaching job because of his race (black). The one Hispanic woman did not articulate any concerns regarding ethnic or racial discrimination.

Religious Preference

Protestantism was identified as the predominant religious affiliation for both mothers (34%) and nonmothers (57%). The next most frequently cited religious affiliation was Catholic (28% of the mothers and 27% of the nonmothers). Twenty percent of the mothers and 3% of the nonmothers reported other religions; 18% of the mothers were Mormon (included in "other" group). One mother (2%) reported she was agnostic, and two nonmothers (7%) reported being agnostic. Two mothers (4%) reported no religion, and one nonmother (3%) reported no preference.

Rural and Urban Settings

The social and societal context of the individual can have significant impact upon that person's development. One deliberate differentiation we chose in recruiting the women for participation in this study was between rural and urban settings. While on the surface an easy differentiation, it proved to be more difficult than we thought. As noted earlier in this chapter, the women were a mobile group. Few were residing in the areas in which they had been born and grown up. These population shifts provided problems in differentiating rural from urban settings, because, one must remember, we were having to decide rurality or urbanity for a time much earlier than the date of interview. Women were categorized as coming from rural or urban settings based upon their place of residence during their childhood and adolescent years, the time when identity formation is a major developmental task (Erikson, 1959).

The women were almost evenly divided between rural and urban backgrounds: 43 were from urban backgrounds, and 37 were from rural areas. Forty percent of the nonmothers and 50% of the mothers spent at least their childhood and adolescence in a rural area. Sixty percent of the nonmothers and 50% of the mothers grew up in urban areas.

The rural women came from larger families; the average number of children in their families of origin was 5.2, compared to 3.2 for the urban women. The rural women married at a slightly earlier age than those from the urban areas, 24.2 years of age compared to 26.7. Eight of the rural women (18.6%) had no children, 12 of the urban women (27.9%) were childless. The rural woman tended to have her first child later than did the woman from an urban setting: 19 years of age compared to 17 years of age. Both groups of women had comparable numbers of children: 1.7 children for rural women; 1.3 for urban women. Divorce rates were similar for both groups; 16.2% (rural) and 14.3% (urban). Almost half (46.5%) of the women from urban backgrounds were widowed, whereas only 37% of those from rural backgrounds were widowed.

The greatest difference observed between women living in rural and urban areas during their formative years was in educational preparation. Fewer of the women in the rural group (16%) had achieved at least a college education; whereas 47% of the urban group had achieved that level of education.

The rural women came from larger families, married earlier, and had less education than did the urban women. More of the urban women never married. For those women who did marry, there was little difference in the success rates of marriages or in the size of their marital families. The reader should keep in mind that 50% of the mothers, all of whom were married, were in the rural group, contrasted to 40% of the nonmothers, 47% of whom never married.

FAMILY OF ORIGIN CONSTELLATIONS

Of the 80 women, only one was adopted, a mother who was reared as the only child. Only one of the participants was a twin; she was also a mother.

Family Size

The average family size was 4.0 for nonmothers and 4.2 for mothers. Nonmothers came from families with one to 10 children. However, the most common number of children in families from which nonmothers came was only one child: 23% of all nonmothers were only children, 17% were from two-children families, 17% were from three-children families, 10% were from families with four children, 7% were from families of five children, 7% from families of six children, 7% from families of seven children, 3% from nine-children families, and 10% from 10-children families.

Mothers typically came from larger families: 10% were an only child, 22% were from families with two children, 24% came from families with three children, 10% from families with four children, 10% from families with five children, 6% from families of six children, 8% from families of seven children, 4% from families of eight children, 4% from families with nine children, and 2% from families with 15 children.

Birth Order

Birth order also differed for the mothers and nonmothers. Among nonmothers, 63% were first-born children, compared to 38% of the mothers. Sixteen percent of the nonmothers were second born; the remainder were third (13%), fourth (3%), and seventh (3%) born. Twenty-eight percent of the mothers were second born, 14% were third, and 14% fourth born; the remainder were fifth (2%) and ninth (2%) born.

Age at Parent's Death

The final set of characteristics of the family of origin was the age of the respondent at the time of each of her parent's deaths. Many women did not refer to their parent's deaths as transitions when giving their life histories. Data were available on the majority of women, however, and differences were apparent. The average age of nonmothers at their mothers' death was 44.5 years, with a range from 8 to 61 years. There was no pattern to these data; however, 14 of the 21 nonmothers (67%) for whom we had this information lost their mothers at age 45 or older. Only 10% lost their mother prior to age 20: one at age 8, one at age 13, and one at age 18.

The mother's average age at the death of their mothers was 41 years, with a range from 3 months to 65 years. Fifteen of 25 mothers (60%) for whom there were data lost their mothers when the women were 45 or older; 6% were under the age of 20 when they lost their mother (one at 3 months, one at age 14, and one at age 16).

Nonmothers also experienced the deaths of their fathers at a somewhat later age than did mothers. The average age of the woman at the time of death of her father was 43.8 for nonmothers and 31.5 for mothers. The range of ages for both groups was broad (2 to 65 years for nonmothers and 4 to 65 years for mothers); however, 12 of 20 nonmothers (60%) were over 45 when their fathers died, whereas only 9 of 22 mothers (41%) were that old.

MARITAL/NUCLEAR FAMILY CONSTELLATION

As we examined the marital family constellations of the women who participated in the study, it was evident that we had three groups of women, rather than the two groups that were initially conceptualized: mothers, ever-married nonmothers, and never-married nonmothers. This section will describe the marital and nuclear family constellations of these groups, first as mothers and nonmothers, then as never-married nonmothers. Fictitious names are used to provide illustrations from the women's life histories.

Marriage

The majority of the women's nuclear families remained stable over their life course. There were, however, disruptions and reconstitutions among some.

Mothers. Among mothers, all of whom were married, 84% were married just once, 12% were married twice, and 4% were married three times. Eight mothers (16%) had been divorced; their average age at first divorce was 37.6 years. At the time of the interview, 66% of the mothers were widowed or divorced/separated and 34% were married.

Divorce was not always easy for these women, although it was not as uncommon as we had expected it might be. Susan Simms, a career-oriented mother, described the situation surrounding her divorce:

> It was the only divorce in my family or his; yes, it was very hard. And in those days, not everybody was getting divorces either. In our acquaintance, I don't think there were any divorces. So that was rough. It drug on in the courts for a long time, because, as I said, we were all personal friends, and everybody thought he'll straighten up, give him a little time.

Twenty-seven mothers had been widowed; the average age at first widowhood was 62.3, with a range from 31 to 81 years. Widowhood was indeed a more socially accepted state, although it presented a number of problems for the women, most often financial. The impact of widowhood is addressed in more depth in Chapter 8.

Mothers reported a range of 1 to 6 children. Forty-two percent reported having two children, 24% had three children, and 18% had only one child. Five women (10%) had four children, and one each had five and six. The average age at which the first child was born was 25.8 years (range 16 to 39), and the average age at which the last child was born was 31.3 years (range 19 to 43). Although 20% of mothers were married by the age of 19, only 10% had a child by that time; the average age for the birth of the first child was 25.8 years, with an age range from 16 to 39.

The women who were in their adolescent years at the onset of the Depression had fewer children than did women who were in their pre-teen or postadolescent years at this time. Chapter 3 deals with the impact of the Depression on the women in our study.

Nonmothers. Among nonmothers, 47% never married, 40% married only once, 10% married twice, and 3% (n = 1) married four times. At the time of the interview, 47% of the nonmothers were never married, another 33% were widowed or divorced/separated, and 20% were married.

Five nonmothers had been divorced; their average age at the first divorce was 36 years. Nine of the nonmothers had been widowed; their average age at widowhood was 62.8 years, with a range from 38 to 82 years.

NEVER-MARRIED NONMOTHERS

Almost one-half of the nonmothers never married (47%). As this was such a sizeable group, we examined whether they differed from married

·nonmothers or married mothers. All of the never-married women were either only children, oldest children, or the eldest daughter. These women were frequently responsible for caring for their parents. Over half of these women (eight of 14) remained in one job or position from their early 20s until retirement (Mercer, Nichols, & Doyle, 1988). Eleven of the fourteen (79%) were born between 1901 and 1909; that is, they were in their 20s at the onset of the Depression. The remaining three women were in their preteen years, aged 6, 9, and 11 at the onset of the Depression. Additional description of never-married nonmothers is provided in Chapter 4.

CASE EXAMPLES OF A MOTHER, MARRIED NONMOTHER AND NEVER-MARRIED NONMOTHER

As can be imagined, it is extremely difficult to select a "typical" mother or nonmother, for each woman had a unique life. However, to allow the reader to meet the women we interviewed, we have selected three women to profile: a mother, a married nonmother, and a never-married nonmother.

Nancy Newton: A Mother

Nancy Newton was born in 1924 in a small community in the midwest. She had one brother, seven years older than she. Her father had come to the United States from Northern Europe as a child; her mother was a second-generation American. Nancy's father was a school superintendent; her mother was a teacher. When Nancy was 9, her father lost his bid for reelection. She noted that as a turning point in her life.

> A change. A definite change, and although I did not know it then, they lost that power when he lost (the election). But my life changed at that point because he became depressed. I felt like I became an adult. I felt very old during the period of time when my dad was depressed. I felt like I was as old as I would ever be. . . . I don't think I ever felt that depth of adultness probably until, probably until my mother died. . . . that sense of responsibility. [With the exception of this episode, she remembered an active adolescence although her parents were somewhat strict.]

Nancy graduated from high school at age 17 and entered college in 1942, at the beginning of the American involvement in World War II.

She did not complete college at this time, rather she and her family moved to California where she held odd jobs until entering college again to prepare for teaching. She identified entering college as a transitional point in her life. Upon graduation, she entered the work force and "really liked it." At this time, she met her husband and married him at age 22. Neither her parents nor her husband's parents were particularly anxious for the couple to marry, as her husband, an army officer, was planning to attend college and graduate school:

> And we wrote back and said we wanted to get married, and the letters that came back were from his mother, "You don't want to do that to poor Nancy, I mean, you have seven years of school to go after you finish the army." And my parents said, "You don't want to do that to poor Charlie." Both of them meaning, "Don't do it."

Nancy had three children, the first at age 23. She also noted that as a transition:

> A definite change, because it took me from work into the home, being a wife and a mother. Probably more into being a wife. I think before then we were lovers. Our courtship just kept right on going.

Nancy had problems with her pregnancies: thrombophlebitis, headaches, and convulsions. She also had several miscarriages. The pregnancy that resulted in her third child, a daughter, was maintained through administration of thyroid and Diethylstilbestrol (DES). DES was administered during the 1940s and 1950s to prevent miscarriage. Females who were exposed to DES in utero are at a greater risk to develop adenocarcinoma of the vagina, and males who were exposed have a higher incidence of urinary tract abnormalities and infertility. The pregnancy was uneventful; however, she again had severe headaches, convulsions, and blood clots, and ever since the pregnancy has had a continuing concern about the effects of DES upon her daughter, who is now also a mother.

Nancy had reentered the work force after the birth of her second child, even though her husband was very much against women working. Her husband completed seminary training and when she was 28, she began the role of minister's wife:

> I seemed to fit into it easy, but it definitely was a different role. It was like going to the first women's society after never belonging to a women's society and having them say, "You'll play the piano, won't you," and then somebody else said, "You have the devotions?"

Nancy described her 30s as turbulent years: her husband entered the active army, and her family moved several times. One move, when Nancy was 34, was particularly noteworthy:

> I think in that church was the first place where I became overwhelmed by both being a minister's wife and trying to do everything right, and I went back into teaching. I created my own position. [She also had a number of other stressors; physical problems that led to surgery for her, and her father died.] He died in my home. I took care of him. . . . I had promised that he would never suffer. . . . My mother hadn't told him (that he had cancer). He had a very quiet death, painless death.

During her 40s, the family moved to another state where Nancy became very active in teaching, accomplishing a number of significant achievements. She then reentered university to work on a baccalaureate degree, but this was interrupted by her mother's death. This was another transition in her life. "It's like I always felt responsible for them. So when she died. . . . it was not being responsible for her that did something, maybe, said, 'Now I can go on with my own life.'"

Nancy's two sons were in the military during the Vietnam War; both returned unharmed. However, this affected the family greatly as one continued to have emotional problems due to the war upon his return.

At 48, Nancy completed her baccalaureate degree. She then went right into a masters program, completing it two years later. Once again her husband was transferred, and she moved into a new role, that of university faculty. The 50s were another time of change for Nancy. "I changed a lot during that whole period. I became more assertive, almost got a divorce, really changed. . . . And the times were changing."

At 60, Nancy had recently completed a doctorate and had two grandchildren. She described her life at the time of the interview, "It feels like an added blessing. There is a feeling of continuity that comes with that [grandchildren], of life going on."

Winona Woods: A Married Nonmother

Winona Woods was born in 1918 in a central midwest city. She lived with her parents, one sister and several aunts and uncles who "gradually left—got married or died." She entered school at the age of 6 and "loved it." During the Depression, the family lost their home and made a series of moves to less and less desirable locations. "The 1930s are a part of my life that I would like to erase. It was a very bad time." The family fortunes did not change until around 1942 when her father finally obtained a good job once more. Winona attended college after high school, working her way through with jobs supported by the Works Progress Administration (WPA) as well as a job at the local drug store. Despite the financial problems, she enjoyed college very much. She reported that college was probably pretty dreary socially, although she did not realize it because of the number of jobs she was holding down to meet expenses. She also reported that it was during her college days that she first really felt like an adult:

> I had to save that money to pay the tuition. I had a lot of choices to make. [After graduation in 1940, she taught school for one year.] And it was such a dismal year. It was a small school, nothing academic about it, you know. . . . I said, I am not going to go there, even if I have to go back to work in the factory on the line canning fruit. [That summer she was offered another teaching job and stayed for a year. In 1942 she joined the Women's Army Corps (WACS), a major transition in her life.] I got more exposure. Here I was a little mid-western girl who worked hard and had all these [people] from all over. . . . Everybody in that office. . . . came from an ivy league school but me. . . . And I met so many different people and different values and it was almost a free . . . here you opened up a whole lot.

Winona was transferred to England and France, managing artists commissioned to paint pictures of the war effect. She was in London during the period when the Germans were sending over the "buzz" bombs," which she described as "really nerve wracking." At 26, she was transferred back to the United States and decided she really wanted to return to teaching. She used her GI Bill benefits (GI Bill of Rights of June 22, 1944 provided for eligible veterans to receive education and training at Government expense) to attend a midwestern university for a masters' degree. She continued on in her education, passing the qualifying examinations for her doctorate.

During a visit home for Christmas, she met her husband, and they were married shortly thereafter. Marriage, she reported, was a turning point; it had a stabilizing effect in her life. She was 28 at the time.

Winona's childlessness was planned, "My husband is handicapped and I was 28, which was considered a pretty good age for children. And that was a conscious choice on our part."

Winona experienced significant prejudice as a married woman student:

Of course I couldn't be married and go to school. And the professor up there . . . he thought that it was a very good idea that I quit, because he said, "Winona, you are in a class with all men who are going to get their Ph.D.s at the same time you do, and you won't get a very good job."

She tried to enter a doctoral program at another university and met the same type of prejudice against married women. She returned to teaching and "loved it"; however, she found the same prejudices existed in the public school system.

Winona continued classroom teaching for 15 years, then "got talked into moving downtown in the role of a consultant to the main office." After 15 years in the consultant role, the "politics finally got me." She returned to the classroom until she retired 8 years later. In her third year of retirement at the time of the interview, she noted that she was having "a fine time." She and her husband were involved in a variety of activities such as raising money for music scholarships, going on opera trips, working for an educational foundation and the local historical society, walking, swimming, and reading. Her plans for the next year included taking a course in Greek at the nearby university.

Retirement was the third major transition Winona described in her life, "Because I really like that. . . . Like one year at Thanksgiving I went to Walden Pond and walked around like Thoreau and saw the squirrels and things like that."

Bea Bullock: A Never-Married Nonmother

Bea Bullock, an only child, was born in 1907 in a midwestern city. She remembered rolling bandages and making cotton swabs for the Red Cross during World War I. She described herself as being indulged as an only child and being quite popular. She described her teenage years as ones of having fun.

In 1924, she graduated from high school and enrolled in a secretarial course so that she would be employable. In August of that year, she obtained a job on a local newspaper. After 9 months she was offered a position as assistant to the women's editor on another paper and remained with that paper for 47 years.

The Depression had profound impact upon Bea and her family:

In 1929, my folks went bankrupt, and lost the house and business and the whole shebang. My father returned to wallpapering, which did not pay well, and my mother, who was 50 at the time, was in no condition to seek employment. [Despite financial problems at the paper, Bea managed to retain her employment and was retained over a more senior employee.] She was married and didn't have to work. . . . I wasn't getting paid as much; she got $33.00 and I got $22.00, and we also did all the women's clubs and society news. Then it was all put together, and for the same $22.00 I had the whole thing. But I didn't lose my job.

In order to make ends meet during the Depression, Bea did a lot of things outside her job: made lamp shades, curtains, and slip covers, knitted, did needle point, did comparative shopping for department stores, and sold Christmas cards. Some of these activities continued throughout her working life.

At age 23, Bea was very much in love, yet felt she could not marry and still care for her family. While the decision had been difficult for a long time, Bea had become sanguine about that choice:

> I carried a torch for a good many years. . . . But the last time I saw him, he had had a stroke and walked with a cane. . . . I had him and his wife for cocktails . . . and all I could do was sit there and think, "Thank God you got him instead of me." Which isn't a very charitable way to look at it.

Bea continued to support both parents for 20 years, until her father's death in 1948. She supported her mother until she died 20 years later at the age of 91.

After her father died (she was 41), the financial state eased a little, she no longer had the expense of caring for an ill father, and, as she noted, salaries had improved. While life became "normal," she became aware of a somewhat restricted social life:

> Well, by the time you get 35, there aren't many people to date. They're all married and your married friends don't want you around. The men don't mind, but the women don't want you around. . . . But I never was one to feel sorry for myself, and I don't think I realized at the time how terribly lonely I was.

During her 50s, Bea became involved in union activities, "partly because I was interested, and partly to get away [from caretaking responsibilities]." Her concern over working conditions and salaries for women led her to run for and be elected the president of the union.

In 1968, at the age of 61, she had an emergency appendectomy. Because of problems of finding qualified caretakers, her mother was also hospitalized. Although Bea recovered, her mother did not and died just seven weeks later. After her mother's death, Bea noted:

> And that's the first time I'd ever stayed alone at night. And I sat down and talked to myself and said, "Look you're no different than millions of other women. They live alone, so can you."

Following her mother's death, Bea began planning for her retirement, saving "like mad." She retired one week after she was 65. She continued to live in the house she and her mother rented:

> We had lived there 18 years, and she had a big heavy oak bedroom set, and I had been born in that bed. And I didn't want to get rid of it but I couldn't go into that room. It was still mother's room. And it began to bug me.

Bea then applied for an apartment in a retirement complex, and 2 1/2 years later she moved to the apartment. However, after two years, she decided it was too expensive and moved to a retirement center. Since her retirement she had become active in the Senior Citizen's Center and with Foster Grandparents; both of these activities have been somewhat disappointing because of financial and management problems within the organizations. Bea had also written one book, was collaborating on another, and was continuing to write two or three features a month for a newspaper. The two major transitions she noted were the 1929 Depression when she went from "having anything my little heart desired to having nothing" and retirement. World events were not of great significance to her, "I was too busy trying to keep my head above water."

SUMMARY

This chapter has presented a profile of the 80 women who participated in the study. In addition to the two groups recruited for the study—mothers and nonmothers—a third group was identified, a subgroup of the nonmothers, the never-married women, who differed by family of origin constellation. Each group, mothers, married nonmothers, and never-married nonmothers, presented a different profile. Mothers more frequently came from larger families, less often had graduate education, and more often had only high school or vocational education. Nonmothers, on the other hand, came from smaller families, were better

educated, married later in life, and had relatively long and uninterrupted career trajectories. Never-married nonmothers were the oldest
child, oldest daughter, or only daughter. They frequently assumed
major financial responsibilities for the family; they also had significant
career involvement.

The remaining chapters of this book will deal with various aspects of
the women's lives and the patterns that have emerged from their life
histories.

■ 3
Political and Historical Influences

People do not grow and develop in a vacuum. In attempts to discover the universals of human development, the influences of history and society are often considered extraneous variables. More recently, developmental psychologists are acknowledging the interactive nature of the human being and the environment, and viewing historical events as one component of that environment (Baltes et al., 1980; Klineberg, 1984; Schaie, 1984). The lives of the women who participated in this study crossed several major historical events: the first and second world wars, the Great Depression, industrialization of rural America, the Korean War, and the Vietnam War, as well as women's suffrage and changes in attitudes towards women's employment out of the home. It was evident as we listened to these women tell their stories that their lives had interacted with the social and historical events of their times. Several of the women were instrumental in the development of governmental programs that were initiated in response to labor needs of the second world war. For some others, career paths were selected because of governmental programs developed to ease the grip of the Great Depression. Rural women were affected most strikingly by the industrialization of America. This chapter presents the stories of these women as they were influenced by, or they influenced, the course of historical and social events of the United States.

WARS AND THEIR EFFECT ON WOMEN

The Great War (World War I)

Few of the women reported events of significance that related to World War I. The majority of our respondents were too young at this point in history to have been consciously affected, although some of the women reported brothers and cousins going off to the war. Lillian Love remembered the first world war affecting her family:

> . . . but during the first world war, the prices fell . . . [we] had to sell. My father decided with no help, see, there was four girls in the family and no boys, and it was hard to find work, or anyone to work for you. So my father decided to sell that farm.

Anne Abbey also remembered the first world war; however, her memories reflected the sense of adventure and crusading spirit that America took into this war (Allen, 1952):

> Oh, how I tried to enlist. In fact, I put my name in and said I was 18, and my manager said that I wasn't. . . . All my boyfriends went, and I didn't get to go. My oldest brother, he wanted to go to the service, he wanted to go so bad, but it was just the year after my father had passed away.

Bea Bullock remembered World War I:

> Well, I remember World War I because our class at school went to the Red Cross every Saturday morning and rolled bandages and cotton swabs, made cotton swabs. And once the Blue Devils came. I think they were flyers from France . . . and I knitted them . . . scarves (for the service men).

Yvonne Yost had a significantly less idealistic memory of World War I:

> Well, we were Germans . . . there was a family too with quite a lot of children, who we used to play with before. Then they found out we were Germans, then they said everything about us, you know. Sang songs and just everything, I can remember that. So we weren't allowed to go down and play with them anymore . . . and of course my father had to give up his guns. [Yvonne related an incident which now seems amusing, but indicates the sense of prejudice operant in the community at the time.] . . . Someone gave my father a rabbit. He put the rabbit there [upstairs] until he made a place out in the yard for them, because he had

several rabbits. Then a policeman came to the door and said he had a warrant to search the house. So he came in and he went throughout the house and upstairs he saw this rabbit and he came down laughing. See the rabbit, when it jumps or hops and scratches itself, makes a noise and they [the neighbors] thought we had a machine gun.

Violet Varsity, a nonmother, offered perhaps the most characteristic description of the effect of Word War I upon the majority of these women:

Well, it was rather distant from me. I had no one in it. I remember the other two wars, because I had brothers. . . . Of course I remember events and how interested we were and when the Germans went through France, I can remember that excitement . . . and things like that.

Nonmothers, who were an average of 3.5 years older, made more reference to World War I than did mothers. Seven of 30 (23%) nonmothers had memories about this event, whereas only 6 of the 50 (12%) mothers had such memories. The reports of the impact of the war were similar for both groups. The women remembered the patriotism and community efforts; they also remembered the hardships of rationing, the negative effect on the economy, and the labor market.

World War II

World War II had a much greater impact upon the women in the study. Many of the women had husbands, fiancés, family members, and friends in that war. Iris Inning reported that her family had nine men in the war. Pauline Palmer noted, "Everyone I was in high school with was in it. Everyone." Virginia Vorgue had a husband, brothers, father-in-law, and brothers-in-law all overseas: "It was a scary time." Several of the women entered the military, and many served overseas.

For several of the women, the war coincided with times that they were particularly active in their careers, and the mobilization of the United States for war brought them to the forefront of activity. For some women this activity was time limited; when the war was over, family called, and they returned home. However, for others, it heralded the beginning of new independence or the strengthening of already well-developed careers, having positive effects on their self-esteem.

World War II led to many kinds of life transitions for the women—those involving loss as well as those contributing to career and self-development. Deaths of fiancés and boyfriends caused major changes in the lives of some of the women. Women were pulled into the work force, and, at the end of the war, many were spat back out, as men returned and were given priority for employment. Women and families moved frequently as husbands in the military were transferred across the country. There was not the sense of crusade that had accompanied the American involvement in the first war, but rather a sense of business (Allen, 1952). Those who married shortly before or during World War II moved frequently during their early years of marriage, as the husband was posted to various military bases.

As with World War I, nonmothers more frequently than mothers reported effects of the second world war. Twenty-three (77%) of the 30 nonmothers indicated this war had a significant impact upon their lives, whereas only 22 of the 50 (44%) mothers indicated such impact. The nature of the impact differed for the two groups. The nonmothers reported more influence on society and the work place, probably because more of them were heavily involved in this aspect of life, and less than half (47%) ever married so fewer had husbands in the war. Also many nonmothers held a worldview of life, so that they talked more about the effects of events beyond those occurring to their families. Deloris Davis and Bea Bullock both described a change in the character of the cities in which they lived as people moved into the cities for war-related jobs. Dana Doolittle noted that there was less competition between men and women during this time. Contrary to the work environment of the Depression just a few years earlier, women were now sought as workers, and there were jobs to be had if one wished to work.

For several of these nonmothers the war provided an opportunity to advance or consolidate careers. Avis Arbeit, Josephine Jones, and Gladys Gilbert all increased their commitment to their careers. All three of these women became major influences in their fields of endeavor. Three women reported making the "final break" from their birth families at this time; two of these women joined the armed forces, and one switched her career from nursing (which had been selected by her mother) to photography and art (her true loves).

The examples of the impact of the war reported by the mothers more frequently involved their husbands. Husbands had joined the service and were transferred about the country. The women also moved; for several this was the first time they had truly been away from home. For some this meant that they began to make decisions on their own, for even if the husband was not overseas, he was often out of the home for extended periods. As Virginia Vorgue reported, "It was a pressure time . . . fun . . . exciting." Evelyn Eems reported, "I began to make decisions on my own. He [my husband] found out I could handle it."

Some mothers also noted the impact of the war upon the status of women in American society in that many women worked, and there was no longer the expectation that women would stay home and raise the family. Felicia Fawn stated, "The war had a big effect on everybody. There was this feeling that I'm helping out on this tremendous effort—a feeling of involvement as a group."

Some women enjoyed the extra benefits that came with husbands in the service and availability of war-related jobs and income. Sarah Sanger reported that leaving the military was quite a shock, "We lost all our benefits." Irene Inning also reported postwar problems with income. She and her husband had both been working in war-related industries and were laid off at the end of the war: "We had a lot of bills, and no jobs." Gayle Goodman, a nonmother, also reported that returning from overseas was more difficult than going, "I had changed more than the setting [to which I returned]."

Both groups of women reported the impact the war had upon the labor force. As noted above, many people relocated for war industry jobs in the large cities, changing the nature of the work force. In the rural areas, labor was hard to come by, as farm salaries did not rise as had industrial ones, and able-bodied men were scarce. Wilma Weeks, a ranch wife whose husband had felt it was wrong for a woman to engage in the hard farm labor (tractor driving, etc.) and a woman who was "afraid of chickens," learned quickly to drive the tractor and help her husband bring in the hay crop:

> We had this hay down, oh, so much of it. We had picked up a couple; that's what you did during the war . . . begged them to come work for us. Well, they came and stayed two weeks . . . and on Saturday, they decided they wanted to go to town to get a haircut, and they both were winos, and you know, we never got them back on the ranch. So Monday morning, my husband came in and said, "Wilma, you've got to go to town. I can't put that hay up alone. If you can just get one man that can drive that tractor." . . . I went to town, and I've never been so furious in my life! There was men all over the streets, and they just laughed at me. They said, "We can make more money by accident standing around on the streets than we can going up and working on the ranch." So I got mad, and I went home and told my husband to go out in that big pasture, and put the tractor out there, and leave me alone. And I went out in the pasture and I learned to drive that thing. And then we took our little girl, she was very little, and put a shade over the pickup and made her a playhouse in the

back of the pickup, and Winston and I spent the next couple of weeks stacking that hay. As our daughter grew older it wasn't long until I was on another tractor, bucking that hay in, and she was driving the tractor to pull it. And then it got so that when my husband mowed, my daughter raked. The three of us put our hay up after that.

Both mothers and nonmothers indicated that the war was a maturing experience for them, whether it was because of personal involvement in the conflict, because they were required to make decisions and manage a household on their own, or because of the unsettling situation of never knowing if one's husband, brother, or other relative would be called up or sent overseas. Both groups also spoke of the inconvenience of rationing and gasoline shortages.

Other Wars

None of the women mentioned the Korean war, and only three reflected upon the Vietnam war. Two of these women, both nonmothers, described feeling sad and worried about the men in the Vietnam war. Nancy Newton had two sons in the Vietnam war; she was saddened because one had resultant emotional problems. As with first world war, it seemed that for the majority of women, the Korean and Vietnam wars were removed from them.

THE GREAT DEPRESSION

A variety of publications exist chronicling the effect of the Great Depression upon women (Elder & Liker, 1982; Ware, 1982; Westin, 1976). The impact of the 1929 Depression on the women in our study differed by age at onset of the Depression, whether they were mothers or nonmothers, and whether they lived in rural or urban areas.

Age at Onset of the Depression

Because the women in our study all lived during the Great Depression and because that event had such a profound impact upon the United States, we categorized them by their age at the onset of the Depression. The categories were preadolescent, adolescent, and postadolescent. The ages 13 to 19 inclusive were considered adolescent years. Twenty-five of the women were preadolescent at the onset of the depression, 16 were adolescents, and 39 were postadolescent. All but five of the postadolescent group of women were between the ages of 20 and 33.

Nonmothers were concentrated in the group that were between 20 and 33 years at the onset of the Depression: 60% of the nonmothers were within this age range (3% were older than 33). Only 23% of nonmothers were preadolescent and 13% were adolescents at the onset of the Depression. The group of women who were 20 to 33 years at the onset of the Depression had the highest percent of women who did not marry: 26% compared to 12% of the preadolescents and 6% of the adolescents. Among those women who did marry, women who were adolescents at the onset of the Depression were older than other age groups (mean age 26.3 years) at marriage. The women who were 20 or older at the beginning of the Depression had an average age of 26.2 at marriage, not significantly different from the other group, but slightly younger, and the preadolescent group averaged 24.7 years at marriage.

Among the group of mothers, those women who were adolescents at the beginning of the Depression were the oldest upon birth of the first child, 28.7 years, compared to 24.7 for the postadolescent group and 24.8 for the preadolescent group. The number of children per family also differed between the groups; women who were adolescents at the beginning of the Depression and who were slightly older and had their first child later also had fewer children (mean of 2.0 with a range of 1 to 3 children). The group who were preadolescents at the beginning of the Depression had the most children (mean of 2.72 with a range of 1 to 6). The postadolescent group of women had a mean of 2.55 children with a range of 1 to 6. This pattern of childbearing is in keeping with data presented by McLaughlin et al. (1985) in their report on the life course of women during the twentieth century.

The women's educational levels also differed according to their age at the beginning of the Depression. Fifty-six percent of the preadolescent group had a college or graduate education, and 44% had high school or vocational education. Forty-four percent of the adolescent group had a college or graduate education, and 56% had vocational education or less. Of the postadolescent group, 36% had college or graduate education and 64% had a vocational education or less. These data are contrary to date reported by McLaughlin et al. (1985), who indicate that the educational levels of women were higher prior to World War II, rather than lower as was the case for our women. Those women who were between 13 and 19 years of age at the onset of the Depression had the lowest overall level of educational attainment; only one of this group achieved graduate education, two had less than high school education, and 5 had a high school education.

Nonmothers generally had higher levels of education than did mothers for all three age groups at the beginning of the Depression. This was particularly striking in the postadolescent group; 42% of the nonmothers in this age group had graduate education compared to none of the mothers. In the preadolescent group, 57% of the nonmothers had graduate education compared to 27% of the mothers.

It is likely that the Depression accounted for part of these differences in educational achievement. Women who were adolescents at the onset of the Depression faced pressures to contribute to the support of the family as soon as possible and so entered the work force, such as it was, straight from school. Women in the rural areas also reported pressures to leave school prior to graduation from high school, either to assist with family responsibilities or because there was no money to continue to attend school. These women were developing self-identities and preparing to enter adulthood at a bleak time.

Although the experience, and perhaps even the outlook of the preadolescent group of women was not much better, families learned from the Depression. Ursula Unger described it well, "My father was very serious about our futures, and he had no money, and he was determined that we would be self-sufficient. We had to make it—or I had to make it, I felt." There was more impetus to obtain further education, because of the continued poor prospect for employment out of high school, and so women who were youngest at the onset of the Depression were more likely to continue in the educational track.

The women who were 20 and older at the beginning of the Depression had in large part obtained their education prior to the Depression. Advanced education for women was not an unusual occurrence during their time.

Possible longer range effects of the Depression by participants' age at onset were also studied. In each of the age groups, women's statements were studied to determine whether they could be classified as having achieved integrity, the eighth stage of development defined by Erikson (1959). Women who were considered as having achieved integrity had achieved satisfaction with their successes and disappointments of life and viewed their lives as appropriate and meaningful (Erikson, 1959).

Among the group who were preadolescents at the onset of the Depression, 56% had achieved integrity (50% of the mothers and 71% of the nonmothers); 69% who were adolescents had achieved integrity (75% of the mothers and 50% of the nonmothers). Among those who were postadolescent at the beginning of the Depression, 70% of mothers and 77% of nonmothers had achieved integrity. Because the postadolescent group covered the age span of 20 to 33 years, this group was also examined by three age groups equivalent to the span for the preadolescent and adolescent group. Eighty-three percent of the women who were 20 to 26 years had achieved integrity (78% of the mothers and 86% of the nonmothers); 82% of the women aged 27 to 33 years at onset had achieved integrity (86% of mothers and 75% of nonmothers), and 60% of those who were 34 to 40 years at onset had achieved integrity (100% of mothers and 50% of nonmothers). Thus, mothers who were older at the onset of the Depression were likely to have achieved integrity, but those who were preadolescent at its onset were less likely; the converse was true for nonmothers.

Overall, 66% of the mothers and 77% of nonmothers had achieved integrity at the time of the interview; Mothers in our study were younger, however, and since integrity achievement or wisdom (Erikson, Erikson, & Kionick 1986) seems to come in the later decades, this probably accounts for fewer of the women who were in the preadolescent group having achieved integrity.

Elder and Liker (1982) observed that hardships experienced during the Depression by women as young married adults seemed to have provided learning that fostered their ability to achieve a balance between losses and gains during old age; 86% of the mothers in our study who were 27 to 33 years at the onset of the Depression had achieved integrity. More nonmothers who were 20 to 26 years had achieved integrity (86%) than those in any other age group; more of the nonmothers in this age range also had college and graduate education. Ages 20 to 26 years encompassed the later launching into adult period (which is described in detail in Chapter 4), and it is conjectural whether the nonmothers, more of whom were caretakers for their parents, were enhanced in their ability to care for loved ones and also in their wisdom in later years (Mercer, Nichols, & Doyle, 1988).

Additional Differences Between Mothers and Nonmothers

Qualitatively there was a differential impact of the Depression upon the mothers and the nonmothers. One-half of the nonmothers indicated a significant impact of the Depression upon their lives, as opposed to just two-fifths of the mothers. More nonmothers reported entering the work force early in their lives to contribute to the support of the family. Yvonne Yost, a nonmother, described her situation:

I always kept thinking I wished I had a job to help my mother and father. Always wished for that you know. Then when I did get a job . . . always give them enough money. [Yvonne quit school after the eighth grade and helped care for her sister, then obtained work as a housekeeper, a job that was close to home so she could continue to help out there. She continued in that employment situation until her retirement.]

Bea Bullock, a nonmother, graduated from high school in 1924 not knowing what she wanted to do.

Well, I didn't know what I wanted to do and nothing was said about college. I don't think it occurred to my folks. Most of my friends went away, but they weren't about to let me go away from home. And so I thought, well, I'll be a secretary. There weren't many jobs for women then . . . and I got a job on the *Times* [a newspaper]. Well, in 1929 my folks went bankrupt and lost the house and business and the whole she-bang. And I was making $22.00 a week and my dad went back to wallpapering which he hadn't done since he was a young man. And they were in their 50s and so I said, well, I would take care of them until they got on their feet. Well, they never got on their feet. I was very much in love once, of course couldn't get married. I thought if I married and still had the family [her parents] . . . Well, what do you do . . . I couldn't just walk out on them.

Winona Woods, also a nonmother, had a very negative view of the Depression:

Well, see about that time the Depression came and we lost our home in the Depression and I remember having to move. And I also remember there were more frequent arguments between my mother and father at that time. And my father lost his job, and I remember that and not having as much as we used to. Now, I wouldn't say that was the worst, it got much worse later on, but, I remember, bit by bit. Christmas wasn't elaborate as it used to be because we used to have big Christmases and it got less and less and the tension in the family and concerns in the family. . . . They didn't have time to spend with us and I think as I got older, I can see now that it bothered my father's self-image a great deal. And he withdrew more and more and spent more time away from the family. And he went to other parts of the state to look for work. . . . The 30's are a part of my life that I would like to erase, because you saw the decline of all values. And as it went, you know, we used to have two cars and then we had one and finally we had none. The values you had been taught to maintain went. You didn't talk about money, and religion and politics. Pretty soon all you were talking about was money. . . . Well, then began a series of moves, all in more declining neighborhoods. To rental property and then that got to be too much, to lower 'til soon we were living in what was really a rather bad neighborhood. But we never felt poor, but my mother must have been worried to death. I knew if I didn't have a job I just couldn't go to college.

Winona managed to put herself through high school and college through a special program. She graded papers for 25 cents an hour. Despite her negative experiences during the Depression, Winona felt those experiences affected her marriage in a positive manner:

> I'd say it's been very rewarding. Probably not as exciting as it might be, because both of us came from a background that had suffered during the Depression . . . and we've been financially very successful and we do lots of things together . . . and we both wanted security.

Mothers also felt the impact of the Depression; however, effects were focused more on family relationships than on themselves. Mothers saw more positive effects coming from the experience of the Depression. Beatrice Bowen moved with her husband from Idaho to Salt Lake City to what they considered to be a "better" environment; however, they lost their business in that city and then moved to San Diego where things were supposed to be even "better." Beatrice stated that she was glad her children experienced the Depression: "It had made them appreciate every little thing; it kept the family close." Karen Koff also felt that the experience of the Depression brought people closer together:

> That was about when I was 11, and things were very, very depressed. There just wasn't, nobody had anything, hardly . . . and it made us more friendly and more compatible and kinder to one another, and understanding, and all that sort of thing.

Pauline Palmer described the impact of the Depression and its effects on her family:

> Well, really, being desperately poor was not uncommon because everybody else was too. And of course, my mother's background was to live off the ground and you always could find some way to pick berries on shares or too, we'd get salmon when salmon was in season, and we'd can it. . . . I learned to make bread when I was about 11 years old; we always had a garden and raised our own produce, and bottled it. Sometimes we couldn't afford to buy bottles, but we could always go out to the garbage dump and get old mayonnaise bottles and things like that; as long as they'd

seal we'd get them. [Pauline also spoke of the impact of the jobless state of her father upon her selection of a husband.] It was very important for me to have a husband who was working, because I had growed up with a family where Dad wasn't.

Generally the mothers spoke more of the inconveniences of the Depression, difficulty obtaining staples, working their way through college, and worrying about parents and family. The Depression did not seem to have had the same lifelong impact upon them as it did the nonmothers who had to support their parents and as a result did not feel they could marry.

Rural and Urban Residences

Besides impacting upon mothers and nonmothers differently, the Depression affected rural women differently from those in urban areas. Rural women who lived in the intermountain west (Idaho and Utah) particularly reported more impact of the Depression. These rural women were unable to continue past high school or could not attend the college of their choice because there was not enough money to leave home. Women like Pauline Palmer were able to stay in high school because of government programs. Pauline's selection of a career was based upon government funding and repayment expectations.

The rural women identified government programs having a more direct impact upon them than did the urban women. The urban women talked about the WPA program (part of the New Deal initiated in 1935) that had provided work for their fathers; however, none of them discussed programs that paid for school books or programs that supported higher education, as did the rural women. The rural women spoke more frequently of the general philosophy of employment places not employing married women and the impact that this practice had upon both their mothers and themselves.

More women in the rural group discussed the importance of the church in their early lives. The church was a major source of social activity for them, as well as a source of religious solace.

Although the rural women were more impacted as far as career choice and educational attainment were concerned, many of the women who lived on farms reported little impact of the Depression. Despite the fact that we had study participants from three parts of the country and that the women who participated in the study were a very mobile group, none of the women lived in areas that experienced the severe droughts of the 1930s. Thus, our farm women had adequate food and clothing, although they did admit that times were tight as far as money was concerned. It seemed when the family was able to raise their own food then the need for money was lessened, and so the impact of its scarcity lessened. Rural women also reported seeing the impact of the Depression as people passed by their houses with all their belongings in makeshift cars and wagons; they reported their parents giving food to the homeless.

The women from the rural settings were generally older on entry into the Depression; 54% were over 19 years of age, whereas only 45% of the urban group were that old. Fifty-four percent of the urban group, as opposed to 45% of the rural group, were adolescent or preadolescent upon onset of the Depression. The age factor may have been more important in the impact of the Depression than the environmental factor, as was noted above.

DISCRIMINATION IN WORK AND EDUCATION

Almost all of the women who participated in the study were employed out of the home at one time. Employment patterns followed those noted by McLaughlin et al. (1985), with women with children having a less continuous presence in the labor force than those who had no children. During the course of our study participants' life spans, the attitude towards women in the labor force changed considerably. Several of the women attributed this to the changing labor demands and needs during World War II, as was discussed earlier in this chapter; however, several of the women, both mothers and nonmothers, experienced discrimination in the work setting, a situation that has been documented elsewhere (McLaughlin et al., 1985; Olson, 1985).

A common policy throughout the United States, it seemed, was not to continue employment for married women teachers prior to World War II. The assumptions being, of course, that married women did not need to work, as they had husbands to support them, and that they would soon have children and so would be unable to teach. Wage differentials and working condition differentials were also reported by the women. Bea Bullock described a number of discriminatory situations:

> Well, she [a co-worker who was fired] was married and didn't have to work. . . . It took me 5 or 6 years to get up to the men [comparable salary]. . . . Not only that, I had to stay on a 6-day week when they got

a 5-day week. . . . I worked every holiday for 18 years. . . . And of course, you didn't get overtime; even when the union came in, I had to stay on the 6-day week and get the lower salary.

Winona Woods also experienced several instances of discrimination. She was well on her way to earning a Ph.D. when she married:

> Well, at that time you couldn't very well do some of the things women do now. . . . The prejudice was very great against married women any place, and of course I couldn't be married and go to the [private] University. And the professor up there . . . he thought that it was a very good idea that I quit, because he said, "Winona, you are in a class with all men who are going to get their Ph.D.s at the same time you do, and you won't get a very good job. . . . You're going to be overtrained for the public schools and you're going to have a hard time getting in a university." [Winona then tried to transfer to a local state university.] The Chairman of the Department [in which she would be enrolled] said to me, "I can't keep you out, but I sure as hell can keep you in." Who is going to enter under those terms? . . . And the state university hired two men up here who had been in my class at the [private] University. I was superior to them in every way, and so you had to have a hard time with that. [Winona returned to teaching in the public schools, but was asked to resign at the end of the year.] I says, "Why?" "Well," he says, "You won't want to work if you're married." And I said, "We're not planning on having a family . . ." "Well," he says, "I can't fire you, but I think you'll want to resign."

Winona managed to keep that teaching position and eventually was asked to teach at the university; however, she attributed the offer to more recent affirmative action mandates than an admission of her qualifications: "The guy who asked me to come up and do it said, 'I need a woman.'"

Other discriminations were more subtle as the women reported career choices and life patterns. For many of the women, this was simply how it was. For others, such as Bea Bullock and Winona Woods, discrimination presented a challenge to be overcome in the hope that conditions would be improved for future generations of women.

THE INDUSTRIALIZATION OF THE UNITED STATES

Those of us born during the past four or so decades take for granted the conveniences of the modern industrial world. We accept as standard, in-house toilets, electricity, all of the electric-powered appliances, the telephone, and the automobile, to mention just a few. Many of the women in the study were born into a world before the general availability of these conveniences. The industrialization of the United States was more apparent when talking with women from rural areas. Rural women talked of the change in the community when the railroad came to the valley: the difference in perceptions of distance when automobiles became common and bridges were constructed across rivers to facilitate automobile traffic. Distances of 45 miles became manageable, whereas, in many of our participants' childhood, the rigors of such a journey by horse and buggy made it a major expedition.

The women from the rural settings discussed the coming of modern conveniences as making their lives easier. For example, having indoor plumbing, the time the town obtained a generator for electricity, and other signs of the industrialization of the United States were major landmarks. These rural women also described "skirmishes" with Native Americans.

As the women recounted their lives, we could not help but be struck by the changes in travel. From the days of the horse and buggy and horse-drawn farm equipment, from times when distances that now are short were of major consequences, these women became world travelers. It no longer took a week to cross the Atlantic or a day to traverse 30 miles. They moved back and forth across the world as part of the course of a vacation or business.

CONCLUSIONS

On the whole, the nonmother's lives as they were related to us were more obviously intertwined with social and historical events during their life spans. Events that occurred when the woman was in her early adulthood, a time of great transitional activity, had more profound effects upon the woman. Those women who were in their 20s at the onset of the Depression and the onset of World War II tended to marry later or not at all, had children later, and often were more involved in the work world than were those women who were younger or older at those points in time.

The personal closeness of the event also affected its impact upon the women. As the women reported, World War I, the Korean War, and the Vietnam wars, while major events in the course of the history of the United States, were generally removed from these women as they did not have personal involvement. They were either younger or older during these wars, such that boyfriends and husbands were not drafted. Unlike the times of the Great Depression and World War II, these three wars did not significantly impact upon the choices available to these women. They were generally too young to be affected by shifts in the labor force during World War I, and the limited nature of involvement in the two wars since World War II resulted in little involvement there.

Women noted the changing values and expectations of women; a significant change was attributed to the second world war when women moved into the labor force in great numbers. While many women pulled back out from labor forces after the war, these women felt that the change in attitude continued. There was increased opportunity for women, at least in perception, if not in fact.

The Depression affected the largest number of women, although some of the women felt that the Depression really had very little impact upon their lives. The assessment of the impact of the Depression varied greatly. Some women felt that they were better for having survived those times, as they felt people gained a sense of values, of camaraderie, and of closeness of family. Other women felt it was a time that split families, a time of stress and tension. Women with a worldview saw the consequences of the Depression from a broad social perspective, whereas others related to it in very personal terms, focusing on the impact that event had on them personally; women with a family view focused on the impact on their families.

The span of time covered by the lives of the women we interviewed was great, particularly in terms of societal and technological change. Although the women did not really attribute many of the changes in their lives to these advancements, it was evident that their lives were significantly altered. The decrease in deaths due to infections after the advent of antibiotics, the change in access to hospitalization, and the prognoses for such diseases as appendicitis and cancer were really taken for granted by the women. Yet many had experienced early losses of family members because of the status of medical knowledge.

Changes in modes of transportation were great over these women's life times. Perhaps the mobility of the group as a whole mitigated their viewing this change as dramatic; however, the older women were very influenced by distances, transportation, and weather, particularly those who lived in rural areas. Several of these women became world travelers upon retirement, a situation possible only because of the changing technology of transportation.

The Depression led to significant changes in social policy and social responsibility in the United States. Social security and unemployment insurance were initiated to prevent the recurrence of the large scale and devastating poverty brought about by massive unemployment. These programs have to some extent reduced the financial pressures on children of unemployed parents. Increasing affluence, as well as an increased range of social services, has resulted in the availability of purchasable care for family members (home care, day care, institutional care) again reducing some of the pressures on adult children. It must be noted, however, women remain the major source of caregiving for older parents (Brody, 1981).

It might be conjectured that in the 1990s women choose to postpone marriage and childbearing, or stay single, for reasons other than those of the women we interviewed. Careers for women are more acceptable, expectations for achievement are greater, and there is more emphasis on consumerism, earning, and spending power. There is greater social acceptability of single mothers and lesbian women. At the same time, there continue to be social pressures for women to marry and have children, thus the phenomenon of the "super mom" who attempts to have it all. It seems that in times of economic stress and in an environment with few formal social supports, women were forced to set priorities. Today in a society with a variety of social programs, and with high personal expectations and acquisitional norms, some women do not perceive that they have a choice. Some try to combine marriage, motherhood, and career, whereas others choose to pursue careers and alternate life styles.

Whether the transitions the women experienced would differ with different social and historical times is difficult to know. On the whole, the women who were interviewed experienced similar transitions with the timing varying between groups. The nature of the transitions were not particularly influenced by history, but the choices women faced in adapting to the transitions were.

■ 4
Identifying Common Transitions in Women's Lives

Although commonalities were identified over the developmental course of the women's lives, each woman had led a distinct and unique life. Life histories of these women, who were born as early as 1888, also reflected the history of the United States. One woman was the first white woman born in Native American territory. Another had a great, great, great grandfather who had signed the Declaration of Independence; she proudly shared the historical documents verifying this. One woman had performed for President Franklin Roosevelt and later danced with Sally Rand at a World's Fair. Another woman's grandfather was in jail for illegal cohabitation when her mother was born into a family with two wives and 18 siblings. From such rich and varied backgrounds the search for developmental transitions and age periods at which the majority of the women experienced these transitions was made.

Many of the women had enormous insight into their developmental transitions over their life trajectory, agreeing with Ryff's (1984) observations that adults have a subjective sense of personal change and stability over time. Increasing individuation (achievement of a clearer boundary between self and environment) and autonomy (ability to function independently as well as interdependently), discussed as the underlying developmental thrusts over adulthood in Chapter 1, were evident in most of the women's life histories. Two brief histories are presented to illustrate contrasts in progression in individuation and autonomy over the life course. The first illustrates the process of increasing individuation and autonomy over a lifetime with readily identified incremental periods that culminated in the achievement of integrity during the seventh decade (an acceptance of one's life as overall positive and that it has had meaning and value). The second life history illustrates how the failure to achieve the tasks of adolescence and early adulthood in relation to individuation and autonomy at the expected time handicapped the final achievement level of both, such that a sense of despair was felt in her tenth decade of life.

Following the two case histories, the developmental trajectory for the total sample of women by chronological age is presented, followed by a comparison of women who had experienced motherhood and those who had not. A discussion of three different groups of women with different views of life—world, family and amorphous—concludes the chapter.

AN EXAMPLE OF DEVELOPMENT INTO THE SEVENTH DECADE

Felicia Fawne, a mother, astutely stated, "There are different layers of adulthood." She described having felt different developmental changes, but that she did not feel as if she were an individual until age 67. She had difficulty describing the transition from childhood to adulthood such that the interviewer asked, "Has it occurred yet?"

> Sometimes yes and sometimes no. Not completely, no. I had a very strong feeling of protectiveness and of rapport with my mother, because our personalities were much more alike than my sister's. . . . I guess when I felt an adult the first time was during my apprenticeship [for selected occupation, age 22 to 25]. It was the first time I really felt competent and accepted as myself for my competence. . . . I also made one or two very good friends. They were *my* friends; they weren't anything left over from my parents or sister; they're both still very good friends.
> . . . When I married [age 26] I was sort of transferring my feelings for my father [father had died when she was 17] partly to my husband. There were a lot of similarities between the two. He had been in the Marines and this had been a 99% letters' relationship, so we really had a hell of a lot to learn about each other. . . . We really didn't know each other. I knew he was a decent, serious guy. There was a very strong sexual attraction and I assumed that love was everything. The first few months were very, very hard, and I assumed it was all my attitude. For many, many years, if something's wrong, why it's the wife. And I didn't have anybody to talk to. So I swallowed a lot of it. . . . He was also a very shy person, and then I began to realize that as socially inept as I was that my skills were much more than his—when I saw him not interacting with neighbors or work

colleagues, and not wanting to do things because he didn't know them. That was a real shock, and I realized that I was going to have to be in charge of our social life. I really wanted—I was from that generation who wanted somebody to make everything all right and to take care of you.

[By age 37] More and more I was realizing that a lot of the communication that you dream of when you are starry-eyed with the one wonderful person in the world, that it was never going to come, because he's just not that communicative and really comfortable with intimate feelings. I began to realize it. . . . I had always had strong premenstrual tension and moods, and I recognized that, and we talked about it and I realized my husband did too, and that a lot of my mood swings were that . . . .

Felicia Fawne's lifelong work at individuation did not flow smoothly for her: Her self-esteem was threatened by feelings of inferiority during childhood in relation to an aggressive, older sister whom she saw as more talented and socially sophisticated, and later, she transferred feelings she had for her father to her husband, as well as dependency and an incomplete separation from her father. Her father had died during the peak of her adolescence when a girl typically replays parts of the earlier oedipal conflict from preschool years and gains reassurance of her self as a young woman in interactions with her father that allows her to then turn to a selected mate. It is also possible that her grief over the loss of her father was not completely resolved when she married her husband, who she realized was in part a replacement for her father. Scarf (1980) referred to such lack of resolution as "unfinished business" that is carried over to influence later years and often leads to depression for many women. Felicia, however, experienced a series of transitions along her life course that enabled her to manage her "mood swings," along with an unusually high level of insight to continue to search for her unique self, separate from all others. She individuated from her sister to some extent when she was around 26 to 27 years of age when her sister had married and had children. She was able to see that she had unique characteristics that her sister did not have in relation to dealing with children. Felicia said about her own first child at age 29:

This was real heavenly. It was a very welcomed child. I just had the same sort of feeling that I remember I had when I got my driver's license. This is something I've heard about all my life and I've actually done it. I just enjoyed every minute.

When her second son was 1-year old [she was 35], she was asked to return to an earlier position she had held:

I really needed an ego boost and I didn't go out seeking it, but when I got it, I realized that it was a good thing for me. It made me feel like a human being, although it was only temporary for six months.

Another major turning point occurred for Felicia Fawne at age 50 when her family went to Europe to live for a year:

I felt a little—very isolated at first. It was the first time that I could remember that I just had time to vegetate and do some thinking. I came up with a lot of changes in values and things. For one thing, I was isolated the whole time from American values of what you ought to do. Much less pressure from advertising types of things. I was in a little bit of a limbo to be able to look at myself, and then also to be able to look at the culture I was in. . . . One of the things that came out of that was—everyone that we met was in context with my husband, and then during the course of the year, I realized that some of the people wanted to do something with me as a person.

Felicia had been extremely close to her mother, noting that she had felt guilty when she married and moved to a different city away from her mother at age 26. She said that she did not really separate from her mother until age 53 when her mother died:

She lived with us for 6 months before she died. Again, it was a turning point; we had a lot of good talks, and I saw how accepting she was of death and how ready she was. That made me have a whole different attitude about death.

Josselson (1987) emphasized that during adolescence, separation-individuation requires a revision of daughter-parent relationships that maintains connection, leading to revised rather than abolished relationships. She also described an outstanding characteristic of identity achievers as being able to tolerate guilt and anxiety; Felicia is very much like the identity achievers described by Josselson as feeling guilty upon turning their backs on parents, even slightly.

Felicia had three sons and, although she was somewhat disappointed that she did not have a daughter instead of the third son, said, "They're all great children." She described her older son's getting married as her "getting a daughter-in-law," and this was a turning point in her life. The birth of her first grandchild in her early 60s was described as "super":

I realize that I really do like little kids and I guess I have some of my mothers' way with them, and just let myself indulge. It's [birth of grandchild] probably just a species feeling that you have completed a certain cycle in what you do for your species. And you're home free. You've been the link in the chain and the chain is carrying on. . . . I've talked with so many people who've had this wonderful feeling and they don't know why they felt so good about being a grandparent. I came up with the solution that part of it was instinctive.

Even following her mother's death, Felicia reflects an integrated part of her identity from her mother's "way with children." In Josselson's (1987) study of 60 women aged 20 to 22 years who were college se-niors, she noted that "women never fully separate from their mothers" (p. 190) and that women separate from their mothers by transferring from their mother's influence to their boyfriend's and husband's influ-ence. A communication workshop that Felicia attended precipitated her feeling as if she were a unique individual at age 67. There she gained insight that her interpersonal style and organizational approach to life were different from her husband's; prior to this she felt that she was either a "rattle-brain" or inferior to his style. At age 67, she achieved an identity different and separate from her husband, one in which she could value herself as a unique individual, whose personality style was different, but not inferior. The reconciliation of differences between herself and her older sister also seemed to be well on the way to comple-tion by age 67:

> In looking at it in retrospect, and I've talked to my niece and nephew a lot about my sister and how different we are and how differently we see things and remember things, I realized that it was not only an emotional attachment, but that we really were very compatible in many things.

Thus, Felicia Fawne's work at establishing boundaries between self and others in her environment was accomplished in developmental layers that she could articulate at ages 22 to 25, 26 to 27, 35, 50 to 53, and 67. Her internally motivated age-40 transition had been of much lesser impact (she went back to her professional work after a 5-year period away from it) than her age-50 transition, which began as a result of external factors (the family move to Europe for a year) and continued by the external event, the age-normative transition of her mother's ex-pected death. Age 53 was later than the age range 30 to 40 that Lebe (1982) postulated that women separate completely from their mothers, but Felicia had begun this individuation when she married at age 25. Chodorow (1978) maintained that since the girl's mother is both her primary love object and the person with whom she identifies, women's separation from their mothers is only partial, as Josselson observed, women also experience themselves as more connected to others than men. Felicia saw the differences in ability to initiate and maintain interpersonal relationships between her husband and herself and saw that she would have to assume responsibility for maintaining social relationships early in her marriage.

Felicia's transition at age 67, however, was internally motivated; she sought mechanisms for greater self-understanding and, because of her readiness for this, appeared to integrate her new understanding of self in a way that enabled her to reflect a sense of integrity. One may assume that Felicia will continue her process of individuation the remainder of her life course. The history of a woman in her 90s who described the resolution of conflict with an older sister many years after the sister's death (Painter & Valois, 1985), indicates there is no age limit for such development.

AN EXAMPLE OF FAILURE TO ACHIEVE INCREASING AUTONOMY, IDENTITY, AND INTEGRITY

In contrast, Claudia Call, a 91-year-old mother, did not appear to successfully achieve an identity during adolescence; she was physically separated from her parents early, "I was the first grandchild; grandmother was partial to girls. She claimed me as her own; I spent half my life living with her," and Claudia married at age 19, but she remained under her parents' authority. There was no evidence that she had established clearer-cut boundaries between herself and her family or that she had achieved the psychosocial and economic independence usually achieved during the early 20s. This woman's family had intervened during times of hardship and made decisions for her all during her early and middle adult life, so that rather than having progressed through developmental levels to achieve integrity in old age, she illustrated despair with her life in her inability to be autonomous.

Claudia's family first intervened in her adult life when she was 20, and her grandmother took her first child as she had taken Claudia several years earlier. Claudia's grandmother kept her daughter who was born with a congenital anomaly, until after the daughter's corrective surgery at age 2. Later, when Claudia was 23, her parents visited her, and upon finding evidence that her husband was an alcoholic (she denied any awareness of this prior to their visit), packed her belongings and took her and her two children home to live with them. Claudia's second marriage was precipitated by her 6-year-old son who asked the husband-to-be if he was going to be his Daddy. She stated:

> I was lonesome at that point. But the proposal struck me as funny. But I accepted. I never had a real deep love for either of them [husbands]. I liked the idea of being in love more than them, if you know what I mean. We learned to love each other. Our attachment was genuine after awhile.

At the age of 28, the time of her second marriage, her own words are those that are commonly heard from middle adolescents, "I liked the idea of being in love more than them, if you know what I mean." At age 30, she had her third child, a daughter. Claudia elaborated little about her mother's death, which occurred when Claudia was 33; her mother had had a stroke and was unable to recognize family members for 4 months. However, Claudia had lived with her grandmother "half the time" as a child and adolescent; her grandmother did not die until Claudia was in her 70s and continued to control Claudia much of her adult life.

Her divorce at age 46 from her second husband, who sang in light operas and with whom she traveled around extensively, was manipulated by her grandmother through her uncle without her knowledge. Her uncle informed her husband of 18 years that unless he disappeared from the scene, she would lose her inheritance from her grandmother. The husband left without telling Claudia why he was leaving, and she did not know his reasons for leaving her until many years later. There seemed to be a total lack of communication around critical events; events happened, decisions were made, and there was no attempt to explore why.

During Claudia's 50s, she had a love affair with a married man, "the only man I ever really loved; I felt I was really alive for the first time and really free." This age period is the first indication of emotional separation and autonomy from her family; in addition, this affair was described in a way similar to that which an adolescent would use to describe an intense love relationship. She married her third husband (who was not her married lover) at age 62 and was divorced at age 66 because of different interests. The love affair in her 50s, third marriage, and divorce from her third husband seemed to have been the only major decisions Claudia had made without family interference, but the divorce decision came from her third husband as much as from herself. Over an entire, lengthy life span, this woman never achieved complete autonomy from her family; her grandmother provided money for her support, and, in her later more fragile years, she depended on her younger daughter to manage her affairs. Her attempts at autonomy in her 50s, usually achieved at adolescence, seemed hampered by her lack of decision-making skills, which should have been developed over 30 years earlier. This finding is supportive of the epigenetic principle of development and Erikson's thesis that failure to achieve tasks of earlier periods impedes the achievement of tasks of a later period.

Unfortunately, Claudia Call's psychosocial immaturity and dependence were transferred to her older daughter who was an alcoholic. The older daughter (who had been born with a congenital anomaly and had lived with her grandmother her first year or so of life) at age 71 remained financially and emotionally dependent on her mother. She experienced much conflict in her ability to totally separate or individuate from her mother and was a pleasant companion to her mother when not on an alcoholic binge. Both were living in separate rooms in the same retirement home at the time of the interview.

The control exerted by Claudia's family, particularly her mother and grandmother, appeared to have affected her ability to achieve her own autonomy and independence; in turn her older daughter was never able to break away from her—the pattern was repeated from generation to generation. Her other two children did not escape the effects of the family milieu without lifelong repercussions. Her middle child, a son, apparently had no problem breaking away from the immature mother. The son had attended boarding school during his high school years at his mother's insistence. The son, however, continued to have a nervous tic (deep muscular twitching of the upper torso) under stress throughout adulthood that he had developed as a 6-year-old when his mother made him practice the piano. The third child, a daughter and successful professional woman, had separated from her mother, but with great conflict. Their relationship remained strained according to the mother, and the daughter had a chronic stress-related health problem. Claudia reported that she saw this daughter, who lived an hour's drive from her, monthly.

Adams and Jones (1983) observed that advanced identity achievement among adolescent females was associated with a parenting style that encouraged independent and autonomous behavior and seldom used controlling or regulating behavior. Diffused female adolescents in their study tended to be from homes with controlling and regulating mothers who offered little direction and fathers who, although praising and approving, were unfair in disciplining. Claudia Call spoke little of her father, but her mother and grandmother evidenced an extreme form of controlling and regulating behavior after she was married and had children. Claudia, by Josselson's (1987) definition, evidenced identity diffusion throughout her entire life: Claudia experienced life events without learning or integrating the experiences or changing internally as a result of the experiences. According to Josselson, diffusions separate and individuate too early, and as such fail to internalize enough identity-forming structure from parents to be able to achieve an integrated sense of self or identity; their sense of self fluctuates, with very little of the environment being rejected as "not me." One can only conjecture that Claudia's early physical separation from her parents to spend half of her time with her grandmother contributed to her diffusion. Josselson also raised the question about how diffusion women's children would experience them as mothers. Claudia's life history provided some information about this; however, the children were also influenced by their grandmother and great-grandmother.

The question might be raised about Claudia Call's cognitive abilities, since events precipitating several transitions at various periods of life occurred without her knowledge or her seeming questioning or protest. However, she had a sharp mind, had delved into oil painting during her 60s, and continued to write poetry until her death. She said at the end of the interview, "I absorb my surroundings; poems just come to me— I'm susceptible to beauty and atmosphere." Thus, in a sense she felt merged with her surroundings. How much of this merging was a creative force is unknown.

DEVELOPMENTAL PATTERNS FOR TOTAL SAMPLE BY CHRONOLOGICAL AGE

All 80 women's reported transitions were examined for possible developmental stages by chronological age by summing and grouping them into 5-year periods from age 11 through 80; those reported up to and including 10 years of age and those reported after 80 were grouped as two separate periods. Beginning with the 61 through 65 age period, percentages were based on the number of women at each of the age ranges who were old enough to have experienced transitions.

From early childhood through the age of 15, 28% of all women reported one or more transitions that changed their life's direction. A dramatic shift in the number of developmental transitions followed, however. The middle to late teenage (16–20) and early adult (21–25) years represented the greatest activity in developmental transitions over the entire life course for all women; 81% and 83% reported transitions during these age ranges, respectively. Viewing the life cycle trajectory apart from this major transitional period from 16 through 25 years, four additional developmental peaks were observed for the women overall: age 26 to 30 (68%); age 36 to 40 (58%); age 61 to 65 (62%), and age 76 to 80 (56%). Based on the thematic nature of the transitions occurring for women during these major developmental periods they were classified as follows:

- 16 through 25 years: Launching into Adulthood/Breaking Away
  - 16 through 20 years: Early Launching/Breaking Away
  - 21 through 25 years: Later Launching/Breaking Away
- 26 through 30 years: Age-30 Leveling/Young Versus Old
- 36 through 40 years: Age-40 Liberating/Attachment Versus Separateness
- 61 through 65 years: Regeneration/Redirection
- 76 through 80 years: Age-80 Creativity Versus Destructiveness Period

Levinson et al. (1978) described four bipolar forces that they saw as major forces leading to structural change over the entire life course, but having particular salience at the mid-life transition at 40 years: Young/Old, Destruction/Creation, Masculine/Feminine, and Attachment/Separateness. They maintain that full resolution of these bipolar forces is never accomplished. Erikson (1959) also emphasized the continuity of bipolar forces over eight stages of live in which increasing differentiation occurs over time, noting that each task of each stage is related to all other stages, depends on the proper developmental sequence, and that each major task or developmental challenge of each stage exists in some form before the critical time for its emphasis arrives. Erikson's bipolar tasks and the stage of life at which they have primacy are Trust versus Mistrust during infancy, Autonomy versus Shame and Doubt during toddlerhood, Initiative versus Guilt during preschool age, Industry versus Inferiority during school age, Identity versus Identity Diffusion during adolescence, Intimacy and Distantation versus Self-Absorption during the first stage of adulthood, Generativity versus Stagnation during the middle stage of adulthood, and Integrity versus Despair and Disgust during the third stage of adulthood. Both sets of these bipolar forces were in the back of our minds as we studied the life histories; however, while at times using the same terminology that other researchers have used in order to build on what is known, we have also tried to be true to the unique quality of data we studied.

Launching into Adulthood/Breaking Away

Viewing the clustering of transitional events over the life course of women with their resulting adaptation processes and resolution as development, the major developmental period for women was from middle to late adolescence through early adulthood. There were no changes in the numbers or qualities of transitional events occurring during the age span 16 through 25 indicating this was one period as a unit rather than the two arbitrarily assigned age groupings (16 to 20, and 21 to 25). This prolific and consistent activity toward increasing individuation and autonomy was also an indication of continuity rather than discontinuity from the commonly separated stages—adolescence and early adulthood. Attachment versus separation, identity versus identity diffusion, and intimacy versus self-absorption were dominant polarities in operation during this period. The major driving force was the breaking away from parents and leaving home. Comments reflective of this initial breaking away from the family of origin to get out on one's own were as follows:

- "I knew I wanted to go to college and break out of that environment."
- "The superintendent of nurses told me when I went to nursing school, 'I accepted you because I knew there's a girl that needs to get away from her mother.'"
- "I got out on my own; my mother and father weren't right at my side to tell me what to do and how to do it. That's when I grew up."

The anticipated, socially defined transitions such as graduating from high school, going to college, finishing college or vocational training, going to work, and getting married predominated during these years in which the women were clearly working on their identities, autonomy, and intimate relationships with others. Choices or demands of life situations, however, during these launching years had long-range impact on the rest of the life trajectory.

Gould (1972) also observed a "we-have-to-get-away-from-our-parents" theme from 16 to 18 with a continuation of the theme from 18 to 22 years among psychiatric outpatients and 524 nonpatients. The finding of the tremendous developmental activity during the launching/breaking away years from 15 through 25 is also in agreement with the findings of Levinson et al. (1978) that a major early adult transition occurs during the age range of 17 to 24. Women, however, did not address all of the early adult tasks of establishing a dream for the future, preparing for and beginning a career, and finding a mate and marrying to establish a family (Levinson et al., 1978) during the launching into adult period. The task of forming mentor relationships to facilitate the achievement of other tasks was also less notable and to a much lesser extent than that identified for men. These tasks of early adulthood were approached serially and in different orders by different women, so that some of these tasks were not dealt with until later in life.

Josselson (1987) stated: "The configuration of a woman's identity at the close of adolescence forms the template for her adulthood" (p. 168). She found in her follow-up study of 34 women 12 years after they were college seniors that women who had been characterized as foreclosures, identity achievements, or diffusions tended to remain so. Moratorium women had made individualized choices and moved ahead with creative ways of living that offered surprise and change. The world of these women at early adulthood was the familiar world of their adolescence, indicating the continuity that was observed in our study reported here.

Age-30 Leveling Period

Just as there seems to be consensus regarding the launching into adulthood period, our findings support the age-30 transition as a developmental period. Our observed transition from age 26 to 30 is in agreement with findings of Reinke, Holmes, et al. (1985) in which 78% of the women reported transitions during the 27 to 30 year range, the Levisonian studies of women's adult development (Roberts & Newton, 1987), and with those Levinson et al. (1978) for men.

Although continuity was evident from the turbulent years of early launching to later launching into adulthood, discontinuities became evident in the age-30 period, which was also a quieter period. Although over two-thirds of the women experienced an age-30 transition, the events seemed to be a series of individual occurrences or tasks, rather than patterns of common occurrences across the sample, such as was the case during the launching period with graduation from high school, vocational school, or college, etc.

Marriage, separation, and/or divorce were more common occurrences. Thus, the discontinuity of roles as wife or as single working woman were evident. Intimacy versus self-absorption and attachment versus separation were more dominant polarities at this period.

Age-40 Liberating Period

A departure from the men's developmental patterns that was the most striking was the age-40 transition that occurred for women from 36 to 40 years. Levinson et al. (1978) reported a transitional phase from 36 to 37 to 40 or 41 in which men focused on becoming more senior and expert in their positions toward "Becoming One's Own Man." The reported transitions from ages 36 to 40 for many of these women did not reflect becoming more senior or expert, but reflected their *first* opportunity to reformulate their life's goals and dreams to begin a new career or other focus (although women who were in their 20s in the 1970s might fit more closely to the male model of career development, this due to increasing societal approval of women's employment outside the home). Thus, because of different early choices during the launching into adulthood that reflected both societal pressures and family need, these women worked at some of the early adult tasks during their late 30s that men had worked on during their early 20s. This was dependent upon women's earlier choices and environmental situations and is in agreement with others' findings (Roberts & Newton, 1987; Stewart, 1977). Jones (1988), in writing about the changing seasons of a woman's work life, described the late 30s and early 40s as "a time to be yourself" and the mid-forties as "a time to start over."

Sarah Sanger illustrates the difference we observed in the age-40 transition for women. She graduated from college at age 21 and married at age 23; "Everything I did centered around what he [husband] did." Her first and second daughters were born by the time she was 26, and a third was born at age 31. During this period, the family made many moves due to the husband's transfers. However, at age 36, she decided to go back to college after very satisfying part-time work, "I needed to be my own person." She reported a "wonderful" period of employment following her additional college preparation until the age of 46. Thus, while she "became her own person" to parallel the similar process that occurred for men, this was her initial thrust toward becoming a person apart from wife or mother.

Regeneration/Redirection Period

A period of regeneration and or redirection of one's life occurred during the ages 61 to 65. This period of women's development after initial retirement from a first career reflected a new opportunity in the women's lives for new careers or activities that had been deferred earlier because of lack of time or freedom. There was no sense of retiring to sit in a rocking chair or to disengage from social interactions. Overall, these vibrant, active women pursued many plans and activities. Erikson's bipolar generativity versus stagnation may be more descriptive of this developmental stage in which women pursued second careers, community work, and self-fulfilling activities.

A less satisfying or creativity-inducing transition also occurred for the first time among some of the women. The generativity in care of others was no longer limited toward providing a better world for the younger generation, as described by Erikson, however. The care of others extended to include the older generation and was neither easy nor welcomed. Emma Ewing at age 63 stated:

> The thing in my life now that is the most damaging is care of my mother. She is 95 and lives alone. This is not nearly as pleasureable as taking care of children.

The Young/Old polarity was also operative for many as they dealt with this retirement age for the first time:

> I died at 60; you're the older generation once you reach that age. (Terry Tobias)
> I probably think of myself as young today as when I was 30 years old. I don't feel 62; it doesn't seem possible I am. (Oma Onyx)

Age 80: Creativity Versus Destruction

The final transitional peak observed among the total sample of women was the age-80 transition. This was a time for second or third retirements, illnesses, creative pursuits, and the loss of family members and friends through death. Thirty-four of the women (43% of the sample) were old enough to report transitions during this age range. Because of the extraordinary activity reported by women aged 76 to 80, the age-80 transition may also be viewed as the transition to wisdom for women that were in our study. Their strength and creativity in dealing with life at this stage were outstanding.

From the ages 76 to 80, the majority of the women having reached or lived through this age range faced an enormous developmental challenge. The age-normative ravages of chronic illness and other debilitating physical conditions occurring with increased age were experienced personally and/or by family members. Destructive forces in the bipolar creativity versus destruction were real. However, for many, creativity brought a peaceful calm to this developmental phase of life. Werner (1967) noted that with higher individuation, persons become more creative and less egocentric; this was true for the women's age-80 transition. Deaths of loved ones also mirrored the reality of moving toward the last years of life. In addition to the creativity versus destruction polarity, or perhaps an adaptation to this dominant force, was the polarity of integrity versus despair. The outcome of achievement of integrity is wisdom; "Wisdom is detached concern with life itself, in the face of death itself. It maintains and learns to convey the integrity of experience in spite of the decline of bodily and mental functions" (p. 37, Erikson et al., 1986).

Summary

By studying all women's transitions during arbitrarily established 5-year periods, developmental periods emerged in which the majority of women (over 50%) reported one or more transitional events. The years 16 through 25 were turbulent and active as the women experienced a breaking away from families of origin and a launching into adulthood. The age-30 period ushered in a leveling off of activity as women experienced a variety of transitional events. The age-40 transition was a time of liberating or freeing up time for self to pursue activities that men usually attack during their early 20s. A regeneration/redirection developmental period brought an additional gift of time after retirement to again pursue self-fulfilling activities.

The generativity versus stagnation polarity was central at the regeneration/redirection stage. However, the generativity Erikson described of caring for or contributing to the younger generation takes on a new role in the 1980s; women become caretakers for the older generation as well as for their mates in their own generation. The age-80 transition was characterized by creativity versus destruction; disease and ill health of self and loved ones were major destructive forces. However, self-fulfilling creative activity, which is discussed in greater depth in Chapter 9, brought much satisfaction and a sense of integrity at this age.

An examination of these same 5-year periods by whether women had experienced the mothering role was then done. When this was done, the age-40 period did not hold true for the majority of nonmothers, and the age-80 developmental period did not hold true for the majority of mothers. New developmental periods also emerged for one or the other group of women and are discussed in the next section.

DEVELOPMENTAL PATTERNS OF MOTHERS AND NONMOTHERS

The powerful influence of environmental and historical factors, particularly family situations, became readily evident when differences between mothers and nonmothers were studied. Differences in peak transition periods were also seen when women were separated according to whether or not they had experienced the mothering role.

Although mothers and nonmothers differed by whether a majority (>50%) reported a transition at each of the age periods, there were no significant differences in the percentages reporting transitions at each of the 5-year age periods over adulthood between the two groups (Mercer, Nichols, & Doyle, 1988). The only time period in which differences were significant was from 11 to 15 years.

Early Childhood

Early childhood experiences seemed to set the milieu that was to restrict choices and opportunities for approximately one-third of the women who married and became mothers. (We did not have any unmarried mothers in our sample.) Twice as many mothers (34%) as nonmothers (17%) reported transitions from the age of 4 through 10 years. During early childhood, mothers reported transitional events such as assuming responsibility for younger siblings, death or divorce of parents, family moves, death of other close family members, serious illnesses such as rheumatic fever, living in an orphanage, music lessons, or birth of siblings.

Nonmothers also reported non-normative transitions from ages 7 through 10, but in addition reported somewhat different incidents during this early period such as the day World War I ended, rolling bandages for the Red Cross during World War I, and starting to school. Their teachers' empathetic responses to their wetting their pants and crying led two of the nonmothers to make the decision at age 6 to become teachers. They followed through with this early decision. One nonmother reported that she could not remember an age when she was not responsible for her sisters, "The responsibility was always there."

Puberty and Early Teenage Years

An unexpected finding was the number of traumatic, non-normative life events during the years 11 to 15. Significantly more mothers (36%) reported transitional events during this period than nonmothers (13%). The majority of mothers' early transitional events were traumatic non-normative transitions. Their mothers' serious illness or death, death of siblings or father, family moves, father out of work during the depression years, and father forcing them to quit school were among transitions reported by mothers during this age. Thus, the template for these women's adulthood was laid down in early adolescence.

Nonmothers' transitions during puberty and the early teenage years included illnesses of self, death of sibling, mothers' serious illnesses, poverty of Depression, quitting school, big picnic as a coming-out party, and World War I Armistice celebration. The small number of nonmothers (n = 4) who reported a transition during this age indicates that fewer influences from this age were remembered and, possibly, that more of their life events at this time were positive. Persons tend to remember the more catastrophic events in life. However, development occurs as a result of crises and catastrophes. Riegel (1975) maintains that social development is "founded upon and finds expression in conflicts, disagreements, debates, and dialogues" (p. 101). Terr (1987) has presented arguments to support that trauma during childhood may be reflected later in themes in creative works.

Middle and Late Adolescence: Early Launching into Adulthood

The percentage of mothers (84%) and nonmothers (77%) reporting transitions during the ages 16 through 20 were similar, but the transitional events differed qualitatively. Thirty percent of the mothers married during this 16 to 20 year age period, and one had married at age 15, contrasted to only one nonmother who had married at age 18. Another nonmother reported that her father had refused to let her marry the only man she ever loved when she was 18. Twenty percent of the mothers had a child by the age of 20. Thus, we see a different life trajectory emerging for mothers, more of whom had also experienced catastrophic life transitions during the childhood and early teenage years. Their precocious, earlier development from these earlier events had deprived them of a complete childhood; they assumed adult roles earlier than nonmothers. Or perhaps, they saw marriage as an escape from their early heavy burdens and responsibilities.

Nonmothers described graduation from high school and going to work as transitional events during the early launching into adulthood period. Other transitional events described by nonmothers included getting first car, becoming church organist, obtaining an illegal abortion, mother's death, responsibility to family as oldest girl, travel to Europe, illness of self, family move, and entering college or other training program (nursing or secretarial). With the exception of the large number of mothers reporting marriages and births of children, transitional events were somewhat similar except that no mother reported an illegal abortion.

Ages 21 to 25: Later Launching into Adulthood

The percentage of mothers (82%) and nonmothers (83%) reporting transitional events during the later launching into adulthood period (21 to 25 years) were virtually the same. However, events leading to developmental change were dissimilar.

All but two of the nonmothers had some type of paid employment during these early adult years. This suggests that nonmothers worked on a career trajectory prior to establishing a family, a sequence observed among men during early adulthood (Levinson et al., 1978). In contrast, just over half (58%) of mothers were employed during the ages 21 to 25 years. In many of the teaching positions, women were required to quit teaching upon marrying.

Only one nonmother married during this age period, contrasted to 44% of the group of mothers. Nonmothers married an average of 10 years later than mothers (33 years and 23 years).

We have been talking about a developmental period ranging from 16 to 25 years that indicates the launching into adulthood period. We examined the one event that the women identified as signaling the transition to adulthood, a time of leaving their childhood behind. During the launching into adulthood period (ages 16 to 25), the majority of the women reported these single transitional events after which they no longer were children (54% of mothers and 70% of nonmothers). However, a total of 87% of mothers felt as if they were adults by age 25, with one-third having stated they had made the transition to adulthood by age 15. The earlier non-normative catastrophic transitions experienced by more of the mothers had deprived them of part of their childhood.

Only one (3%) of the nonmothers felt she was an adult by age 15, bringing their total to 73% having achieved adulthood by age 25. This woman could not remember a time free of responsibility for her sisters. Thus, over one-fourth of nonmothers achieved adulthood much later than the group of mothers, from the ages of 26 to 45. The nonmother who reported becoming an adult at age 45 had been born with clubbed feet, and her parents had been highly protective of her all her life. She went to visit in another city and made the decision to make the move to that city, away from family, on her own. This example illustrates how unusual circumstances delay the breaking away from family at the usual age. Overall, the group of nonmothers experienced a longer carefree period of childhood as compared to the group of mothers.

The events women cited as indicating adulthood also differed some-what between mothers and nonmothers. One-third of the mothers described the early, heavy family responsibility in contrast to 13% of nonmothers. Nonmothers tended to describe their first job (37% in contrast to 22%) or graduation from high school (13% contrasted to 4%). Nonmothers did not differ from mothers in citing being independent or marriage (10% of each group in both situations). For 12% of the mothers, the birth of their first child was viewed as the transition to adulthood. The first sexual intercourse was named by 7% of nonmothers; one was 36 when she had her first sexual intercourse and considered herself an adult, and although she said she "loved sex," she never married. Another nonmother stated, "I had my first affair at 25, and that's when I no longer had a mother or father. I felt as though I had shucked them off through having the affair." She married at the age of 41; however, two of her suitors were killed in action during World War II when she was in her 20s.

Age-30 Leveling Period

During the ages 26 to 30, 70% of the mothers and 66% of nonmothers indicated an age-30 transition. This third highest peak of transitional activity by age period represented a leveling off of activity to a more quiet period, and although differences in the percentage of women re-porting transitions at this age period were not so great, different types of transitional events were reported by mothers and nonmothers. Twenty percent of the nonmothers were married during this period, contrasted to only 6% of the mothers. One feisty nonmother who married at age 26 bragged:

> We belonged to the old school, father knows best where women were supposed to be seen and not heard. The only thing is, I didn't promise to obey. But I had that understood before I went to the minister; that was something I had never done, and I wasn't going to start it then.

Later marriages did not assure better decisions or choices, however, One of the nonmothers who married during this time was divorced in her 40s because her husband was a homosexual pedophile; two others were later divorced for other reasons.

One nonmother said she became an adult at age 30 when her hair turned grey. Nonmothers described helping to put younger siblings through college or supporting their parents during the 26 to 30 year age period. One nonmother became a Dean of Women during this time; others went to school to work on masters' or higher degrees.

The majority of mothers reported births of children, illnesses of self or husband, or divorce; others, however, were going back to school, work, or getting involved with community activities. For this latter group of women, family situations for the first time were such that they could focus on activities for self-development.

Age 31 to 35 Years

The majority of nonmothers (57%) reported transitions from ages 31 to 35, contrasted to 40% of the mothers. Parental illnesses and deaths, marriage, graduate school, winning a lottery, World War II events, and moves were the transitional events reported among nonmothers.

Mothers largely reported births of children; moves; husband's, children's and self illnesses; community activities; second marriages; and parental deaths. Husbands' moves were difficult for many of the women who had to search for new friends and a new support network.

Age-40 Liberating Period

This period from age 36 to 40 had been identified as a developmental period for the majority of all women. However, when groups were examined according to experience of the motherhood role, it was the mothers (64%) who were in the majority; less than half (47%) of nonmothers reported an age-40 transition.

Thus, this developmental period was more liberating for mothers who had married earlier and had begun childbearing at an early age before nonmothers even reported a transition to adulthood. The types of transitional events reported by mothers included career changes or returning to school, although the majority were child-related (births, graduation from high school, marriage, illnesses). Levinson et al. (1978) observed that part of the settling down process for men involved the bipolar conflict of young/old: the struggle to fulfill older adult values of society, while the boy in them wanted to attain goals without the necessary work. Mothers did not seem to question the difficulty in work toward early life dreams; they showed no evidence of the childlike magical dream of power to achieve any goal without hard work that Levinson et al. observed in men. The mothers' earlier formative years that were remembered by the non-normative transitional events were harsh in their reality and had deprived many of them of early creative activity of such dreams of childhood.

Among nonmothers, marriage, graduate education, and career change were predominant transitions during 36 to 40 years. Thus, they were becoming more senior and more expert in their career roles toward becoming their own person, analagous to men's developmental trajectory (Levinson et al., 1978).

The 40s

The years 41 to 45 were more quiescent, with less than half of the women experiencing transitions and with virtually no difference between mothers (48%) and nonmothers (47%) reporting transitions. One-half of the nonmothers and 46% of the mothers reported a transitional event during ages 46 to 50.

During the 40s, moves, career change, graduate education, parental deaths, illnesses of self, accidents, birth of niece, love affairs, and marriages were major transitional events reported by nonmothers. Mothers reported being widowed, being divorced, parental deaths, child-related transitions (illnesses, marriages, deaths), self illnesses, moves, buying homes, beginning a business, nervous breakdown, trips, creative writing, marriage, farmer's depression, house burned down, graduate education, and career change.

The 50s

From ages 51 through 55, only one-third of the nonmothers reported a transition, in contrast to half of the mothers. The transitional events that contributed to more mothers experiencing a transition at this time seemed to be child-related (children's marriages, becoming a grandmother). In addition, fewer nonmothers reported job changes.

From 56 to 60 years, 43% of nonmothers and 46% of mothers reported a transition, indicating that most of the women did not experience this time as a major developmental period. Other researchers have reported the 50s as a peaceful and satisfying period (Black & Hill, 1984; Reinke, 1985).

However, Scarf (1980) reminds us that women's middle years revive unresolved and unsettled issues of adolescence; Claudia Call's history presented at the beginning of the chapter illustrates this. Scarf goes on to discuss how women face the problem of creating their own identity far later in life than most men and that changes required of women in their 50s have far greater repercussions than those required for men. Women's role changes that occur present many more discontinuities than for men.

Regeneration/Redirection Period

Retirement of self and/or husband were major transitional events during the ages 61 to 65 years when 57% of nonmothers and 65% of mothers reported transitions. Deaths of friends and family members along with illness of self and family members were also age-normative transitions that predominated during this period for all women. For some, death of a loved one was a welcomed relief: "It was horrifying to care for him [husband] in addition to working, so his death and widowhood were no problem; I felt relieved" (Queenie Quincy).

Many nonmothers began new careers in their early 60s: opened an art gallery to display her art at 61, began a day camp for children at age 63, and switched from teacher to librarian at 65. One nonmother was so depressed that she planned her suicide, but was prevented by a friend who came and saved her. Another was very lonely and said, "When I turned 65, I really started thinking what will it be like to get old?"

Overall, the destruction/creativity bipolar conflict described by Levinson et al. (1978) as peaking at the age-40 mid-life transition for men seemed predominant during this later regeneration/redirection transitional phase for women. Death had become real, and with less time left, there was an increase in creative activities.

Age-70 Transition

The majority of the nonmothers (56%) reported a transitional event between ages 66 to 70, contrasted to 42% of the mothers. Therefore, the age-70 transition was more of a developmental period for nonmothers.

Four nonmothers retired during this age period, while one assumed an Associate Deanship at a large university. Three went to Europe, and two moved to retirement centers to live. One 67-year-old nonmother observed, "Society is not supportive of aging women. . . . So you don't look in mirrors very much."

Husbands' deaths were the major transition reported by mothers during this age period. Two mothers described group activities that were instrumental in their development and growth, one mother did substitute teaching during this time, two engaged in extensive travel, and one experienced the tragedy of her home burning down.

The 70s

From 71 to 75 years, 38% of the nonmothers and 35% of the mothers reported largely age-normative transitions. Nonmothers traveled to Europe, had a stroke/broke a hip, bought and decorated a home, moved to retirement homes (n = 3), and gave up her car (n = 1). Mothers reported deaths of husbands, world travel, creative writing, and movement to a retirement home (n = 1 each).

Age 80: Creativity Versus Destruction

The age-80 transition observed for the total group was more applicable to nonmothers when the two groups were looked at separately. Two-thirds of nonmothers and 44% of mothers reported transitional events from 76 to 80 years.

One nonmother retired from a third career at age 80, but remained extremely active. She was treasurer of a retirement organization and a member of an appointed committee to deal with problems of aging. She was one of the active initiators who had a worldview of life. This woman who had successfully negotiated the professional career world and who continued to be active in her societal accomplishments was no doubt influenced by her worldview and clear-cut identity achievement over her life course. Another nonmother was a lay reader at church and responsible for publishing the weekly church bulletin; she also traveled extensively. She also could be classified as having a worldview of life. Other women had more of a family view and, in fact, said they were family oriented. Women who had a family view of life reported largely transitional events related to family members; their world centered around what happened within the family. Their lives, in fact, centered around caring for family members.

A very creative mother was teaching violin lessons at age 76, attending a creative writing class, and was publishing short stories and poetry. Chronic illness took its toll, as mothers also reported having a stroke or having multiple sclerosis verified. Another mother's husband committed suicide when she was 77, and the events surrounding the suicide indicated he had intended to kill her also. Thus, destructiveness/creativity was manifest even greater at the age-80 transition.

Age 81 and Older

Just over one-third (38%) of nonmothers and half (56%) of mothers who were 81 and older reported transitional events. In reflecting about their lives, there was evidence of achievement of integrity for all but one (Claudia Call, whose history was presented earlier). One 81-year-old nonmother indicated that she had just recently achieved integrity:

> I've wondered and wondered why I didn't find somebody to love me that I loved and have a family, and the answer has just come to me lately. That my goal was to be who I am and to teach school. And the lives that I have had under my care. . . . I've realized that clothes, men, and things aren't the most important. Now, living on my own, an independent life is much richer and more meaningful.

This woman had married and divorced at age 37 because her husband was impotent. She had a married lover during her 40s, and when she was 47 the lover died. She described going down the street crying, "Thank God, it's over; If I can't have him, no one else can." Serious surgery at age 78 probably precipitated her achievement of integrity; she described having made peace with God at that time.

Other nonmothers described pursuing worldviews through reading, including history and philosophy. Poor health, including chronic illnesses and hip fractures, made up other transitional events for all women. A mother had had a book published at 87 (she paid to have it published) and was bright and alert at 95. A 94-year-old mother's reflections indicated her integrity:

> We were happy where we lived. That's my philosophy of life. We stayed close together during the Depression. I'm really glad the children went through that because now they appreciate every little thing.

This woman proudly told us that she had 12 grandchildren, 28 great-grandchildren, and 4 great-great-grandchildren. Her husband had died when she was 81.

ACHIEVEMENT OF INTEGRITY

The eighth stage of development defined by Erikson (1968) is the struggle to balance one's sense of integrity with earlier disappointments in life. The person who has achieved integrity has adapted "to the triumphs and disappointments of being"; integrity is "the acceptance of one's one and only life cycle and of the people who have become significant to it as something that had to be" (p. 139).

Using this definition, we categorized the women according to their achievement of integrity or despair. Integrity was reflected by statements such as, "I had a good life. . . . I loved my music, the church, and my teaching. . . . I really felt I was helping," and "Looking back, I think my life has been a happy life. I try to be optimistic and look forward to better things." Despair was reflected by statements such as, "I've had a hard life; always a hand-to-mouth existence," and "I don't have this happiness inside me now. . . . I resent all those things."

Overall, 70% of the women had achieved integrity at the time of the interviews: 66% of the mothers and 77% of the nonmothers. When nonmothers were divided by marital status, an unexpected finding emerged: 86% of the never-married nonmothers had achieved integrity, in contrast to 69% of the married nonmothers. Thus, the wife role appears to be related to the achievement of integrity more so than the mother role; the percentage of married nonmothers who achieved integrity is similar to the married mothers. Women who marry may remain dependent in part on their husbands for their identity and as a means of achieving their goals and satisfactions in life (Mercer, Nichols, & Doyle, 1988).

Among the total sample, 16% reflected a sense of despair; we were unable to categorize 13%. One mother was vacillating between integrity and despair. However, based on the achievement of the task of the final stage of the life course, the wife role appeared to have a much greater influence than the mother role.

PREPARATION FOR DEATH

Achievement of integrity by finally resolving any conflict about the worth of their lives and preparation for death was a parallel developmental process that was observed. Women who were 81 or older almost always made some reference about readiness for death. Agnes Amherst's comments illustrate this. She was an 81-year-old nonmother:

I feel like I am sitting, waiting to die. I had a vision of a beautiful woman in white who made me feel so peaceful, so I am looking forward to death. I hope they soon find me dead. I have no fear of death. . . . On my 80th birthday, they had a special mass for me; 62 people were invited to a special dinner.

Bea Bullock, nonmother, elaborates:

My friend and I discuss death because time is running out—not in a morose way, but because time is running out as a reality and you don't feel as well. . . . I like myself. I did what had to be done . . .

WOMEN BY THEIR VIEW OF AND APPROACH TO LIFE

After rereading all of the life histories many times, there seemed to be three somewhat dissimilar groups of women. One group of women never questioned their autonomy in controlling their lives. These women had a worldview of life, as opposed to a more narrowly constricted family view that was held by many. Women who held a worldview had internal drives that propelled them onward in pursuing school or changing jobs: "I wanted more control over my life, and I felt what should be done." This extraordinary sense of independence was gained early in life through family relationships and values, and in large part from their fathers:

- "Education was a significant value in our family; my father was always the principal of the school I attended. . . . I had a broad view of the world, which I had begun by my father."
- "Like my dad told me, 'You have to work your way to get there sister, and if you get an education you will have earned it.' Hell, I got mine by trial and error."

This group of more internally controlled, assertive women were "movers and shakers" and were like the active initiators described by Evers (1985); they could be classified as identity achievements during their launching into adulthood stage and remained so during their life course.

A second group of women went through a series of employment experiences, and their self-reflections and transitions were precipitated as much by others as by internal forces. For this group, an optimistic versus a pessimistic view of life seemed important to their ultimate level of development. They neither had the vim and verve of the assertive worldview group, nor were they as passive as the third group, whose development seemed to be spurred on by a series of environmental situations. This second group held a more family view, and their life commitments reflected this family orientation. Those who were more optimistic withstood many traumatic family tragedies, including severe illnesses, deaths, and great disappointments in children; their optimism nevertheless prevailed, and their family network supported their endeavors:

- "So I'm secure and enjoying these years very much."
- "I've always maintained a lively interest in sports, music, and reading. I enjoy . . ."
- "I've been pretty happy in spite of awful marriages. Dad said if I burned my butt, I'd sit on the blister [regarding her marriage at 18]."
- "I've always had good times; I've never really had bad times."

This group reminded us of Fern from Josselson's (1987) study, who had a foreclosed identity and who Josselson noted could not be prodded to talk about life outside of her family and religion.

A third group of women appeared to live their lives in response to situations with no inner force operative; they held an amorphous view of life (formless, vague, no regular structure). They had characteristics similar to the passive responders described by Evers (1985) and to the identity diffusion group described by Josselson (1987). As was the situation among passive responders in Evers' sample, some of the women in our study whose development progressed by these external forces had been involved (or trapped) in caregiving through much of their life. Many began caregiving for the older generation during their launching into adulthood period. Examples of their summaries of their life course are as follows:

- "I think I just had my own course and I followed it. . . . I suppose I've been fortunate in a way that I have been able to do that."
- "I've had a blah life. . . . Life has all blended together."
- "I find there's a change in my life every 10 years. . . . I didn't feel picked on. I always felt I had things just as good as anyone else. [At 62, she has many financial problems, is a widow, and describes herself as in 'limbo.']"

Although the diffusion group of women Josselson studied reported satisfaction with their lives, those with gratifying commitments had allowed another person to take over for them.

MARRIED NONMOTHERS' DESIRES
REGARDING MOTHERHOOD

We were interested in reasons for the married nonmothers foregoing motherhood. Their later age at marriage was a factor for some of the nonmothers in not becoming mothers. Some indicated that they would have liked children, for example, Edna Ebert:

> Now I wish I had had children. . . . Everyone else has children to comfort them. But I've seen so many things I wouldn't have if I had children.

Others who did not desire children:

> I had to do a lot of pinch hitting for two families when they were having all those children. Enough so that I made up my mind that I didn't want any. (Florence Filbert)
> It wasn't my lot in life [a child] . . . But God almighty knew I would never make a good mother I guess. (Kathryn Kane)
> I'm really happy I never had children; never wanted any; and never used birth control. (Queenie Quincy)
> I just never had that desire [to have children]. (Ruth Rogers)
> I have an obsession against having a baby. [See Chapter 5.] (Eve Edwards)

While the nonmothers recognized that they may have missed something by not being mothers, this had been reconciled by validating their achievement of integrity. They reviewed the facts in a philosophical way or chose to rationalize the role of motherhood as coming from a higher power who knew they should not be mothers.

MARRIED AND NEVER-MARRIED NONMOTHERS

Of the 30 nonmothers, almost half (n = 14; 47%) never married. We turned first to their families for possible differences. The first, major difference was the woman's ordinal position among siblings. All never-married women were either the oldest child, only child, or the oldest daughter. The women in this position in their families were most frequently responsible for care of one or both parents during their 20s and 30s, the more opportune times for marriage. The one never-married nonmother who could not remember a childhood without responsibility for her sisters (Amy Andrews) felt this responsibility until the sisters all had a college education. During the Depression, her father had lost his job and she contributed to their support until both parents died when she was 45 to 49 years old. Inez Inkles noted, "I was going to be married just at the time my father took sick, and then my mother took sick, and things just didn't work out."

A second never-married woman's (Deloris Davis) father died when she was 21, and she was sole wage earner for her mother and two siblings. Laverne Lewis fell in love with a married man during World War II and never was so profoundly in love again. Another never-married woman's (Ruth Rogers) mother died when she was 18, and she became "lady of the house." She cried when she told about her father's death some 35 years prior to the interview, indicating that while she had been a very productive active initiator with a worldview, she had not resolved her grief following her father's death or completely separated from her father.

Violet Varsity had responsibility for her mother after her father died when she was 38. Her brothers were in the Army during World War II, and she said, "I had responsibility for taking care of her. It was a responsibility as well as a pleasure." Her mother died when she was 47; however, in her 60s, she was also helping to care for a very ill sister. World War II also played a role in Dana Doolittle never marrying; her fiancé was killed during that time. Sally Salmon noted that the man she would have married died when she was 21.

Agnes Amherst was "afraid of boys" when she was 18. Her father was out of work when she was 25 (during the Depression), and she was the "only wage earner for awhile." Pamela Parsons never cared much for men, but "the married ones always liked me." Bea Bullock also was a major earner for the family at age 22 when her family lost their home. Her father died when she was 41, and her mother died when she was 61. Bea was philosophical about her unmarried state:

> By the time you get 35 there aren't too many people to date. They're all married, and your married friends don't want you around. The men don't mind, but the women don't want you around. . . . I like myself; I did what had to be done, and I don't think I griped about it. And I'm not sorry. I don't think I missed anything. If I'd have had children, they'd probably have been brats. If I had a husband, he'd probably beat me every Saturday night.

Thus, we see that the woman's gender and birth order led to her becoming caretaker for her family when outside forces—the historical event of the Depression—intervened. In addition, another historical event influenced the marriage decision when a fiancé was killed during World War II. Josselson (1987) reported that women at age 32 to 34 who had not married were more sharply defined and had explored their selves more extensively than those who had married. Lutes (1981) found in her study of married and single college students that married students were more likely to be identity foreclosed than identity achieved.

SUMMARY

Developmental periods were identified over the life trajectory of women, with differences observed for mothers and nonmothers. Nonmothers' life course trajectory was similar to men's trajectories as identified by Levinson et al. (1978) in some ways, yet strong social biases were evident. Nonmothers who married, married later in life, but many seemed predestined to never marry because of their gender and birth order. The older daughter, only child, or only daughter had the responsibility of helping parents during the launching into adulthood and age-30 leveling periods. None of these women reported their brothers as ever assuming financial or physical support of parents during the early adulthood years! History-graded influences such as the 1929 Depression and World War II interacted with family constellation to place women into adult caretaking roles; however, it is curious that women did not tell about their brothers contributing money for parental support over the years. It is of interest that 86% of nonmothers who were 20 to 26 years old at the onset of the Depression had achieved integrity. Nine out of 14 (64%) of these women were also never married.

The unmarried status and being 20 to 26 years old at the onset of the Depression were more strongly associated with the achievement of integrity than was the mothering role. The percentage of married nonmothers and mothers (all of whom were married) who had achieved integrity were similar (69% and 66%), contrasted to the never-married group of women (86%) who had achieved integrity.

The family milieu was the strongest influence on directions that all women's life course would go. Early tragic non-normative events deprived mothers more so than nonmothers of an early childhood, predestined some into early adult roles, and, in fact, appeared to influence much of their life course. Early within the family and from their fathers' influence, the women tended to gain a worldview as opposed to a family view, which may have also operated as an internal motivator to take control over their own lives. Those women who clearly had a worldview and felt in control of their lives were the active initiators who were social leaders in addition to directing their own lives.

Transitional periods are pivotal developmental periods in which persons are more open to intervention or help to facilitate their adaptation and development. The launching into adulthood period ages 16 through 25, the age-30 leveling period, the age-40 liberating period, the regeneration/redirection period, and the age-80 creativity versus destructiveness period seem to be critical periods in the life course of women. Interventions during transitions are critical because of the potential long-range positive effects of minimal help given at the period of need.

■ 5
The Awesome Mother: Her Influence on Her Daughter

When we began to study life histories of women, we were concerned with the impact on women of the motherhood role. What became evident was the impact of the women's mothers on their lives; they talked more about the mothering they had received than the mothering they had done. These mothers were awesome: on the part of the daughter, there was either a great deal of admiration or outright rejection of their mothers. Mingled with this admiration or rejection was an underlying fear—fear that they would not measure up to their mothers or fear that they would be like their mothers. Nonmothers also had much to say about their mothers; in one situation it was evident that the mother's repulsion toward sex and childbirth contributed to the daughter's decision to never have children:

[Eve Edward's father had committed suicide when she was 2, and her mother never remarried.] She always said she could take care of one, but she would never marry and run a chance of having more children because she didn't like sex and she knew she could make a living for one but she wouldn't take a chance again. . . . There wasn't anything that I could do as a child or as an adult that pleased her. I knew that all my life.
      . . . There was a lot of conflict in the family; I had an aunt who had a no-count husband, and she had a little girl 6 months older than me. If they were shut out of their house, Grandma would take her in and use my mother's money and my clothes for them . . . So my mother just took me out of school and to a boarding school, and it was $16.00 a month. And I

was the only baby in the boarding school . . . I cried at nights. . . . I
left and went back home for awhile when I had diptheria and scarlet fever
around Thanksgiving, and they couldn't keep me at school . . . I had
convulsions.

   . . . Mother didn't die until I was 53. I had her as a responsibility from
the time I was in my 30s. . . . I was very depressed at 56 and planned
my suicide, but a friend saved me.

   . . . I have an obsession against having a baby. And I've had lots of
affairs with men, but I never loved any man enough and anybody that I
thought that I loved, I never loved him well enough that I'd be bothered
having a young one. I thought the awfullest thing in the world was to have
a young one. . . . I've had people say to me, "Were you an unwanted
child?" And I can remember saying, "Well, my mother said if she'd have
known she was going to have a baby she wouldn't have got married." He
promised her they would not have any children. And they were married in
April, and I was born in January of the next year. And my mother was so
ashamed of her looks that when she'd go through the house, she'd put her
apron up over the dresser mirror so she couldn't see herself. And if she
had to go to the grocer, she'd go at night . . . She told my dad when I
was born that she didn't get enough fun out of having one so that she'd
never have the second one.

Thus, Eve Edwards is an example of how the mother–daughter relationship may determine the daughter's reproductive experiences—in this
situation, the decision to not have a child. Uddenberg (1974) found that
mother–daughter conflict contributed to conflict around reproductive
factors. Others have also observed that conflict stemming from women's
rejection of their mothers as adequate role models led to conflict in
assuming the mothering role and to depression. As a teenager and young
woman, Eve Edwards did a lot of acting out and almost lost her job at
age 19 for going to bootlegging joints where they sold illegal liquor
(during Prohibition); she had flunked out of school seven times.

   The question was raised whether there were differences between
mothers and nonmothers in their mother–daughter experiences. This
seems particularly relevant since motherhood is considered a stage in
adult development (Schectman, 1980). Benedek (1970) reminded us
that "parenthood as psychobiologic process ends only with the death
of the parent" (p. 185); thus, transactional processes between parent
and child lead to developmental change within each (parent and child)
over the life cycle. The daughter as a mother has conscious and unconscious memories of her experiences of being mothered, which she
relives with her own child (Benedek, 1959). Reidentification with
one's own mother occurs as the daughter notices that her behaviors

with her child are reminiscent of her mother's behaviors with her (Schectman, 1980).

Ballou (1978a, 1978b) observed a process of women's reconciliation with their mothers occurring over the course of pregnancy. The mother is viewed increasingly as someone good and giving over the course of pregnancy, and pregnant women come to view their childhood as good; if the woman has many ambivalent feelings about her mother, this process is more difficult. Ballou (1978a) also noted that for most of the women becoming a mother was synonymous with adulthood and adult competency. Adult competency and resolving childhood conflicts and gripes also represented adult rights with adult privileges, with their mothers displaced from a position of "maternal authority to one of benign motherhood" (p. 404, Ballou, 1978a).

DEVELOPMENT AND REPERCUSSIONS OF THE MOTHER-DAUGHTER RELATIONSHIP

Daughters do not have to break away from early identification with their mothers as do men. This lack of early differentiation from their mothers leads to a diffuseness of boundary between self and mother, and, according to Chodorow (1978), this diffuseness continues throughout a woman's life. Women, according to Chodorow, reproduce their mothers' mothering, because their psychological capabilities for mothering develop through their ongoing intense relationship with their mothers.

Over the life course, psychological development of individuals continues through internalizations of facets of relationships with others that are significant to them. Internalization leads to increased separation-individuation and indicates a developmental resolution of the polarity between longing for greater intimacy versus striving for greater autonomy and mastery (Behrends & Blatt, 1985). Separation refers to the psychological process of differentiation, the distinguishing of self from another person (Blos, 1985). Individuation refers to the complementary and closely related process of consolidation and integration within a newly differentiated person (Blos, 1985). Behrends and Blatt define internalization as a process in which persons recover lost or disrupted, regulatory, gratifying interactions with others by making facets of those interactions a part of their own enduring functions and characteristics. Internalizations occur at progressively more complex levels over the life cycle, with psychological development the result of the steps of repetition of gratifying involvement and experienced

incompatibility. Experienced incompatibility means that an earlier established relationship no longer meets the needs of one of the participants; gratifying indicates only that the relationship meets basic needs
but is not necessarily healthy, pleasureable, or satisfying (Behrends &
Blatt, 1985).

Daughters identify with their mothers from infancy, and, when they
become mothers themselves, their earlier identifications with their
mothers precipitate the emergence of unresolved individuation issues
(Blos, 1985). Reproductive attitudes and problems apparently are unconsciously transmitted from mother to daughter, as was the case with Eve
Edwards. Daughters of reproductively maladjusted mothers were observed to have a higher incidence of obstetric complications and either
longer or shorter childbirth experiences than daughters of well-adjusted
mothers (Uddenberg, 1974). Among another group of women, prolonged
labor due to inefficient uterine activity was associated with a poor relationship with their mothers (Kapp, Hornstein, & Graham, 1963). Others
reported that mother–daughter conflicts were related to prolonged labor
and slow cervical dilatation (Uddenberg, Fagerstrom, & Hakanson-
Zaunders, 1976). These findings support Deutsch's (1945) warning that
a woman's refusal to identify with her mother may weaken her capacity
for mothering.

The motherhood role is developmental from the perspective of providing an opportunity of reworking mother–daughter relationships to establish clearer boundaries between mother and self. One of the major tasks
of pregnancy is the woman's resolution of mother–daughter conflicts and
the establishment of a clearer sense of autonomy and differentiation from
her mother so that it is possible for her to move to a peer relationship with
her mother (Bibring, Dwyer, Huntington, & Valenstein, 1961). Ballou
(1978b) observed that women who resolved dependency conflicts with
their mothers could allow themselves to be dependent on their mothers
during pregnancy and childbirth; they were also able to then accept their
infants' dependency.

Fischer (1981) found that when daughters became mothers, the
mother–daughter pair reevaluated each other and each became more
involved in the other's life as each redefined and renegotiated their new
relationship. Fischer suggested that although the developmental stake
of the daughter was to break away from her mother during adolescence,
the developmental stakes of mothers and daughters are more convergent
following the daughter becoming a mother than at any other period
in the life cycle. Developmental stake refers to both individual and
relationship development, including current personal needs of lineage

members and the history of the relationship (Thompson & Walker, 1984). Thompson and Walker (1984) studied student women, their mothers, and their grandmothers. Among mothers and grandmothers, grandmothers reported greater attachment to their daughters; however, attachment scores were higher when general aid to each other was similar. Younger mother–daughter pairs viewed attachment to the other similarly when the relationship for general aid was reciprocal; however, in nonreciprocal relationships, the dependent partner was less attached to the partner giving more general aid.

We still lack a coherent knowledge base about adult mother–daughter relationships, but we know even less about women who do not opt for the motherhood role. Are nonmothers' relationships with their mothers different, and if so, how are they different? Differences were found both in the family situation of overall need and in selection of mothers as role models; the mother–daughter relationship appeared to affect the selection of career trajectory or motherhood trajectory during the breaking away/launching phase of their development.

MOTHERS AS ROLE MODELS

Only 10% (n = 3) of the nonmothers said their mothers were a role model or mentor for them. Of these three, all listed another person in addition to their mothers. In contrast, 35% (n = 13) of the mothers for whom we had this information named their mothers as a role model. Over half of the mothers (n = 7) listing their mothers as role models also named another person. Grandmothers were role models for six (12%) of the mothers.

Among women who did not list their mothers as a role model, it was evident that for many, their mothers were negative role models, for example, they elected to be unlike their mothers; the women had not consciously named their mothers as role-models, but they had rejected their mothers as someone they wished to be like.

Jackson (1984) studied the self-esteem of 12 persons from a life history perspective, using the constructs ideology, idealization, and central conflict to show how self-esteem functioned in the resolution of dilemmas in each respondent's history. Ideology was defined as the individuals' general conceptions of beliefs and ideals about their social world and their place in it. Idealizations were memories in which an important person in the individual's life history served as an "exemplar of some particular ideal in action" (p. 40), and a central conflict was defined as "a set of

memories and concepts in which an individual expresses painfully con-
tradictory themes" (p. 45, Jackson, 1984). The individual's self-esteem
evolves as resolution of the central conflict or problems in specific situations occurs. Sholomakas and Axelrod (1986) found that women's self-
esteem and role satisfaction were enhanced when their relationships with
their mothers were perceived as loving and accepting.

In our research, examples of the women's mothers as idealizations and
as central conflicts were evident. Women's idealizations of mothers as
positive role models will be discussed, and then these will be followed
by discussion of situations in which there was central conflict between
mothers and daughters, for example, mothers as negative role models.

Positive Role Models: Mothers as Idealizations

Joyce Jenkins. The first example of the mother's powerful, positive
influence resulted in a well-adjusted daughter who had also had a well-
adjusted family:

> My mother was home of course, but she, I guess, was the most influential
> role model. However, I did look up to my sisters and to my aunts a great
> deal. Our activities were around the home. Having big dinners and having
> people in on the weekend was much of our social activity. And I especially
> used to like to have people with children.
>   . . . I didn't feel so sorry for myself [at age 11, when her father died];
> I felt sorry for my mother. I can always remember this, and I watched her
> to see how it would affect her although I felt terrible, but I felt for her,
> just terrible. . . . So any little thing I could do to earn money, I'd always
> give half to my mother. I always felt sorry for her, and, of course, she was
> at middle age; she was not able to go out and get a job. It was almost
> impossible. People looked down, no matter what the situation, they
> looked down on women who worked. . . . But life went on because she
> maintained the farm with us kids and my grandparents. She was very
> close to her mother. Her mother was very important in her life.
>   . . . I also remember my mother didn't sit around in a depressed state.
> I was watching her, you know, so that she would be able to carry on, and
> she did. . . . And I was the youngest (of three daughters), and I was
> always the most sensitive to my mother's situation. And I also resented my
> sisters asking for so much because I felt, "Aren't you sensitive to what
> my mother's going through?" . . . and I resent my sisters for doing this.

Joyce's close empathy with her mother and her not grieving for her
father except in empathy with her mother suggest the diffusion of the
boundary she maintained as a child with her mother. She also had

difficulty breaking away from her mother to go to nursing school when she was 18:

> And that was traumatic, leaving home because we had had such a warm family life, you know. And again, I felt for my mother. But after all, I was in the same city, but still it was traumatic. I became an adult then. I had to make some very definite decisions. I had to make, wrench there to get away from my family, and I was going to start nursing and I never started anything I didn't finish. I was determined. You really almost had to be, had to become an adult in those years.

Despite some diffuseness of boundary with her mother, Joyce was able to make the decision and proceed with breaking away/launching into adulthood, although she remained in the same city. Joyce married and had three children, just as her mother had. Unlike her mother, she worked; but like her mother, she became a widow when she was a young woman (31 years of age); and like her mother, she never remarried. Her idealizations of a mother who did not sit by and become depressed after her father's death but who could carry on were incorporated into her self-esteem in a positive manner. Joyce was also able to carry on. At the time of the interview, at age 66, Joyce had seven grandchildren. Her mother had died at the age of 90 when Joyce was 52:

> Of course that was difficult. To lose your mother, it really leaves a space in your life.
> . . . I have a very full life. Enjoy—the big thing still is my family and my grandchildren. The pattern goes on.

Joyce Jenkins, a woman who definitely had a family view of life and the world (as discussed in Chapter 4), had bought a home in the same neighborhood where her mother and aunt lived. She said, "I stayed in the same neighborhood. My mother stayed in the same neighborhood. My aunt stayed in the same neighborhood. My grandparents stayed in the same neighborhood."

Thus, this mother merged with the idealizations of her mother to maintain somewhat unclear boundaries between self and her mother, although she managed to "wrench away" from the family to go to nursing school. However, she remained in the same city, and when she could buy a home, she elected to remain close, in the same neighborhood. Nevertheless, the diffuseness that may have existed in the boundaries between Joyce and her mother did not inhibit her development in other areas. Her close empathy with her mother indicated a very close identification. There was no question of her acceptance of her mother as an ideal. Her mother's strength in dealing with her father's death was something she could emulate with comfort and pride.

Inez Inkles.   Inez, a 78-year-old never-married nonmother at the time of the interview, described her mother:

> My mother was a perfect lady, and she was a hard worker, and she was kind-hearted. She was always doing something for the poor, and the sick, and the needy. I said, "We'd have been millionaires if we'd had some of that money she spent on others." She was definitely a model for me, and in doing the right thing and the proper thing. She taught us at home. We didn't dare sit down at the dinner table without using our table manners. I remember one time my brother, there were guests in the home, and he liked something very well, and he just took the plate and said, "More ham, more ham, more ham." And from that day on for months, there was a board at my mother's place at the table, and boy, if he didn't say "please," and "thank you," and "may I," he got cracked on the hand. But she taught us some things that we needed to know, behavior that we needed to have. She saw to it that we had a happy home. There wasn't a lot of discouragement or anything like that. She wouldn't let us go chasing around at night on the streets, but she always saw to it that we were entertained here at home. We'd play cards and games, and then she'd have a surprise for us—a cookie bowl or a treat of some kind.
>
> I was going to be married just at the time my father took sick, and then my mother took sick and things didn't work out. My family came first. I had made a promise to my father when I was very young. He was in the hospital for 9 months and 14 days with a ruptured appendix, and he made me promise for years and years that I would never put him in the hospital. . . . So when he got sick [Inez was 42], I knew what I was up against, and I'd made that promise and I kept it. That's the same with my mother. I couldn't put her in a rest home or anything. I came home and took care of her. She was critical for 5 years [and died when Inez was 57].

Inez, who was the only daughter, had achieved a sense of integrity at 78 and said about her life: "I have no regrets at all. I think life has been pretty good to me." She had earned a baccalaureate degree at age 26 and had a career as a school teacher. She had retired at age 68, did substitute teaching for a couple of years, and had enjoyed traveling, Eastern Star, and other social activities during the intervening years since retirement. The fact that her mother, a stern disciplinarian, served as a role model and as one who always helped others along with her early promise to her father left Inez with no conflict in her mind about her self-sacrificing role in forfeiting marriage to care for her parents. Thus, Inez also idealized her mother without conflict, but the family situation of need preempted her marrying. The home environment in which her mother was central enabled Inez to have positive self-esteem; the firm discipline and apparent encouragement (there was never any discouragement) had provided secure guidelines. Inez had clearer boundaries between herself and her mother than was the situation with Agnes Amherst.

Agnes Amherst. Agnes, a never-married nonmother, stated that she "wanted to be something like my mother when I grew up, I knew that." She lived with her parents and took care of them until their deaths (her mother died when she was 47, and her father died when she was 49). Agnes had a nervous breakdown when her mother died and had to take a leave of absence from work to nurse her mother before her death and afterwards because of her own illness. Both exhaustion from the caretaking role and the forced separation from her mother because of her death may have contributed to her nervous breakdown. She had achieved integrity at 80 to 81 years of age, noting that her main satisfaction in life was, "I do for other people."

Negative Role Models: Nonconflictual and Conflictual Relationships

Mothers as Negative Role Models in Nonconflictual Relationships. For some of the women, there was no conflict in rejecting their mothers as someone they wished to emulate. Amy Andrews is an example of the acceptance of a mother whom she did not wish to be like:

> My mother was a friendly, outgoing person, but unlike my aunts who could cook and sew, my mother was a helpless person. Her mother had always told her, "I can do it better," so she grew up and never had an opportunity to do anything. We children always took over; I wasn't very old and I was making my sister's clothes. At 11, my youngest sister was born, and I remember bathing her and taking care of her from the beginning. I felt responsibility. I didn't feel responsibility for my sister who was 13 months younger, but I did for all the rest [Amy was the oldest of 5 girls].

Amy Andrews, a nonmother who was 78 at the time of the interview, had accepted her mother's helplessness, and saw it as a result of how her mother was mothered. Rather than being merged with her mother, through role reversal she became the mothering person. She assumed her mother's responsibilities with her younger sisters and did what her mother could not do. Her father had not been a strong role model for her either; "Father was never good at finances. My sister [13 months younger] and I paid off their mortgage on their farm in 1920 and helped them financially until they died [her father died at 91 when Amy was 49, and her mother died at 85 when she was 45]." Role reversal of parent-child responsibilities was a challenge to Amy. Responsibility to Amy was seen as an opportunity to do things. This view that she learned so early in life propelled her through a dynamic, escalating career trajectory of national and international reknown from which she retired in her late 60s. She remained highly involved in national and international organizational work. Amy's mentors were persons (women and men professors) who led to her getting masters' and doctoral degrees. When asked why she left a professional position that she described as enjoying so much, she said:

> I was always challenged by something new. If someone says, "We don't know what it's going to be—it'll be tough," I'm attracted and scared too at the same time. . . . If someone told me a job was tough, it was always a challenge for me to lick it.
> . . . There was never time to regret a [career] move. So much to do . . . Those were exciting years—I wouldn't take anything for the excitement.

Amy Andrews also had an overall worldview as opposed to a family view of life. She was of European heritage, and her father's family had denounced the state church in their native European country. She also had grown up with a mixture of ethnic groups, which no doubt had contributed to her worldview. She also had an identity achievement status during her launching into adulthood and continued this status throughout her life course.

Mothers as Negative Role Models in Conflictual Relationships.   Gladys Gilbert, who was 67 at the time of a very complex interview, related that her parents divorced when she was almost 7 and that she and her younger brother were placed in boarding school. When asked who was the most significant person in her life at that time, she replied, "Nobody. That might be the story of my life in many ways." The complexity of her life was revealed as she continued:

A lot of fear was implanted in me early. "What's going to happen to me," seems to have been a focus. My mother told my father if he went overseas he needn't come back to her. . . . You know in those days we didn't talk about such things but whether Mother, Mom was looking elsewhere, she was a very attractive woman and only went to the second year in high school but had a native intelligence. . . . When I was 9, my father came and got me and I went to live with him, and he was on and off employed and not employed. My brother didn't go with me . . . My father was a child beater [beat her brother only—not her], and so my brother at the age of 8 ran away from him. . . . When I was 15, my mother remarried and she came and got me. I had not seen her for almost 6 years. My mother was a thwarted person. She felt thwarted. And when I say that she was miserable, I say that she . . . to do some of the things that she was to do and yet we had wonderful food, good home, or what the world's society calls a good home, and she wasn't interested particularly in education. It was a defense with her because my father was a college graduate. . . . My mother was a great person for dragging things into court. . . .

I graduated from high school at 16. Mother'd go away with my stepfather because he traveled, and he was a very fine man. He should have given my mother a good punch in the nose. But he didn't. He was rather a gentle person, and I censor him for not participating more and not accepting the father role at all. But my mother was the kind that said to me,"You go out and get a job or don't come home." And here is this half-baked, insecure person without typing or any skills. . . . With no skills you were a maid, which I was. So one day when I was about in my 17th year, they came home from a trip and said, "You're going to be a nurse." And the undertaking parlor was on that side of the street; I went around the block to avoid it. Nursing meant dead people, and it meant other things, and I didn't think I could do it but they said I had to do it, and so I went for an interview and they accepted me. The superintendent of nurses told me later, "I accepted you because I saw that there was a girl that needed to get away from her mother." I thought that was pretty sharp. . . . Living with my mom, supportive measures were nonexistent, although she taught me many things. But I'm a great believer in heredity coming through. In all honesty, I was probably lacking in that drive some people have, and perhaps she didn't know what to do with me, you know.

Gladys finished nursing school, and contracted tuberculosis while working in the tubercular ward. She was hospitalized for over a year, and got out of the hospital when she was 25.

I don't think I knew a secure day in my life. I met my first husband, and we developed a friendship. He also had tuberculosis, and I went to live with my mother after I got out of the hospital, and she told me if I was too much work, I would have to leave. It boggles the mind. Don't think this was any slob. Far from it. That's the punch. But there was something wrong for years I'm sure, and besides which she was an alcoholic—I believe one of the worst I have ever seen. I married at 29.

He died with TB after we were married 11 years. . . . Socially by the way, I've always felt adequate. I mean friends came easy, and I don't really think that I can say that through my life I suffered social deprivation. . . . I had two daughters . . . the first born 9 months and 15 minutes after we were married, and the second 2 years later. After my husband's death . . . I had lived with insecurity for so long I think I was kind of anesthetized. . . . My mother used to show up once in a while, and then she finally wrote me. I sent her a gift at Christmas time, and she sent it back and said that I needed it more than she did. It was money. And that was it. So I wrote her and told her that I didn't think we needed to engage in this sort of thing and that I was 30 whatever I was and she was in her late 40s. I never saw my dad after the 30s. There was a very ugly court trial, and so I never saw him after that. Thank God for that.

. . . My one daughter, the second one, seems to have a lot of animosity toward me. "Mother" was a holy word you know, but it no longer is a holy word, as you know. And so she [younger daughter] and I went to Europe; it was a debacle. She just told me off. I couldn't believe it. She was an inner person, and my older daughter was outgoing. So I'm sure she kept many, many things boiling. She goes to a psychiatrist. She had a teenage marriage when she was 19 that ended in divorce. But it's sex, just as it was with my parents. . . . Both of my daughters were very, quite attractive. My mother used to inform me periodically that I was not. She couldn't understand how I got such good-looking kids.

Gladys's mother died when she was 56 and left her a small inheritance. She had remarried when she was 42, had a son at 43, and retired at 62. After years of insecurity, she was able to say at 67, "So I'm secure and enjoying these years very much."

As much as Gladys tried to reach reconciliation with her mother, even to the extent of describing herself as one without much drive, her mother's rejection of her Christmas gift was the final rejection she could tolerate from her mother. Gladys could not idealize her mother and implied that she was sexually promiscuous, for example, "looking elsewhere" while her father was overseas. She believed in heredity, and, when her relationship with her younger daughter erupted on what was to have been a pleasurable vacation, she was bewildered. It is quite possible that without counseling to help her resolve her feelings of emotional deprivation from her mother, she unconsciously reenacted some of the same mothering behaviors toward her daughter, as Blos (1985) observed young mothers with such conflicts do. She rationalized that her mother's genes were responsible for her daughter's teenage marriage and divorce: "But it's sex, just as it was with my parents."

Gladys was able to reconcile her life and to accept where she was, so that she had achieved a sense of integrity at 67. Despite her life of fear and insecurity, she had learned to adapt to each crisis and emerged as a more secure person. Her stepfather, who she remembers as very gentle, probably provided her with more love and security than she recognized, but could not entirely make up for the void in her mother's affection. The pattern of mother–daughter conflict extended to her own situation.

The patterning of behavior from generation to generation was also observed among others; for example, Phyllis Painter described her own mother as a very domineering, possessive woman who made her wait on her and her friends rather than allow Phyllis to make friends of her own. Her daughter, who was born when she was 35, was greatly troubled; she ran away and married at 18 when Phyllis was 53. Phyllis suffered a stroke at age 77 after a very unpleasant episode with her daughter. The daughter died at the age of 43 of alcoholism when Phyllis was 78; she was dead for 2 weeks before being discovered. Nevertheless, Phyllis at 82 had made peace with her life (i.e., achieved integrity): "My outlook hasn't changed so much as the world. I have never been afraid of dying because I had a beautiful life and I can't regret it."

Unresolved Conflict with Maladaptive Consequences. Noreen Nunnally, a 74-year-old nonmother, unlike Gladys Gilbert had resolved little of her conflict. Reviewing her life history led to her having an asthmatic attack.

> My mother ran away from my father when I was 5 or 6 and took me to a boarding school. I was in boarding schools most all my life, one or another. And when I first went there I was frightened to death of everything and everybody, and at night the last thing after study hall you have to turn around and kneel, and I'd kneel in the seat and I'd wet my pants. . . . All through childhood, my mother would call and say she was coming up to see me, and, on the following weekend, say on a Sunday, I'd look for her all day long and she never appeared. And then a few days later during the next week here would come this box full of candy bars or here would come a beautiful pair of shoes, which I couldn't wear, I'm wearing uniform shoes you know. . . . To this day I don't really like candy. . . . I always had money; she saw to it that I had the material things, but I didn't have anything else. Even in the summer time I would be with—

sometimes I'd be with friends of hers, but they'd be perfect strangers; other times which were wonderful, I would be with one of her brothers and family, which was wonderful for me . . . My mother saw to it that I had dancing lessons, but she wouldn't let me have art lessons, and that's the only thing I wanted to be . . . I went to public school 1 year in Texas, a half year in California, I was in boarding school in Washington and in Texas. My mother was married and divorced three times by the time I was 21. And she was one of these really beautiful people, really a beautiful-looking person, but this tremendous personality, so she was just, you know. She could have used a few more brains for one. I was the only child, so she had to keep me some place; she was gone with her husband most of the time. My whole thing was traumatic anyways. I graduated from a boarding school in Oklahoma. . . . My mother had figured out that it was the thing for me to do was to become a teacher. . . . And although I didn't want to be a teacher, the dutiful daughter went all through school . . . Then I moved to another state to work and enrolled in art school. [She left teaching and painted from that time.] . . . When I lost my mother it didn't really bother me too much. I could never take care of her, I'm just responsible for her and all. But it didn't really bother me all that much because I never was that close.

Noreen Nunnally had married during her 20s, but divorced 6 months later. She married her second husband when she was 29, was married for over 40 years, and had been widowed for 3 years. She described her second husband as a wonderful man who had spoiled her terribly. She was distressed that she had not been able to begin painting again (3 years after his death) and that the grief for her husband was so much more profound than she had anticipated. Noreen was deserted by her mother when she was at a very young age, and at 74 reported that she still didn't like candy, which her mother sent to her instead of coming herself. One could speculate that she continues to reject candy as a representation of her mother. She described her husband of 41 years as her mentor; he appeared to have provided the emotional void that her mother had been unable to provide. Supportive relationships provide attachment through intimacy, conveying a sense of security (Weiss, 1974). For Noreen, her husband provided the anchoring to enable her to work on her own identity (Josselson, 1987). Rubin (1979) found that many women at mid-life had let their husbands represent them as a person: "she exists only through him, is counted and counts herself in the world only in relation to him" (p. 125). Noreen's husband-mentor had also provided her with a stable identity as wife who was taken care of and loved, and he encouraged her in her painting.

Noreen's mother had provided only material things, which she resented, and controlled her life by sending her to teachers' school instead of art school. Noreen was in group therapy at the time of the interview in an attempt to deal with her grief over the loss of her husband; however, she in reality was also grieving for her mother. She changed tense in speaking of her mother's death: "I'm just responsible for her and all." Noreen's feeling of responsibility for her mother seems not to have ended; she rejects her mother as her mother rejected her, but in her lack of having an earlier identification with and later differentiation from her mother, she is also rejecting parts of herself. Her husband was several years older than she and had children by a previous marriage; she did not indicate whether her childlessness was deliberate or not. However, he had fulfilled an important role of nurturing and support; with his death, Noreen's earlier loss of nurturing and support from her mother was also grieved. Sarason and Sarason (1985) suggested that feelings of isolation and loneliness may be associated with childhood losses of support and related feelings of inadequate or insecure relationships.

Summary

Unresolved mother–daughter conflict continues to affect the other's adaptive abilities after the death of one of the partners. Our findings also agree with the empirical evidence that anger and hostility along with love and admiration continue to plague the mother–daughter relationship as long as it lasts (Friday, 1977). The intense initial tie between mother and daughter, which may continue as one of the most joyous relationships, may also lead to the daughter's devalued self-esteem. There is also evidence that an unresolved conflicted mother–daughter relationship inhibits the ability for achieving intimacy with others, and a pattern of conflict extends to the third generation.

Separation from their mothers at an early age had an enduring effect on both Gladys Gilbert and Noreen Nunnally. To be separated from the primary person of identification at the age of 6 or so and placed in a boarding school contributed to almost lifelong feelings of insecurity for Gladys and Noreen. Noreen, who had not achieved integrity and was very unsettled, exhibited a profound somatic response (asthmatic episode) to recalling her deep emotional pain that began with being in boarding schools away from family. Her grief was such that she could not be creative. Two other women in the study had also been placed in boarding school during these early years and also had problems in interpersonal relationships (Eve Edwards, discussed at the beginning of this chapter, and Constance Calvin whose mother died when she was 7; Constance Calvin also felt unloved and described herself as a very lonely child).

Women's positive idealizations about their mothers fostered their adaptive capabilities and contributed to their overall more positive self-esteem. Unresolved conflict from relationships with negatively perceived mothers contributed to difficulties in adapting to ongoing transitions; it was as if women, in rejecting the parts of their mothers that they did not wish to be like, also rejected part of self. Women with unresolved mother–daughter conflicts were able to function well when they had someone who supplied the emotional void that their mothers had not supplied. When this person, who provided the emotional support that their mothers had failed to provide, was removed either by death or other separation, the grief at this loss seemed to recapitulate the early grief at losing their mothers—figuratively, if not actually. Ballou (1978b) described the husband as becoming an approving maternal figure who protects the pregnant woman from her mother, while at the same time also representing the oedipal father who encourages her sexuality. Perhaps husbands fulfill this role in many instances apart from a pregnancy, so that women who have deep-seated mother–daughter conflicts can function well as long as they have this support. Josselson (1987) observed that women anchored their emotional attachment on a male partner as a means of separating and individuating from their mothers; this anchor enabled them to continue their identity development.

The question may be raised as to whether Noreen Nunnally might have resolved some of her conflictual feelings about her mother if she had experienced motherhood herself and, in the process, reaped developmental benefits. Eve Edwards, who was cited at the beginning of the chapter, was able to achieve integrity by age 78 to 81, although she had been depressed to the extent of planning her suicide at the age of 60. Noreen, with the help of counseling, will hopefully be able, in time, to also reach some reconciliation with her deceased mother that will allow for her greater self-acceptance.

Although only three nonmothers listed their mothers as role models, most nonmothers spoke lovingly and warmly about their mothers. The overall theme that was a part of achievement and positive development over the life course among nonmothers was of early childhood homes characterized by happiness and protection along with responsibility and discipline. In the absence of these characteristics, not only was their development affected, but their physical and mental health was as well.

When mothers had unresolved conflicts with their mothers, this conflict extended to their relationships with their daughters. Their daughters in turn experienced pain as evidenced by acting-out behaviors (teenage pregnancy, alcoholism), sometimes to the point of premature death.

Cohler and Grunebaum (1981), who studied women in three-generation families, found that the woman's relationship with her own mother influenced how she handled the issues of separation and autonomy with her own daughters. The grandmothers who had encouraged dependency in their daughters as children were frightened by the emotional demands of their adult daughters and attempted to establish some distance, contributing to a more difficult adjustment of the adult daughters to their own daughters. The adult mothers felt resentment and disappointment, and the grandmothers felt annoyed and frustrated.

Wilma Weeks had words of wisdom that need further exploration. When asked when she became an adult, she said:

> Merciful heavens. Probably it occurred to me when my daughter got old enough that I made the decision, "I am never going to be a sister to her. I am the mother, and she is the daughter." . . .
>
> But I think you pattern your life more after your grandmother. Grandmother was one of these pioneer women; that's a funny thing that I've never thought of before, but we do tend to skip a generation. [Wilma married when she was 24 and moved from the city to a ranch where she continued to live. The ranch was without indoor plumbing or electricity and quite primitive for her first 11 years there.] . . .
>
> My granddaughter would of course slash both of her wrists right now if we told her, but she's going to relate to me a lot more than she will to her mother. . . .
>
> At 52, my daughter gave me a grandson, and three years later, a granddaughter. So you can see for yourself what really made me alive on the farm.

Thus, having a strong grandmother and becoming a grandmother were both highlights in the women's lives.

GRANDMOTHERS

Grandmothers as Role Models

Grandmothers were named as having been role models by seven (14%) mothers and one nonmother. Agnes Amherst, a nonmother who had a nervous breakdown following her mother's death, also talked about her grandmother during her childhood, but to a lesser extent. Her mother and grandmother always made a specific dish for the church picnics because they made this dish better than anyone else in the community. Agnes described her grandmother as a long-term role model: "I admired her. She called me her little mouse when I was little."

The larger number of mothers with a predominantly family view may have been a factor in more mothers than nonmothers referring to grandmothers as role models. In some situations, grandmothers were mother figures during their mothers' illness or absence. Daisy Dalton described her grandmother who took care of her and her siblings when her mother was ill:

> Oh, Grandma was great. Grandma ruled us with a rod of iron; I can tell you, you never argued with Grandma. Boy, Grandma said something, and you did it! And she lived to the ripe age of 88.

Beatrice Bowen described her grandmother as her role model:

> My grandmother. If there was anyone angelic, she sure was. She was a Queen Victoria type, short and heavy—wore long dresses, all black in winter, all white in summer. I was named after her; I always looked up to her. . . . My aunt wanted to adopt me, but my mother wouldn't hear to it; she [her aunt] never had any children. She was a sort of second mother and was a great influence for other things.

Becoming a Grandmother

Grandmotherhood was very special to all of the mothers who had experienced this transition. Two major themes emerged from the mothers' descriptions of being a grandmother. Overall, the mothers as grandmothers viewed their grandchildren as gifts, such as Wilma Weeks implied above: "My daughter gave me a grandson." Even Maude Morris who had married at 41 and acquired teenage stepdaughters commented, "I'm interested of course in her children, and I think I feel like a grandmother. I'm not a mother. I don't know what a real mother thinks like."

Avis Arbeit described when at age 68 her grandson came to live with her to go to college [his parents had moved out of the country for an interim]: "He was 18 and with me for 3 years. He was a joy and also a problem. I regained part of my youth when I had him with me; he kept me going. They were happy years."

Sarah Sanger described some differences between children and grandchildren:

One of the interesting things I've seen in these last few years is the relationship with grandchildren. They are really more interested in us as people and as human beings and in our life experiences, than other people in general who are so busy living their lives.

Nancy Newton also described grandmotherhood as an added blessing, but the second theme, that of continuity of generations, was evident in her comments:

There is a feeling of continuity that comes with that of life going on, especially when you see a characteristic smile or something that you remember from somebody on your side of the family.

Felicia Fawne, who was quoted in an earlier chapter, was quite articulate in the theme of continuity: "It's a species feeling that you have completed a certain cycle in what you do for your species. And you're home free." However, grandmotherhood also meant very much emotionally to her. At 61 "my first grandchild was born! And that was, that was super. I had a chance to spend quite a bit of time with them . . . would just pick up and go."

We know little about the developmental impact of grandmothers on grandchildren. In one study, grandmothers were observed to have a significant influence on the majority of children in a psychiatric clinic, both through their influence on the children's mother and as a major caretaker in the mother's absence (LaBarre, Jessner, & Ussery, 1960). As a result, the children received a double dose of attitudes from mother and grandmother. This was perhaps the case with Claudia Call (described in Chapter 4), whose children demonstrated potential psychosomatic effects from their family milieu. Positive effects were also observed among grandmothers of children in the psychiatric clinic; in some instances, grandmothers interacted to counteract the mother's rigidity or severity (LaBarre et al., 1960).

CONCLUSIONS

The mother–daughter tie has lifelong influences on each daughter generation. As a transactional relationship, mothers also continue to develop as they recapitulate their own conscious and unconscious experiences of being mothered and come to view their mothers with more understanding and with greater reality. These findings support the views by others that daughters never completely individuate from their mothers and the process of individuation is a lifelong endeavor.

The daughter's transition to motherhood appears to be a time of heightened involvement in the mother–daughter dyad, enabling both mother and daughter to experience a more mature and gratifying level of relationship.

In this study, nonmothers more often described positive, autonomy-promoting, caring, and disciplined environments, although mothers were not their role models. The kind of milieu fostered by their mothers seemed to also foster greater differentiation of self, so that they reached identity achievement status and, thus, had greater freedom to pursue other goals. A second family factor quite noticeable among the group of nonmothers was the early parent–child role reversal, in which nonmothers assumed heavy responsibilities for their parents and other siblings during the breaking away/launching phase of women's development. Thus, for some, a grooming in assuming responsibility meant forfeiting other roles, such as wife.

Mothers more often modeled their lives after their mothers and/or grandmothers. They also tended to hold a more family-oriented view of life and the world. As will be recalled from Chapter 4, mothers had also experienced more traumatic family lives during their preteen and teenage years. Spence and Lonner (1978–79) found that economic pressures and family problems played a significant role in the early lives of women they studied; many perceived marriage as an escape from the turmoil of family problems. A pattern of mother–daughter conflict spread to the women's family of marriage.

Women who had unresolved mother–daughter conflict were able to function adaptively as long as they had the emotional support of a husband or other significant person. The long-term effects of mother–daughter conflict were evident, particularly when their major source of emotional support and nurturance (such as a husband) was lost. The work of attempting to resolve mother–daughter conflict continued after the death of the mother.

Health care professionals and counselors can play a central role in identifying women who have not resolved conflicts with their mothers. Through counseling, women may be helped to gain insight into the relationship with their mothers.

■ 6
The Importance of Interpersonal Relationships to Women

Each study participant had the freedom to describe her life course as she wished. Universally, the women spoke of important relationships with family, friends, and others, often citing important anecdotes about these relationships that were a part of their life stories. Gilligan (1982a) made the assumption for her research that the way people talk about their lives and the language used reflect their perceived world and the way they act. Gilligan's (1982b) work has demonstrated that gender differences exist from childhood in how relationships and connectedness to others are viewed. From early socialization, women have learned responsibility toward others in important relationships as a priority, as opposed to focusing on individual welfare and concerns (Gilligan, 1982a):

> Responsibility becomes, in its conventional interpretation, confused with a responsiveness to others that impedes a recognition of self. The truths of relationship, however, return in the rediscovery of connection, in the realization that self and other are interdependent and that life, however valuable in itself, can only be sustained by care in relationships (p. 127).

Josselson (1987) also emphasized the importance of relationships for women's development:

> Communion, connection, relational embeddedness, spirituality, affiliation—with these women construct an identity (p. 191).

111

The assumption was made that if the study participant discussed an individual frequently then that individual must have had an important place in her life and played an important role in her development. The decision was made to tabulate actual references women made to other persons in order to obtain a more accurate view of their proportionate importance. Each transcribed interview was then reviewed and women's references to family members and friends were marked and color coded for analysis.

As the interviews were studied, it was evident that the women's relationships with persons who were central to their lives were very important. Their interactions with significant other persons and their feelings about them were as important, if not more important, than the transitional events in their lives. There were exceptions, however, with some women who focused more on the events than on the relationships they experienced during these events.

This chapter presents the viewpoint of mothers and nonmothers as they spoke of the relationships with other family members in both their family of origin and in their marital/nuclear family. This is followed by a discussion of the women's friends, also an important part of these women's close relationships. A discussion of mentors and a summary conclude the chapter.

FAMILY

The family has been studied extensively by scientists from several disciplines. The White House Conferences on Family Life reflect the national interest in families. As has been true with the study of individuals, different disciplines use various approaches and theoretical frameworks to study the family. Some of the frameworks utilized include developmental, systems, interactionist, and social exchange (Friedman, 1986; Mercer, 1989). The interactionist framework (Wells & Stryker, 1988) was more influential in the interpretation here of the transactional relationships that women described as part of their development over the life course. The interactionist perspective, pioneered by Mead (1934), emphasizes people's ability to organize and control behavior and responses by reflecting about options available to them, as well as their ability to give meaning to others' interactions with them. The person's social group provides the social attitudes and meanings that are assimilated as part of self. Therefore, the family's early influence and the influence of the culture of which the family is a part on an individual family member's development is extensive (Mercer, 1989). The family was defined as the individual woman defined or referred to it; those persons living together as a group and providing mutual support and help to its members were considered a family. In some cases, children who were not either siblings or relatives were reared as a sibling with the study participant, but were considered part of her family of origin. The family of origin is the family that an individual is born into—the family of one's birth. The nuclear family consists of parents of marriage or procreation and includes mother, father, and their children, either biologic, adopted, or both, and applies both to the family of origin and to the woman's marital family. The extended family is made up of the nuclear family and all other persons related directly to the family members or one of the nuclear family members. These individuals are known as "kin," such as grandparents, aunts, uncles, and cousins, or sometimes the "nanny," who lives with the family and cares for the children. Most of the study participants were recalling the experience of belonging to two families—their nuclear family of origin and their own marital/ nuclear family.

In addition to identifying which family members that women referred to most often, insights were gained into the memory of the child's perception of the family of origin. Numerous references were made about all family members, including extended family members.

It was common for adult extended family members to live with the study participant's family of origin. Barbara Bloom had several different relatives from her extended family living in her family of origin home and illustrates the complexity of these early families:

> When I was a tiny child, Grandpa would go into the living room, put a pillow on the floor, lie down and take a nap on the floor. He would say, "Tell Barby to come along," and he would put a pillow down for me and would say, "Now, let's take a nap."
>
> Aunt Marion also lived with us. She was living with us when my mother died when I was 13. She continued to live with us, and my father always told me that I must obey Aunt Marion, that I must mind her just as I had minded my mother.
>
> Now we had three generations that lived in this house. My sister May was 10 years older than I was. There had been five other children born to my mother, but they all died.
>
> My uncle had always lived with our family, but when my mother died he married and moved out.

Down the street a couple of blocks lived one of my mother's sisters. She had a family of 11 children. Of those 11 children, two of the boys [cousins] were sailors and one was closest to my age. He wrote me while he was in the war. I appreciated all that he did for his country; he came through the war fine, but was injured in an accident on the highway after he was discharged and died as a result of that.

[Barbara Bloom's marriage did not result in her moving from her family of origin home.] My husband would not hear of us establishing a separate home so we all lived together—he moved in with me. The house was remodeled within about a year of our marriage. One of my husband's mother's brothers was left without a home and after batting around for a while, my husband couldn't stand hearing about it any longer, and he said that he should move in with us. My husband told me to ask my father if it was all right for him to share his bedroom. I agreed to ask and to have him there as long as he was not drunk. So he stayed. When he got drunk, he went to visit other relatives.

Thus, the large family homes with many extended family members provided an environment for many important family relationships. Study participants were able to learn about and adapt to their world through these relationships.

Some women made extensive references to particular family members. One mother referred to her father often, frequently using the term "my father." She also discussed other family members from her family of origin and marital/nuclear and extended families. Some women spoke of parents only when reviewing the early years of their lives when they were living with their family of origin. Others spoke of parents over their entire life span. The participants' perceptions of their families as they were remembered, along with the relationships they encountered, many of which had sustained them throughout their life time, are the views of family that are presented here.

FAMILY OF ORIGIN

Parents

As would be expected, the members of their family of origin most prominent in the women's lives were their parents. Since, according to Josselson (1987), a woman's identity is always viewed in the context of her mother's, it was not surprising that mothers were referred to significantly more often than fathers [$\chi^2(1) = 11.66$, $p = 0.0006$]. Of 1,319 references to parents by the 80 women, 748 (56.7%) were about mothers (range of 1 to 52) and 571 (43.2%) were about fathers (range of 1 to 32). Although the difference in reference to mothers and fathers was significant, the actual difference is not as great as was expected; fathers were very important to these women.

Since participants who were mothers had referred to their own mothers as role models more often than nonmothers had, we expected that they would have made more references to their mothers. However, while mothers made more comments about their mothers, the difference was not significant (p = 0.08). The 50 women who were mothers accounted for 67% (n = 501) of the references to mothers, contrasted to 30 nonmothers who made up the remaining 33% (n = 247). Mothers made an average of 10 separate references to their own mothers, and nonmothers made an average of 8.2 references.

Of the total of 571 references to fathers, 343 (60%) were made by the mothers and 228 (40%) were made by the nonmothers. Mothers averaged 6.8 references to their fathers, and nonmothers averaged 7.6. These differences were not statistically significant.

Since mother–daughter relationships are discussed extensively in Chapter 5, this chapter focuses on other family relationships.

The Role of Fathers in the Women's Lives

With the emphasis on the woman's close identification with her mother, little attention has been paid to her relationship with her father and the role that this relationship plays in development over her life course. Fathers played several important roles in these women's lives. Fathers were seen by their daughters who were in their seventh through ninth decades of life as teachers, disciplinarians, recreation providers, protectors, role models for parenting, and as a prototype for a husband. A few women experienced difficulty in establishing independence from their fathers; an exemplar of successful and unsuccessful resolution of father–daughter conflict concludes this section.

Fathers as teachers introduced the broader view of the world and politics to the women. Under their mothers' tutelage they learned the more mundane chores of housekeeping and childrearing; their fathers introduced the excitement of the outer world apart from family:

> Shortly after World War I began, I remember my father trying to explain it to me with drawings in the sand at the park where we were—Germany and France and Belgium. (Ophelia Owens)

My father was a politician as well as a church leader, and he was involved in those things when I was growing up. . . . It just sort of came naturally to me. When I was a teenager, my dad was campaigning for a political job. I started doing it through the years. I was a 4-H leader, held offices in the County Homemakers organization, and was president of the State Homemakers Association, and was state president [of many organizations] . . . (Jane Junket)

My father had been a pioneer, and he instilled that I should be independent . . . My father was an intelligent person, and many times I heard him sit and discuss the world affairs with people who wanted to debate, and I'd sit and listen, just enthralled with their discussions, because I wanted to know what was going on in the world. (Lillian Love)

Fathers were also remembered as disciplinarians who were responsible for instilling moral, just, and honest values in their daughters. In some cases, fathers were role models for their mothering:

Dad was quite strict. . . . I probably took his way of living, very strict. I was sort of a disciplinarian [rearing her children], and he was too. But then I don't think that hurts children. They've [her children] both grown up to be very responsible people, and I feel like it's a result of that. (Hilda Hooper)

My father was a very strict person, but he was very good to us. I think I patterned myself after both my mother and my dad. He taught me to ride horses. I was always on his heels up until I was 12 to 14 years old. (Anne Abbey)

Fathers also played important roles in providing recreation for their children. In addition to remembering fathers playing Santa Claus at Christmas and helping with decorations for other holidays and special occasions, they encouraged their daughters to learn to enjoy life:

My father was a musician. . . . We had our singing and dancing. My father taught us each to dance. (Evelyn Eems)
Father used to read to us at night. (Clara Cohen)

Fathers were seen by the women as protectors. This was accepted and viewed in a positive manner:

My dad was a very protective man. He thought his daughters should stay home. He wasn't mean. . . . Just concerned. He just wanted to know where we were all of the time. (Diane Dodd)

My father was very serious about our futures. He had no money but he was determined that we would be self-sufficient. In case we didn't marry . . . he wanted us to go to college. (Thelma Tiller)

Perhaps one of the more important roles of the father was his serving as a role model or prototype for the woman's future husband. In some cases, the husband turned out to treat the woman in the same way her father had, and, in others, he did not.

> I had complete confidence in my husband. . . . My husband was a lot like my father. . . . The transition [to marriage] was not all that much because I figured like father, like him [husband], he's going to treat me just like my father did. Heaven help me if he hadn't. (Clara Cohen)
> I was sort of transferring my feelings for my father [who had died when she was in high school] partly to my husband, because he was in the same profession. There were a lot of similarities. . . . [There was not the emotional closeness she had anticipated, however.] There's always this continuing wish that someday I'm going to get this strong, silent person to talk about his feelings. (Felicia Fawne)

Fathers were also viewed as friends who provided special treats or favors and reinforced positive self-esteem.

> I remember how good my father was. I guess I was his pride and joy. He was always getting me little things, little gifts and things. (Ruth Rogers)
> When my father died, I felt as though I lost my best friend [at age 40]. I didn't feel that way about my mother because of the hardship she put me through. She could be warm; it's hard to love someone who beats you [with a frying pan or whatever she had in her hand]. (Avis Arbeit)

Conflict with Fathers

Although it was reported much less frequently than was the case with mother–daughter conflict, some women experienced father–daughter conflict that had long-term repercussions. An example of father–daughter conflict that was finally resolved with the daughter making her own choice to marry and leave her father is that of Edna Ebert, a nonmother. Following this example, a less fortunate woman will be discussed: Ollie Odom, a mother, who was unable to resolve her conflict with her father satisfactorily.

Edna Ebert.   Edna Ebert's references to family illustrate the long-term impact of close relationships between family members. Edna, who was

74 at the time, made 15 comments about her father during the 2-hour interview. Her remarks provide a profile of a father who was loved, yet feared at times and his impact on her life.

> [At age 7] My father had a terrible temper. One morning we got up and went downstairs and the bird was gone out of the cage, and my father was looking for the cat and he was going to throw the cat in the fire because he thought that the cat had eaten the bird. I'm sure that my father would never have thrown him in the stove, but at that point I was positive whatever he said he was going to do, he would do.
>
> [Differential relationships between parents and her brother] I knew all of my life that my mother would give my brother everything and my father would give me anything I wanted. It didn't take too long to figure that out. . . . If he [brother] wanted anything he knew to go to mother, and if I wanted anything I knew to go to my father.
>
> [The differential parent–child relationship also extended to discipline.] And I knew that my father would crack down on him much more than he did on me.
>
> [Other characteristics about her father] My father says he is German. . . . My father sold the store . . . My father had sisters and brothers that I was very close with. . . . Dad did not have to go [to World War I]; I guess he must have been too old for the draft. [Only twice did she refer to her father as "Dad."]
>
> [Caring in personal relationship] My father primarily helped redecorate the car for the annual big high school parade. . . . I think I had a very happy childhood.

Edna Ebert's early memories of when she was a young adult help bring details of earlier years into focus. At age 19, during the early launching into adulthood stage, she took a job teaching and moved away from the family home; she defined this transition as becoming an adult. However, she was fired after a year for dating the high school basketball captain, and she moved back home again. Her mother, a severe diabetic, died 3 years later, and she kept house for her father:

> My father always had been a drinker. He started drinking and had become quite a drunkard. [Pause.] Oh yes, I remember now, that as a child I had plenty of feelings about him staggering around. So he must have been drinking then, but I wasn't conscious of it. When he got drunk on hard liquor he was mean. . . .
>
> After my mother died he tried to quit drinking. He didn't quit drinking, but he quit staying drunk. Because I kept house for him, and uh, I remember that I got so mad at him earlier at his drunkenness and one time I think I was afraid of him. But he never did hurt me.

[At age 37 she again left her father's home.] I left Dad by himself at the house. He had gotten the liquor under control, and he still had this job, so it worked out very well.

[Edna married at age 39.] I didn't know why he [father] didn't get married. But he didn't; he was alone all those years I was away. But as soon as I got married, he got married. But I guess he still thought maybe I might by chance come home again.

Edna Ebert had assumed responsibility for caretaking for her very ill mother upon returning home after a somewhat unsuccessful breaking away from home. Upon her mother's death, she assumed the responsibility of caretaking for her father and did not really break away from her nuclear family of origin until she was 37. At that time she left home. She met and married her husband 2 years later. The age-40 liberating stage, from 36 to 40 years, was her second chance for self-development. To do so she had to turn her back on responsibility to her father. Edna illustrates the statement made by Gilligan (1982a) at the beginning of this chapter that placing responsibility for relationships with others takes priority over self needs for most women. Edna, however, broke away from family responsibility successfully during her late 30s and had a 22-year career following her marriage; she also continued her personal development.

Ollie Odom. Ollie had married at age 21, but was divorced 5 years later and for several years lived alone with her son, rearing him as a single parent. Ollie described a series of hospitalizations for both physical and mental problems; her mother and father were helpful to her during these times. Her father took her son as a teenager to another state to live with him, and Ollie sent $100.00 per month to her father for the son's room and board. At age 39, Ollie moved into her father's home following her mother's sudden death because he had written frequently how much he missed her and that he had cancer, but this turned out to be problematic.

My dad treated me like a little girl. If I went out, it was just terrible; he'd be waiting at the door when I came home. He wanted the best for me. He loved to go out to restaurants to dinner. He loved to go to the theatre, and he loved music. I met a fellow there who flipped over me. . . . Well, the situation just got so bad that my dad ordered me out of the house. He didn't like the man, and my son didn't like him [the man]. They wouldn't like anyone that I did, and he was a fine man. . . . So my dad told me to get out of the house if I was going to see him again. So I got out of the house and moved, . . . and I just collapsed. They took me where they drugged me and gave me electroshock. . . . I had attempted suicide with pills. . . .

I think my dad turned to me more as a companion than a wife, you know the companionship and I was like a little girl to him. . . . And still I wanted my own social life. Makes me shake to think about it.

Ollie's remark regarding "I think my dad turned to me more as a companion than a wife" raises the question of whether in her mind she was fulfilling a wife role, similarly to how a 4-year-old at the height of the oedipal conflict fantasizes. Preschool girls often fantasize that they will grow up and marry their fathers. There was no evidence to indicate an incestuous relationship here. Ollie's repeated mental deteriorations requiring hospitalization and the information that she was able to share in this interview indicate that she had many unresolved feelings about her relationship with her father. He died 1 month following driving her from his home.

Intergenerational Influences Over Time

Fu, Hinkle, and Hannah (1986) observed a relationship between individual dependency and family interdependence within an Appalachian subculture. The dependency and family interdependence were transmitted to successive generations through social reinforcement and parental childrearing attitudes. Fu et al. (1986) suggest that dependency is the mechanism that leads to the development of family interdependence, which in turn reinforces dependent behavior. From Edna Ebert's account, her father waited to marry to see whether she would not again become dependent on their relationship and return home; he had reinforced her dependency on him, but she was able to separate from this dependency finally by age 39. Ollie Odom's father treated her at age 39 as if she were a young teenager, but threw her out when she refused to quit seeing her boyfriend; her father was unable to deal with Ollie's lack of dependency on him.

Intergenerational relationships between mothers and fathers have emerged in more recent research as important during childbearing years as predictors of infant attachment during pregnancy (Mercer, Ferketich, May, DeJoseph, & Sollid, 1988), of mate relationships (Mercer, Ferketich, May, DeJoseph, & Sollid, 1987), and of family functioning (Mercer, Ferketich, DeJoseph, May, & Sollid, 1988). The quality of women's relationships with their mothers was positively related to their developing maternal role behaviors during pregnancy

(Curry & Snell, 1985). Women's positive relationships with their fathers were associated with a satisfying pregnancy experience and an affectionate relationship with their husbands (Gladieux, 1978). Gladieux postulated that a woman's relationship with her father influences her value of femininity and comfort in other heterosexual relationships. Hospitalized pregnant women's early relationships with their fathers were predictive of their perceived family functioning, whereas their husbands' relationships with their mothers as teenagers was predictive of their husbands' perceived family functioning (Mercer et al., 1988). Flaherty and Richman (1986) reported that the perceived quality of childhood relationships with both the mother and father were related to the subsequent quality of adult social support systems. Further research on the early socialization experiences in the family is needed to clarify mother–daughter and father–daughter influences on later adult relationships.

Sibling Relationships

The relationship that has the longest duration of any in a woman's life is her relationship with her sibling; it is lengthier than her relationship with parent, husband, or child (Dunn, 1984). The 68 participants who had siblings referred to them a total of 580 times; they referred to their brothers 277 times and to their sisters 305 times. This slight preferential difference in reminiscences of sisters over brothers was not statistically significant. Overall, participants who had siblings averaged 8.5 references to them during interviews.

The 45 mothers with siblings had 94 brothers and 85 sisters; the 23 nonmothers with siblings had 50 brothers and 40 sisters. There was no significant difference in the distribution of brothers and sisters in each of the groups of women. The number of references made about the 144 brothers averaged 1.9 per brother, and about the 125 sisters, 2.4 per sister. When viewed from this perspective, although brothers and sisters played important roles in women's development over the life course, collectively that role was not as great as that of parents.

The 90% of the mothers who had siblings made 60% of the references to siblings, and the 77% of nonmothers who had siblings made 40%. The differences in the observed percentages referring to siblings versus the expected percentages were not statistically significant between mothers and nonmothers.

Dunn (1984) reported that adults attribute their closeness to siblings to the quality of early relationships within their nuclear family of origin.

Daisy Dalton, a daughter in a missionary family, spoke about her mother, father, brother, grandmother, grandfather, aunt, uncle, father's cousin, father's cousin's husband, cousin of her mother's husband, brother-in-law, sister-in-law, and her own son and daughter extensively. Although Daisy's family of origin had lived in Canada, Iran, England, and the United States and vacationed at the Caspian Sea, Daisy maintained a family view of life as opposed to the worldview held by some women. (See Chapter 4 for discussion of a family view versus a worldview.) Daisy, in addition to having traveled extensively, was fluent in Latin, French, German, and Persian. However, Daisy's relationship with her brother was very special:

> There is a special bond between us; but we hardly see each other. But we get together and it's, you know, it's right back there. . . . It's just something . . . He was my family, but I guess it was the same with him.
> [Daisy spoke of her older brother's sensitivity when she got menstrual cramps at camp.] I remember I went to camp and got cramps, and I'd never had cramps, and my brother was the lifeguard at camp. And I couldn't understand how—he's 7 years older—how he knew to be so good to me . . . He was so good to me, and I couldn't understand how; it seemed like he knew more what was happening to me than I did.

There was also some sibling rivalry that led Daisy to speak up and demand her rights regarding the college that she would attend.

Bank and Kahn (1982) identified three types of the more common sibling relationships: close identification, in which each sibling feels much similarity with the other; partial identification, in which some similarity and some difference is felt; and distant identification, in which each sibling feels much difference and little similarity.

In close identification, Bank and Kahn observed three patterns of sibling relationships: fused, blurred, and hero worship. From the women's viewpoints (without our knowing if the woman's sibling felt similarly), hero worship, a form of close identification, was more characteristic of sibling relationships reported by our study participants than other forms of close identification, as was the case with Daisy Dalton above. It would be expected that those participants whose sibling relationships were of distant identification would be less likely to talk about them. Felicia Fawne, a mother, described her hero worship of her sister when she was 6 years old:

> The friends I had in school were not around to play with. . . . My one companion was my older sister, who was a much more assertive person

than I was and who I thought never could do anything wrong. Whatever she said was right, and she took advantage of me—not deliberately, but as you would.

Sibling rivalry, according to Bank and Kahn (1982), can be a major means of ego development and identity resolution in childhood that continues into adolescence and adulthood. Such an extension of sibling rivalry was illustrated by a nonmother, Maude Morris, into her 60s:

I had one older sister, and we were a year apart. I wanted everything she had. I can remember my first menstrual period and how it started unexpectedly when I was about 10 or 11. It was a big event for me because I started before my sister. . . .

Part of going to high school meant that I could wear silk stockings, and my sister had been able to do this for a year.

Just last year my sister died, very unexpectedly [Maude was 63 years at the time]. She had a heart condition—the type that we thought would go on for 20 years. She died suddenly, and I found that devastating. . . . When we got the notice I remember thinking, "She knows about that before I do too." She always knew everything before I did.

Zoie Zenith also had closely identified with her brothers. This close identification extended from early childhood until she was in her 20s:

When my brothers had the measles and the mumps, I felt bad because they did, and particularly the youngest one. When he had the mumps on both sides, I'd sit and rock him.

[All three of her brothers were in the military during World War II.] I guess I was about 20 when they had to go in the service. . . . I remember trying to keep my mother and dad from worrying too much and trying to take the place of my three brothers—going fishing—which I did not like. But I went fishing all of the time with my dad, and I received letters from the boys about things that they didn't want mom and dad to worry about . . . in the front line, repairing big tanks . . . on anti-aircraft. . . . And John was in the marines, . . . we felt very fortunate that they all came back without any injuries.

When he came home he said, "I don't think I'll ever laugh again." [He spent one night until 3:00 A.M. telling Zoie about the war, then never talked about it again.]

When Zoie was asked at age 65 who the most important people in her life were [she was a widow], she replied, "My mother and my two brothers that are living."

Memories of sibling relationships were important over the entire life course for participants. Eunice Evans, a mother who was born in Norway, at 74 years, spoke about her siblings:

> We all went back to Norway when I was 69. We had a beautiful time. My brother, his wife, and my sister all went to our home town. I saw my family, and I went to the church where I was baptised and confirmed, and it was just great. We went to the place where we were born. I forgot to mention that my Dad was in the United States when he was a young man, and then came home and married my mother. And then he had the three children; he had my brother, me, and my sister. My father passed away, and my sister was born, and so it was kind of sad. My mother was quite ill and stayed ill for most of her life.
>
> I lived with an aunt, my brother, lived with another uncle, and my sister stayed with my mother. . . .
>
> When I was 15, I had to go to the city and get a job and so did my brother. We had some good friends in the city. We both worked. I went to the city where my brother was; I came to the United States at 19. When I arrived, I said to my brother, "Well, here I am." . . . My brother and I were together, and he always saw to it that I was okay and that I didn't do anything or run away with anybody that asked me.
>
> He moved with me to Chicago and saw that I attended school. . . . I met my future husband there, but my brother was my security until I was married.
>
> [She spoke about her sister later in the interview.] You know, in 1975, I had to trek back to Chicago where my sister lives. . . . My brother lives in Southern California. I have not seen him for a long time.

Eunice's brother who looked after her stage of early launching into adulthood may have in part fulfilled the role her father would have, had he lived.

RELATIONSHIPS IN THE MARITAL/NUCLEAR FAMILY

Husbands

Within the marital/nuclear family, among the 66 women who were married, a total of 1,105 references were made about their husbands. A very striking difference was found between mothers and married non-mothers in the number of references made to husbands, however $(\chi^2(1) = 48.86,\ p = 0.0000]$. Mothers who comprised 75.8% of the married group made 965 references to husbands, in contrast to the nonmothers (who made up 24.2% of the married women) who made 140 references to husbands. The average number of responses made by mothers was 19.3, and among nonmothers 8.8.

The group of mothers spoke of their husbands almost twice as often as they did their mothers (each averaged 10 responses about their mothers, contrasted to 19.3 about their husbands). However, among the married nonmothers, no significant differences were noted between the average number of references to their husbands and mothers (each averaged 8.2 responses about mothers, contrasted to 8.8 about husbands).

The differential response to husband between mothers and nonmothers may in part be explained by the nonmothers' later marriages. Mothers who married earlier had a longer span of married life. In addition, mothers' younger age at marriage made them more vulnerable to transferring dependency from parents to husbands. As Rubin (1983) had observed, many women in this study also defined themselves in relation to their husbands. Husbands are also important to mothers in their father role of providing guidance and nurturance in addition to sharing responsibility for children.

Women overall reported their marriages as major transitions in their lives. Wilma Weeks described her marriage as the most significant event in her life, "I married a rancher and it completely turned my life around." Hannah Houser stated, "I suppose getting married was (a major turning point). That's a very wonderful experience. And my life changed radically because I didn't marry until I was 35 and I had been completely immersed in my music."

Other women transferred feelings for their fathers to their husbands when they married. In some instances they married men similar to their fathers, as described above. Thus, without individuating from fathers, they became attached to their husbands. Excerpts from Felicia Fawne's history in Chapter 4 illustrate the women's difficulty in differentiating from their husbands; Felicia was unable to do this until age 50 when they moved to Europe and she made friends on her own, and more completely at age 67 when she gained insight into her own uniqueness, separate from her husband. Ursula Unger is another example of a mother who was unable to differentiate from her husband until his death, "I left my parent's house, became dependent on my husband until his death."

In Chapter 8, many of the participants' vignettes highlight the difference in feelings of loss of husband and loss of mother. Loss of husbands had a greater impact on the women's lives overall than the loss of their mothers.

Josselson (1987) noted that husbands often fulfill the role of mentor for women. Only two of the married nonmothers (12.5%) named their husbands as mentors, and one mother (2%).

Although not all marriages were easy, few ended in divorce. Velma Vaughn was in what she described as a "very, very [pause] not difficult marriage, but he worked constantly and we didn't have a chance to get too well acquainted" for 52 years! She was a widow, and her husband had used alcohol heavily in the last few years of their marriage, supposedly to relieve pain from a fractured spine.

Another mother with a worldview, Thelma Tiller, continued to have some misgivings about what she had given up over a 35 year marriage: "I was reluctant to get married . . . I'd promised him I'd marry him . . . I knew I was going to be trapped." Thelma had sacrificed doing her practice teaching at a better college further away from home when she was in her late 40s at her husband's insistence. Three years after her husband's death she said, "That's a big thorn that I still carry within myself."

Children

The 50 mothers had a total of 122 children, an average of 2.4 per mother, with a range of from 1 to 6. Only one mother had 6, one had 5, 6 had 4 children, 12 had 3, 21 had 2, and 9 women had only 1 child.

Mothers made 741 references to their children, with a range from 2 to 35 references. However, many of the references to children were responses to probes, "How many children did you have, How did you feel when your child left home for the first time, etc." There was an average of 14.8 references to children per mother, and an average of 6 references per number of children. Mothers commented about children less often than about their husbands (average = 19.3).

Mothers' references to children dealt with their births and how soon after their marriages the births occurred, schooling, baby-sitting arrangements if the mother worked, the children's graduation from high-school, marriages, divorces, and births of their grandchildren. As was discussed in Chapter 5, grandchildren were a great source of pleasure to the women.

For 12% of the mothers, the birth of their first child represented the transition to adulthood. Clara Cohen noted, "You're not free any more; you have a responsibility." Karen Koff shared that "It was instilled in my upbringing to be a good wife and a good mother." Karen had 4 children.

Childbearing had its difficult times as many women reported several miscarriages and perinatal deaths. The mother of 6 lost her only son to Sudden Infant Death Syndrome. Three women had lost adult sons, and one had lost an adult daughter.

One mother's only daughter disclosed that she was lesbian when the mother was 56 years old and recovering from surgery for a benign brain tumor. Gladys Gilbert whose mother–daughter conflict was discussed in Chapter 5, had a teenage daughter attempt suicide, a teenage daughter marry, and a son whom she referred to as a "sore." The teenage years were painful years of other mothers with teenage daughters also.

Most of the women expressed relief when the last child left home as opposed to loneliness:

- I was lonely when my son (only child) went to the army.
- I was kind of glad for them to have a chance to be on their own.
- I don't miss taking care of sick ones and doing their laundry; I don't miss that in the least.
- We don't have the worry and hassle if they're not in by midnight or 1:00 A.M. When they were home I worried more about them. When the kids leave home, a couple can have a new life, an independent feeling.

However, overall, the women were pleased with their children and their grandchildren. Their children's accomplishments were related to the interviewers with much pride.

FRIENDS

Friends also had an important influence on the women's lives. This is in contrast to findings by Levinson et al. (1978), who reported an absence of friendships in men's lives. The length of time that some women had maintained friendships was impressive; reports of lifelong friendships were common.

At age 70, Delores Davis, a nonmother, remembered an incident from her childhood friendship that extended into the present:

Everybody was to dress up for a procession around the schoolyard for Thanksgiving . . . I knew my mother didn't have the money to do it. So some other girl's mother made me a Red Cross uniform. So, I'm in the parade around the schoolyard, and I fell and had a bloody nose. Veronica,

two or three grades ahead of me, picked me up and cleaned me off.
. . . You'll never believe that, about 6 months ago, in church I saw her
again. I said, "Are you Veronica?"
  [A supervisor from work who corrected her errors developed into a
friend–mentor.] But she got to be a very good friend of mine. [Told several
anecdotes about jokes they played on each other; this friend died when
Delores was 30.] In the meantime [early 20s], I joined a couple of Catholic
organizations where I met more friends that I still have. . . . I still be-
long to one of them; I'm past president.
  [She described a politician whose father had worked in the same build-
ing that she had worked in for years.] He invited me to his swearing-in and
to his party afterwards. . . . But I made a friend for life. No matter where
he meets me or who he's with. . . . I was at a meeting he addressed, and
this lady told him he could leave by a side door. He says, "I can't, I see a
good friend of mine and I gotta go say hello to her." So he came over and
said, "Hi. How are you? To know you is to never forget you."

Delores, who never married, had both women and men friends that she
enjoyed. Importantly, the friendships helped her during difficult periods later in life, such as during hospitalization following a detached
retina. The supervisor-turned-friend described above helped her get
established in her work.

  Florence Filbert, an 84-year-old widow, had maintained strong,
long-lasting relationships with other women. She had a lifelong
friend and another with whom she had been friends for over 50 years.
At age 31:

> You might say the real turning point was when I came to California over
> 50 years ago. And I didn't meet my number-two husband for 15 years. I
> had been up in Chicago. They had breadlines in Chicago, and I heard
> there was work to be had in California. . . . So I came out with friends.

  Gayle Goodman, a never-married nonmother, remembered childhood friends with nostalgia at age 62:

> His parents had a little store across the tracks. He used to bring me candy
> out of the store, and he would come home with me after school. He was
> my friend for quite a while.
>   [In high school] I had a cadre of friends that I ran around with, and we
> formed an exclusive club—this was one of those secret clubs. We had pins,
> a club house. . . . I suspect I had a number of friends because I was an
> only child. I had several friends that I spent a lot of time with. Our home
> was their home.

Gayle made an interesting observation. She attributed her many child-hood friends to the fact that she was an only child.

Phyllis Painter was expecting a visit from a friend whom she had started to school with some 75 years earlier. Diane Dodd described corresponding with one friend for 53 years who visited her every time she was in the city. She also noted:

> And then I have another group of 10 girls, old ladies now, who still get together every summer. I have a lot of good friends I still maintain contact with.

Lillian Love explained, "Oh, I've learned if you're going to amount to anything in life, you've got to think about other people in the world," which perhaps explains something about the women's long-term friendships.

The friendships did not appear to play a strong role in their ongoing adaptation to transitions, however. The role that these friends played seemed to be in maintaining a historical view of continuity of one's self.

ROLE MODELS

Role models provided important guidelines for behavior and responses as women adapted to the transitions occurring in their life context. Role models or mentors are persons that an individual may wish to emulate and are persons who are interested in helping the individual to select and attain her goals and in molding her future. Role models play an important role during transitions, especially when there is uncertainty about the social expectations for a new role. References to role models were usually in response to the interviewers' probes.

Except for professional women, to whom the terms were more familiar, the women seldom used the term "mentor" or "role model," but spoke of persons who "were important to them," "had taught them the things they needed to know," or "how to respond or behave" in new or changing roles.

Among the total sample of 80 women, nonmothers more often spoke of men as role models; 30% of nonmothers and 18% of the mothers referred to a male family member, teacher, professor, or other professional as one who had influenced their lives in achieving their goals. Seventeen percent of nonmothers and 12% of mothers referred to both men and women as role models. More of the mothers (42%) than nonmothers (37%)

named a woman as a role model. Only 2% of the mothers and 10% of the nonmothers denied having a role model or mentor. Mothers in our study, overall, reported older women relatives or friends as role models, which agrees with Reinke's (1985) observations of women in her study. Nonmothers, however, who had had longer career trajectories than mothers, more often reported the type of mentor described by Levinson et al. (1978) for men. Nonmothers named professors, physicians, instructors, judges, and other professionals holding state and national appointments, in addition to family members.

Remarks made about their mentors indicated the great influence they had had on the women's lives:

- "I think that I owe everything to my older sister."
- "He told me not to move to Arizona because for my own physical health I would be better staying where I was."
- "She pushed me all of the time—she made me manager, and because of that I had to make all of the arrangements and so I learned from that. She pushed me ahead to make my self better."

A mother with a family view of the world described her role models:

My mother was home, of course. She, I guess, was my most influential role model. However, I did look up to my sisters and to my aunts a great deal. Our activities were around the home. Having big dinners and having people in on the weekend was much of our social activity. I especially liked to have people with children in.

Josephine Jones, an 80-year-old nonmother with a worldview of life, had several men mentors. She stated:

Well, I had a broad view of the world which I had begun by my father. He knew lots of people, and they shared our home, our lives and theirs' with us. . . .
Another mentor and friend was [professional in federal office] himself.

SUMMARY

This chapter focused on important relationships in the women's lives. The transitions cited by the women occurred within the setting of family, friends, and role models or mentors who had a part in the women's development over their life course. It was clear that these persons provided the relationships that were the backdrop for life events. Through the eyes of these older women (in their seventh decade of life or older), with the vantage point of maturity, their important relationships had provided them with emotional, informational, and physical support that facilitated their adaptation to each transition.

Among mothers, the marital/nuclear family was more central to their lives. If one accepts that the frequency of relationships mentioned indicates their importance, those relationships most important to mothers were with their husbands (average of 19.3 references), their children (average of 14.8 references), their own mothers (an average of 10), their fathers (an average of 6.8), and their siblings (an average of 5.5).

Nonmothers made an average of 8.2 references about their mothers and 7.6 about their fathers. Married nonmothers referred to their husbands an average of 8.8 times, indicating that their husbands, whom they had married later, were not as central to their lives as husbands were to mothers.

Health professionals' awareness of the importance of women's relationships with others should enhance their ability to provide individualized care. Knowledge of the person's important relationships aids in understanding the responsibilities and social support that the person has. Use of reminiscence may also be a useful adjunct to practice by providing the older person an opportunity to recapture the joys or previous relationships that are no longer available.

■ 7
Geographical Moves: A Catalyst for Psychosocial Development

"Then I said to my mother . . ., there is no work here for anybody, so why don't we go to America? So we went to America." Phyllis Painter, an 18-year-old at the time, was living in England when she made that decision. Her decision, arrived at as a result of personal reasons and her country's economic situation, had long-reaching consequences. The personal reasons included the fact that her father had died 4 years earlier. This led to a financial crisis requiring her mother to find work. The financial crisis also caused them to lose their home and to move to cheaper surroundings.

A cousin, living in the United States, upon hearing about the death of Mr. Painter and the family's ensuing difficulties, had written to them that he planned to come to England to take care of them. The economic conditions in England were poor, and the Painters knew that employment opportunities were limited; it did not seem feasible to have the cousin come to England to help them. A more logical conclusion was that they should go to the cousin in the United States. Phyllis made this decision and convinced her mother that it was the best alternative. Sixty-four years later during our interview, Phyllis Painter described this decision as one that led to an important transition in her life. Upon arrival in the United States, life became even more difficult:

> We were terrible. . . . We were dressed for winter, and it was so hot. . . . My cousin didn't want any part of us when he saw we didn't have any

133

money . . . So we found a place to live in a rooming house. I went into
the telephone company and got a job, and my mother, she didn't do
anything. I didn't get much money, only about $60.00 per month [1920],
and, so then, I stayed with the telephone company about 9 years and I
went ahead [advanced] pretty good. [She married when she was 25 and
had a daughter 10 years later.]

The implications of this important transitional move for Phyllis Painter,
along with many others cited by other participants, give credence to the
importance of using a multidimensional model for studying life span development. The developmental model proposed by Baltes et al. (1980)
emphasizes the relationship between the impact of events and developmental stages in women's lives. Baltes et al. (1980) included transitional
moves among the non-normative life events. Non-normative life events
refer to events that have not occurred in any age-expected or history-
graded manner, such as career change, relocation, and death. The impact
of events such as relocation varies according to many factors such as timing, patterning, and duration of the event; the event becomes significant
because of its impact on human development (Baltes et al., 1980). Thus, a
person's development cannot be restricted into age-graded or historically
graded development, but rather must be viewed from an individualistic
viewpoint of development.

As we pursued analysis of the women's rich life histories, we saw that
the developmental model proposed by Baltes et al. (1980) provided the
best framework for our analysis and reflected our overall viewpoint because of the inclusion of all kinds of transitions—environmental, social,
and biological determinants and normative and non-normative events. We
had expected the non-normative transitions of untimely death or illness
within the family. An unexpected finding was the large number of transitions directly related to relocation (a change of location of residence)
involving a move or translocation of some type. Relocation involves moving from a familiar and often quite comfortable environment with friends
who can provide support to an unknown or foreign environment.

Both mothers and nonmothers indicated that such moves led to their
lives taking new directions that often involved role change. These transitional moves fell into two categories: moves that were motivated or
planned by the woman and those moves that were motivated or caused by
another person—usually a parent or spouse. The self-motivated moves
involved a cognitive and/or emotional decision, that is, the decision to
move came from within the woman herself. Such moves were categorized
as internally motivated moves. Other moves occurred as a result of

another person's decision and were categorized as externally motivated. In some situations, both internal and external influences led to the move. An example of this is Heloise Harvest, who told of influencing her husband in a combination of externally and internally motivated decision making:

> Turning points? One of them was when I aided and abetted my husband to take a job away from the west coast. The first one. He took a 6-month leave . . ., but I urged him to stay on in the midwest.

It was important to clarify the relationship between the actual move and the reason for the move to determine whether the move was internally or externally motivated. There is an extensive range in the extent to which people control their experienced life events. Weisz (1983) summed this eloquently while quoting Brim (p. 1, 1974): "Most of us live out our lives . . . 'somewhere between the conditions of slavery and omnipotence' (p. 234)."

In situations of self-motivated moves, women potentially could feel more in control of their lives and, thus, feel better about themselves. High correlations between sense of mastery (or control of life's situations) and self-esteem have been reported among adults in the community and among new mothers (Folkman, Lazarus, Gruen, & DeLongis, 1986; Mercer & Ferketich, 1988).

A woman's move as the result of another person's decision was often related to "going along" with that decision and more or less agreeing with the decision. Through such acceptance, she maintained the status quo within her family by moving her home to another environment. Other moves were linked to earlier decisions such as those described by Sarah Sanger who knew that her husband-to-be would be relocating to find work and that his line of work would require transfers from time to time. Examples of how these moves that were related to her husband's career led to her own development follow:

> [After a move to a small Southern mill town] I found that I really didn't like living in a tiny little town. I was horrified by the whole social stratification. . . . I didn't like what I saw there at all. We were accepted into the top layer [of the stratification] because we were educated, although we had no money. . . . There was the professional group of people and then this huge group of mill workers. I taught for the first time there because it was when they needed teachers so badly. I had all these darling little mill children because I was given the kids that the other first grade teachers didn't want, and we had to make home visits and I saw how they

lived and it was pretty bad. . . . It was a real realization of what it was like to be really, really poor . . . The two local doctors held a clinic every other week, one afternoon, for the black people in town; that was their sole access to medical care. All children were delivered by midwives—not even accredited midwives. My consciousness was really raised in that place.

[After a transfer to Washington, D.C. from the mill town] I was just delighted to be in a place where there were just all of these wonderful things. I got into a American Association of University Women (AAUW) chapter which had a lot of socially conscious people and I got involved in a study of what was then always known as socialized medicine and became a proponent of that and shocked a lot of my friends. I got really socially conscious in the mill town, and I was able to act on it in the Washington area. My father was a southerner who was very pro-Roosevelt and pro-opportunity for blacks. He realized as long as there were repressive measures that it wasn't good for society as a whole.

I also did the thing that started me on a career path [age 31] during that time. I had my third child, but on Saturdays I went to work in the local branch of the public library. I just loved it and loved dealing with the people who came in. . . . As an untrained person, they were very good to me in terms of recognizing me as a real person in that I might have something to contribute.

Thus, we see much personal development occurring in Sarah Sanger as a result of both of her externally motivated relocations. Not only did the majority of the women report a move as a transitional event in their lives, but several also reported more than one move led to personal change in their lives.

INCIDENCE OF MOVES OR RELOCATIONS

The developmental impact of translocation (moving from one place to another) was strongly evidenced. Forty out of 50 mothers (80%) and 20 out of 30 nonmothers (67%) reported moves as important transitions in their lives. Thus, for most of the study participants, a relocation of residence was a transitional experience leading to developmental change.

Not all translocations resulted in a developmental transition, however. Some of the women reported from 16 to 20 moves without noting the moves as leading to their lives changing significantly in any way.

Table 7.1 summarizes the numbers of moves that were related to developmental change in their lives. The 40 mothers who reported

TABLE 7.1 Transitional Moves Reported By Mothers and Nonmothers

	Mothers		Nonmothers	
Number of moves	n	%	n	%
One	24	48	9	30
Two	9	18	5	17
Three	3	6	4	13
Four	2	4	1	3
Five	0	0	1	3
Six	2	4	0	0
Total	40	80	20	67

transitional moves reported a total of 71 moves. Of these 71 moves, 43 (61%) were externally motivated, 25 (35%) were internally motivated, and 3 (4%) were both internally and externally motivated. Forty moves were reported by the 20 nonmothers reporting transitional moves. However, more nonmothers reported internally motivated moves, with 22 (55%) of the moves coming from their decisions. Only 12 (30%) of the nonmothers' moves were externally motivated, and 4 (10%) had both internal and external influences. Since 47% of the nonmothers never married, fewer nonmothers moved because of husbands' career moves. This factor accounts in large part for differences between internally and externally motivated moves.

MOVING AS A PROCESS

Relocation to a new environment can be traumatic, exciting, or a routine experience. The moves involved translocations to new countries, as was the case with Phyllis Painter, to different parts of the country, as was the case with Sarah Sanger, or sometimes within the same city. Much physical activity and emotional upheaval often accompanies the process of moving. In the move to a new environment, many similarities or extreme differences were found between the old and the new locations. However, there appeared to be a uniform process experienced by most of the women.

Process of Moving

Most moves seem to involve six or seven phases in the process: predecision, decision to move, physical and mental preparation, packing and leave-taking, traveling, unpacking and relocating, and the settling-in phase.

Predecision Phase.   A predecision phase may occur first, as with Amy Andrews: "I always had in the back of my mind that the dean's position would open up, and I wanted to live in that area." She had made a decision about moving prior to the time of actual opportunity to move, so that when this particular position opened she would apply for the transfer (which she did).

An example of an internally motivated move seemingly without much predecision or predeliberation or cognitive preparation was that of Carrie Carmichael's when she was 45:

> I lived in New York for a very long time. When I was single, I did some traveling, but I always came home, and I always would read up before going somewhere to familiarize myself and to decide whether that's where I wanted to go or not. And I came to San Francisco; that was in 1946. I was to be there for 10 days. I had my position back East. Each day I was more thrilled with watching and seeing how all the different groups met and seeing the children you don't see in New York—the Japanese, Chinese, Caucasian. I thought that it was so beautiful, and then I loved the city and I kept saying, "This is a small-scale cultural city compared to New York." I attended the theater and the opera.
>
> I couldn't see myself leaving, and one day I went down to the ticket office; it was the day before I was to leave, and I said to the lady, "I want to change the date. I'm not going to leave tomorrow." And while she was working on my ticket, I suddenly thought, "Well, if I'm not going to leave, I want to stay longer. What shall I do." I didn't have very much money. So I said, "May I have a refund, and when I decide to leave I'll get a ticket."

Carrie went on to say that she stayed in San Francisco, and 2 years later she met her future husband and married him. Later in the interview, she was asked to review important transitions in her life:

> Well, the big turning point was coming to San Francisco, breaking from the family, untying the knot. I think that definitely, because I was very close and I felt responsible for helping my father and keeping house and

all that. . . . When I wrote home that I was not coming home and when I'd spoken to the family, I received a letter from my brother. It said, "Congratulations, you've grown up."

Later in rereading Carrie Carmichael's life history, it became evident that this seemingly sudden decision had been a long time in the making. Years before coming to San Francisco, Carrie had remembered:

It was after my mother died that I felt more responsible towards the home, and I was even considering just staying home and keeping the house and the family. We all discussed it. Some of the family thought "yes," and some thought "no." A friend said, "Carrie, don't do it. You'll ruin your life." Yeah. But it's really when you make an important decision like that. Going to Europe doesn't mean anything [reference to her first trip away from home].

Decision to Move Phase. The decision to move may reflect personal choice and thus is internally motivated, "I have always wanted to move to California. I am not getting any younger, so I am going to move to California now." Billye Bond illustrates someone else making the decision to move for the family (an externally caused move):

We went to church. . . . My son was settled in school, and I belonged to Parent Teachers' Association [PTA]. People seem to get close in small communities . . . and then the bomb fell again. We were to be transferred to the Southwest—my husband had another promotion.

Parents usually make the decision to move and the child/children may not be involved in the decision-making in any way, but they are automatically included in the move to a new home. Although not the case with women in our study, older adults are sometimes treated as children and relocation occurs as a result of circumstances beyond their control. An older person becomes seriously ill, is transported to a hospital where she is in temporary residence, and when she is partially recovered, she is moved to a nursing home, another temporary residence. However, at this point, someone makes the decision about a more permanent residence. The decision about the new place of residence for the infirm elder is made by someone, whether it is the physician, social worker, family member, or the individual. Decision-making and problem-solving enter into all relocations that occur, and there is a fairly rational reason for leaving one place of residence and moving to another.

Physical and Mental Preparation Phase.   The physical and mental preparation phase includes physical and mental tasks related to the actual move. Physical tasks involve packing, discarding useless items, sorting, organizing, and cleaning in readiness for moving. Mental activity includes notification of family and friends that a move is imminent, the selection of a moving company, making arrangements for the actual move, selling and buying or renting a house, discontinuing utility services, and notification of children's schools, churches, and clubs.

The mental preparation includes some grief work in beginning to separate from friends and in relinquishing roles (president of the PTA or other club membership). In grief work, there may be some anger at the cause for the move if the move is not internally motivated, and occasionally some disorganization is present, such that it is hard to get on with the needed chores. Parkes (1971) spoke of relinquishing parts of one's known or assumptive world as painful because of the threat to the individual's security. However, in situations of self-motivated moves, gains are seen, which balance or outweigh the losses.

Packing and Leave-Taking Phase.   The packing and leave-taking phase follows the physical and mental preparation phase closely. Packing includes moving all of the household supplies into the moving van or other vehicle, keeping aside necessities and valuables to be moved by car, cleaning the house, and actually leaving the house. Friends have farewell dinners and parties for those leaving. Finally, the walk through the house for the last time looking for missed items and nostalgically grieving for the happy memories that are being left behind and saying goodbye to family, neighbors, and friends conclude the leave-taking.

Traveling Phase.   The traveling phase may be seen as either an enjoyable time or a frustrating time. This phase represents the time and miles that elapse between the leaving of one home and arriving at the new home.

Unpacking Phase.   The unpacking phase includes moving in and placing possessions and furniture in the new home site. This is followed by quick unpacking of necessities and slower unpacking of other things. Much physical and mental energy is exerted in this phase as utility services are ordered; new neighbors are met; new friends, physicians, dentists, schools, and churches are selected; and the family becomes familiar with the new house and community. There is a gradual incorporation of the new setting and life as this phase blends into the final phase.

Settling-in Phase.   The settling-in phase occurs as individuals begin to feel "at home" in their new environment. New roles in the community are taken on as the individual becomes a part of that community. The grief of moving has resolved as the individual reintegrates her life within the new community. Developmental transitions seem to occur during and following this period.

CHILDHOOD MOVES

Although children are rarely involved in the decision-making process to move, they experience the phases of grief and moving. Many women gave vivid descriptions of early childhood moves. Gladys Gilbert's memories of a move when she was 6 (61 years earlier) were as follows:

> My parents were divorced at this time. They were in the process of a very ugly divorce. . . . so we went to board in a ranch situation, my brother and I. My memories of that is that it was a life-saver. We stayed in a ranch with eight or nine other children. [The decision to send her to the ranch seemed to have been her mother's and perhaps a social worker's.]
>
> [Gladys reported that her father had frequently beat her brother, and she commented on the ranch experience] I think that my brother and I got a little bit more attention than some of the other kids, for reasons that I don't understand.
>
> [When Gladys was 9 she was moved again because of her father's decision. Her dad came to get her, and she moved from the ranch and began to live with him.] They wanted to skip me 2 years in school, but no, I skipped 1 year. Living with my father who was on and off employed and not employed was sort of a pillar-to-post life. No family situation, and I had no girlfriend or anyone. Well, when I was 15 my mother remarried, and she came and got me. I had not seen my mother for almost 6 years.

Each of these externally caused moves for Gladys during her childhood and teenage years represented a transitional event for her.

Any relocation may lead to cultural shock. Cultural shock according to Leininger (1978) is the feeling of helplessness and discomfort that causes a state of disorientation for the outsider in the new culture. The newcomer has no signs or clues as to how to respond in the new culture. Sarah Sanger described a family move from the northeast to the southeast when she was 11 years of age as such:

> It was a culture shock for me. I was a good student, but I was not socially advanced in any way. I had not been interested in boys or clothes, and I

got to Miami and found that my peer group was interested in all those things. I had to do a lot of fast adjusting because I didn't want to be left behind. I remember they laughed at some of my clothes because I was wearing very sensible shoes and that kind of thing, and I had to get into the kind of little flirty-looking clothes they were wearing. I was entering junior high school at that time. . . . I think I wasn't where I really wanted to be in terms of the group of friends and acceptance for 1 ½ to 2 years. About the time I went into the real high school was when I got it all organized.

MOVES AS SEPARATING AND REUNITING FAMILIES

Moves or family relocation involved both loss of close proximity to other family members as well as a reunion for others. For some, the relocation included the loss of much more than family, as was the case with Maude Morris:

> It [the transitional move] meant that I didn't get my doctorate; I got married. It could have gone one way or the other. I was married and that was a tremendous change because it meant that I now said "goodbye" to Canada and I was moving to a foreign country, leaving my family and moving close in proximity to my future husband's family.

Other moves involved uniting families, however, as was the case with Nancy Newton who was 17 and enrolled in college 80 miles from her home. Her family was separated during World War II; her mother was teaching in the home community and her father was working in a ship yard on the west coast. Her brother, who was in the service, was stationed on the west coast. Nancy stated:

> After an especially lonely Christmas during the war when everybody was separated, I wrote my dad and said, "This is not the way to live. Can't we come to California?" I didn't want to be in college. . . . My dad wrote back and said he had all the plans made so we could come to California. So I quit college and my mother resigned, and we came to California.

A CONTRAST OF NONTRANSITIONAL/ NONDEVELOPMENTAL MOVES AND DEVELOPMENTAL MOVES

Laverne Lewis, a nonmother, moved many times during her lifetime. As close as could be determined, she moved/lived in at least 26 different places; she considered only three of these as making a change in the direction her life took, however. All three of these developmental transitions were internally motivated: at age 18, moving to London to take a first job; at age 23, moving to France; and at age 50, moving to the United States. However, other moves, not viewed by her as transitional, indicated the impact of moving, especially for a child. In addition, such moves provide important information for health professionals who are working with very mobile populations. Laverne Lewis remembered:

> Now, we moved when I was 9. My grandmother was living with us; she lived in the top of the house with two nurses because she had a stroke. There was also a nanny and me and my sister who was 2 years younger. My brother came, and I was put into a room of my own, but I was terrified of sleeping alone, because we had the woods where my father would shoot just at the back of the house. And the owls would hoot, and I knew the owls were going to get me. I would sleep with my knees up to my chin shivering, "Nanny please give me a light; please leave the door open." She always shut the door. I [still] think it is awful. And then we moved again— to a smaller house because my grandmother died, and we were very happy because next door there was a family with children.

Both of the aforementioned moves were remembered, but did not alter her life's direction in any way; however, the transitional move at age 18 cited above was a developmental milestone. Although the move appeared to be internally motivated, external factors were also involved in leading to the move:

> So then things were so awful I had to get a job because the business went wrong and my father had to go bankrupt, but he would not. A friend next door said to my father, "You can't do that; think of your wife and children. Sell the home just because you're going bankrupt. Where are you going? Sell your family in the street."
> My father wouldn't take advice from anyone in the world so we had to sell the whole home. My mother was a darling, sweet, gentle little soul, and we three kids. We had to sell everything. We weren't allowed to keep our teddy bears or music or anything. I was 18, and I looked for a job. I couldn't find a job locally, and I didn't want to because all of the friends I had were at school. They had homes and money, and I couldn't face that. . . . So I answered an ad for a mother's helper in London. I wrote my Aunt Elizabeth who lived there and asked if she could help me because I'd never been anywhere you know. Aunt Elizabeth met the train and said, "What are you doing? What are you doing?" I said, "I've got this

job with two little children in London." Oh, she was mad! But at any rate she took me over, and there I was.

Laverne stayed with that family for 8 months. She continued to work as a mother's helper for many different families; thus, the many moves. Then, she noted, at age 23 a developmental move occurred. After the internally motivated decision, she made plans, and after much negotiation and many letters, she remarked,

> I got the job and went to France. I was happy! I was happy! Those were the happiest days of my life. We were all in the chateau together, and it was home. Even now I cry when I talk about it. I was so happy there. I was loved. It was my home.

Although she continued to work as a mother's helper, and her occupational role did not change, her feelings of security and her outlook did. Laverne's next transitional move came 27 years later when she moved to the United States. This move follows all of the phases in the process of moving:

> **Predicision, decision phase:** At midnight, I was alone, living in a suburb of London. I was listening to the church bells and car horns and whistles to welcome the New Year [1955].
>
> I reviewed the past year, which had been very dull. I lived in "digs," which means one room, a small kitchen, and shared a bathroom. For 2 years I had been trying to find an apartment, but with the bombing during the war and a housing shortage, my luck was out. I longed for a home of my own. . . . I lay thinking about the future. I loved traveling and had either lived in or visited France, Spain, Italy, Germany, Switzerland, Austria, Czechoslovakia, Gibralter, and Spain, and wondered where to go. I made a sudden decision to go to America—no idea about how to set about it, but the actual idea seemed great.
>
> **Physical and mental preparation phase:** [After various maneuvers and help from friends, Laverne's plans were made to leave.] All of the permits were cleared, and I was able to get down to travel arrangements. The last month, giving away books and other possessions and saying goodbye to friends and family, was rather tough, for the United States was a very long way from home, and I did not know a soul or even a cat, in that huge country. At times I felt rather afraid, but fortunately I am blessed with good health and guts.
>
> **Leave-taking phase:** I was given a lovely bon voyage party, and the director of the company where I worked presented me with a nice traveling bag. Ten friends came to Waterloo to see me off, and I found it awfully hard to smile and talk and laugh.

Traveling phase: I traveled first class to give me courage, but I suddenly realized how alone, at age 50, I would be in the future. I just managed to keep up and had a weep in the "loo" the minute after we left. From Southampton I sailed in the Queen Elizabeth—goodbye England. [She arrived in the United States.] This had taken from January to October 25, the date I arrived in New York. [She continued across the continent in a bus to a children's boarding school where she was to be employed. All of her luggage was inadvertently sent ahead, and all she had to travel with was what she was wearing for the 10-day trip.] Upon arriving, Laverne moved quickly into the next phase of relocation.

Unpacking/settling-in phases: Arriving . . . I was relieved to find all of my luggage. Was I happy to have a change of clothes! It was a bit scary to live with someone I didn't know, 5,000 miles away from home, but I was fortunate we were a happy household. I arrived in the afternoon, and no one was at home except one of the teachers. I had a shower and fell on the bed and slept to be woken by whispers, "There she is, wonder what she is like," and opening my eyes, I saw two bright faces beaming at me. I had arrived.

It was rather a shock to find out that most of the children's mothers had been divorced two or even three times. . . . I loved the children and the place—winter time and hot sun every day.

The process involved in internally motivated moves (such as Laverne Lewis's) was slightly different than for those involved in moves due to external circumstances. Ursula Unger, a mother, described over 20 moves over her life course. She described the first move when she was 10 years old:

My father realized we needed a much bigger house, . . . and they bought a large house in the country with 72 acres. That was the house we grew up in—from the fourth grade through high school. And that was a dramatic change for me. I remember loving the old house; it was on a wide street with a garden with an island and rocks and trees. I had lots of friends, and we'd sit up there and talk in the evening. Lots of interactions, and when we moved to this big house which was absolutely gorgeous, it had 18 rooms. We had it remodeled. It was very lonely. For the first time I had my own room; everybody had their own room. And my mother had a couple of people that worked a little bit of the land and kept up the house. But it was very lonely for me, because I left all of these friends and I didn't make any new ones right away, and was rather isolated. It was one-fourth mile to the next house. It was not a happy house for me. I remember my mother saying I didn't need friends, that I had all my brothers and sisters.

[Many years later she moved into town and married when she finished college.] Well, I had met my husband actually in high school and dated him the last year in high school, and when I went to college we continued that relationship and were engaged for two and one-half years of college. He was in the Reserve Officer Training Corps (ROTC), which meant that he would go in the service after graduating. So he graduated on Sunday, and we were married on Monday [she was age 20] much to my parents' disappointment, chagrin, and unhappiness. They thought the college years were wasted. It was the only time in my life that I really stood up to them. But it was hard, and still is, even years and years later.

My husband went immediately into the service, and so he went to North Carolina for training, and I joined him as soon as I could. I didn't want to be home, so I kept working at a secretarial job I had. I joined him in North Carolina, and then we went to Georgia, then to Connecticut. Here I was an Army wife; I did have teaching credentials, which I'd gotten because I didn't know what else I really could do or wanted to do at that stage. I taught; there was always a demand for teachers. Then he was stationed in California, and he got orders for overseas, and as he was being processed, the war ended. That was another turn. . . . Before this, I had never traveled or had much independence. Suddenly having to be traveling alone and following my husband to these camps was a totally new experience to me and sort of scary.

[Ursula and her husband moved a couple more times.] We decided that it would really be more fair to our families to try living near them [in the North], although we didn't really want to. So he got a job in August, and by January we were absolutely sick of the cold weather and of not having a car. We finally got enough money together to buy a little car. I think it was the last Ford convertible they made, 1940 [she is 25 at this time]. Anyway, we packed all our worldly goods into the back of this little car and drove across the country to California. And this time our parents didn't really say anything. I think it was a certain sadness, but they didn't object. They sort of recognized that we were going to make our own decision.

[After two more moves, they bought a house. Her dialogue revealed many of the same feelings as expressed when living in the happy home of her childhood in the city.] I had my little house which I loved and we lived in. I guess you would call it a development. Everybody was just out of the service and was getting started—lots of young children and a lot of community projects. It was a very happy time. We lived there 7 years. And then another move.

It seemed like a long drive, and so we moved closer to his work. But he decided to move on. I guess I was a suburban housewife in those years, but they were happy years, the children were jolly, and so for about 10 years it sort of went along. Then my husband was transferred back East. But he went toward a new career, and I knew that I had to be the good wife and go with him and keep up morale on the surface.

[Her husband was asked to go to Europe.] We talked it over, but I felt like I had to go along with him and make life fulfilling, rewarding for him, and that we would adjust the marriage. He went overseas. I stayed with the children until school was out. And then I sold the house and joined him. And that was really a dramatic turning point in my life. [She did not know before arriving in Europe that her children could not live with the family and go to school. They had to be sent to another country to school.] At 43, it was a real crisis for me because we had always had a real compatible family group. I think I fantasized that we'd all be together again in the States and life would be as it had been, but it's never happened because they graduated from high school and went on to college. So essentially my children left home 4 years earlier than anticipated.

I had to start thinking "What am I going to do with my life now?" I went through a lot of depression at that time in my life because it was such an uprooting, and I really missed the children and all the activity.

[Three years later they moved back to the States when Ursula was 48.] I thought about this a lot and talked it over with my husband and decided that I would apply to the University. . . . I was surprised to be accepted at my age. It went well.

[At 51, Ursula had a master of science degree, and the couple decided to move back to California.] So again we packed our car. This time I spent a month packing a lot of other things too. . . . I started looking for a job, and I was really fortunate. It took me 6 months, but it took me 6 months to get settled anyway.

Although Ursula had started a new career at age 52 and it was a turning point in her life, she summed up her life: I think my number one priority always was my home and my husband and family, but I needed the career for my own mental health. I think in some ways, my husband thought of it as sort of nice, it's fun, it's frivolous and all. But he was always supportive and kind. His only comment when I began my career was, "Well, you better get somebody to help in the house; you can't do everything." And so I did.

Ursula Unger moved several times and focused on various stages of the moving process during the different moves. Only four of the moves were transitional, in that her life took a different direction, however. One was internally motivated, and three were externally caused by her husband's career change.

Ursula Unger's transitional moves are representative of many other mothers in this study. Many of their moves were because of their husbands' career changes. Although the women had the freedom not to move, that freedom would have meant leaving their husbands or finding some other solution, thus, not a practical choice for many. However, these externally motivated moves precipitated other events in the women's lives that led to their continuing personal development. Although the moves per se were outside the women's control, what the women could do with their lives as a result of the moves was within their control. So, although Ursula was depressed at having her family separated prematurely by the move to Europe for her husband's career, she thought out what she might do about it in terms of her life. She needed her career, which she began preparing for in her late 40s and moved into during her early 50s, for her own mental health. She rebuilt her life structure in order to become her own person.

Identity Loss Through Moves

Moving from a community of familiar friends and/or family to a community of strangers with different values and philosophies also meant losing persons who up to that point had reinforced the women's identities. Identity emerges through interactions with others in the person's social context, others who reaffirm who one is and what one does (Erikson, 1968; Mead, 1934). This was exemplified by Sarah Sanger in a move because of her husband's career change:

> I had a hard time because I surrendered both my professional identity and any life that wasn't linked with his when I went there. I had to give up a lot of identity then. I had a lot of rejection in terms of the kind of person I was. Women my age in that little town weren't like me. They were much more conservative. . . .
>   One thing that I did with a young friend at my daughter's suggestion was start a women's group, of which I was the oldest member, and the young ones were really young and were having all kinds of early wife and motherhood problems. . . . It was just really a hard place for those women, and because I had been through all that, I was able to be helpful to them in many cases. It made the whole thing worthwhile to me that time in that state. Those young women are still my friends and call me long distance and say, "What shall I do?" That's very rewarding.

Sarah was able to continue her development despite her initial identity loss of interactions with women her own age. She created a new role for herself, that of mentor to younger women who did not reject her more liberal views.

SUMMARY

Relocations to a new residence are viewed differently by individuals experiencing these events. Not all such moves are considered to be transitional events leading to personal development. The process of moving, however, has six or seven phases: predecision, decision to move, physical and mental preparation, packing and leave-taking, traveling, unpacking and relocating, and the settling-in phase. In each move, much physical and mental work and energy are involved.

Transitional moves involve setting up and making choices for a future period of time for self and the family. Gains help to balance the losses that occur in such moves, but individuals grieve to some extent in relinquishing friends, old and loved homes, and familiar environments. If the new environment is so different that cultural shock occurs, the feeling of disorganization is more acute. The newcomer must learn how to act and respond to cues within the new environment in order to adapt. However, in taking on new roles and incorporating the new life, individual development is ongoing.

Health professionals can be aware of the disorganization an individual experiences around the time of relocation. Importantly, families with children may be counseled about the impact of moves on children. A move to a larger house is not necessarily welcomed by a child. Having one's own room may be frightening to the child initially. Leaving friends is particularly difficult for the school-age child and teenager.

■ 8
Identity Change Through Loss

Deaths and illnesses had a great impact on the lives of the women we interviewed:

- When my fiancé was killed in the war [World War II], I decided to go to graduate school; I found it more satisfying than entering another relationship.
- At age 32, I was involved in a serious accident. I had glass in my eyes. After that, I saw things differently.

Few of the women reported death, illness, or other significant loss as the single overriding factor in their lives, yet it was evident that losses precipitated much change over the course of these women's lives, and for some of the women, these losses did, in fact, result in major transitions. All but one woman reported experiencing at least one significant loss during their lifetimes. Significant work has been done correlating life stresses with illness (Dohrenwend & Dohrenwend, 1984; Kjervik, 1986; Moos, 1986; Vingehoets, 1985). We examined these women's lives from the opposite perspective. How did illnesses and losses (generally deaths) impact women's development over the life course? Did the women experience transitions due to losses, and did they identify these times as periods of change?

TIMING OF LOSSES

The chronological age or the developmental stage at which the loss occurred was important in both the impact the event had upon the women's life course and in her ability to recall and characterize the event. Losses early in the woman's life often had a more profound impact upon the overall course of the woman's life, although the majority of the women were more conscious of the impact of losses in later life. It was also evident in examining the pattern of loss experiences that women were more likely to experience losses during certain age periods than during others. Mothers also had a different pattern of loss experiences than did nonmothers.

The Early Years

There were some differences in the patterns of illness and death experiences for mothers and nonmothers in their early years. For example, over twice as many mothers as nonmothers experienced deaths before the age of 20; 20% of mothers compared to 9% of nonmothers. Nonmothers, however, felt a greater influence from illnesses during childhood and adolescence than did mothers; 7% of nonmothers, compared to 2% of mothers.

Frequently the earliest memories reported by the women related to losses—funerals for aunts, grandmothers, or siblings. The women did not attribute great significance to these nonparental losses. In fact, they often shared that they really had not understood why there was such sorrow on the part of older family members. For some women, however, early losses had a profound effect upon their lives. Women whose mothers died or deserted the family early in their lives were sent to live with relatives or to boarding school. Such relocation was difficult and usually resulted in the woman expressing feelings of insecurity throughout childhood and, for a few, into adulthood. As Constance Calvin recalled:

> I had been such a lonely child and I couldn't understand . . . I mean, I felt like I was unloved, and when I came down from boarding school in the middle of these young people and a lot of handsome young men that expressed their love for me, I couldn't understand that anybody loved me.
> [Another excerpt from Constance Calvin's recollections of her childhood] And I happened to walk near the kitchen, and I heard the two colored maids talking, and one of them said, "Poor little Connie, nobody wants her" . . . Yes, and it was true.

Delilah Diamond also moved frequently during her childhood and adolescence as her mother served as a domestic in several households on the West Coast. She recalled the effect of her father's death when she was 5 years old and the subsequent loss of stability in her home life:

Adjustments started early in my life with my mother's coming and going and my father's illness and death . . . but when I married I felt so secure for the first time.

Interactional relationships within one's family of origin are central to the processes of identity formation; these unique relationships are based on a cumulative background of expectancies (Weigert & Hastings, 1977). The loss of a family member means that part of a concrete identity that was a part of the self is lost because that unique interactional relationship no longer exists. Delilah's loss of her interactional self as her father's daughter at age 5 contributed to her feelings of insecurity; she did not feel secure until she married at age 24.

Their 20s and 30s

For mothers, when all decades of their lives were compared, the decade of their 30s was least impacted by deaths, and the decade of their 20s least impacted by illnesses. For nonmothers, deaths were least evident in their years under 20 and illnesses least during their 20s, as it was for mothers. However, although losses were less frequent during nonmothers' 20s and 30s, losses that occurred during these ages were more likely to have a profound impact upon the woman's life. Sally Salmon's fiancé died, leaving her unwilling to make such a commitment again, so she never married. Dana Doolittle, another nonmother, also experienced the death of her boyfriend. Rather than enter into a new relationship, she focused on her career. Maude Morris, also a nonmother, had two boyfriends killed in the war; she was 20 and 25, respectively, at their deaths. After the second loss, she decided to go to graduate school, as she found it more satisfying than entering another relationship.

The deaths of parents during their 20s and 30s pushed some of the women into the role of breadwinner or manager of the household. Deloris Davis was thrust into this role at age 27 when her father died, and she became the sole wage earner for her mother and siblings. Three of four women who were thrust into such positions never married.

Other nonmothers also experienced losses other than deaths during these decades. Although these losses caused significant change in the woman's life, the loss did not result in the woman not marrying. Noreen Nunnaly was nearly blinded in an auto accident at age 32. She noted that after being spared from blindness, she "saw things differently." Ruth Rogers cared for an ill father from the age of 21, then at age 25 her husband was involved in an accident that resulted in the couple leaving the city and moving back to her mother's farm.

Although several of the mothers experienced losses during their 20s and 30s, few attributed a profound change in their lives as a result. One who reported losses as having a great impact on her life during this period was Clara Cohen, whose husband was diagnosed as being diabetic when she was 26. Her husband was required to seek alternate employment; the family, then living in California, returned to Utah, where he was employed in a lower paying position. Clara sought employment to help the family finances. When Clara was 30, her 10-year-old daughter contracted polio. The daughter survived, but with some residual paralysis. Again, Clara felt a major impact on her life with the loss in her daughter's physical health. The timing of a family member's long-term disability appears to relate to the difficulty in the family incorporating the necessary life-style changes (Cleveland, 1980); Clara's age-30 transition was rife with loss that led to upheaval in her life.

Several of the mothers lost parents, but the loss was not reported as being a particularly significant event in their lives. Since mothers had married earlier than nonmothers, they had established a conjugal relationship in their own nuclear family, which in itself emerged through a process of acquaintance, courtship, love making, marriage, homemaking, and, for some, mothering. Spouses share and reaffirm mutually intense affective identities (Weigert & Hastings, 1977).

Later Years

As would be expected, losses and illness were more frequently reported in the later years for both mothers and nonmothers. Two decades stand out as ones in which losses were dominant themes: the women's 50s and 60s.

The 50s: Quiescent but Loss Oriented.   The decade of the women's 50s was one of relative quiescence; however, of the transitions reported in this age period, the greater proportion of them related to deaths. Significant events during this age period often involved death of a spouse, parents, and siblings. It was during this decade that several of the nonmothers lost their own mothers. In recounting the losses that occurred during this age period, the mothers did not indicate great changes in their life courses as a result of these losses, although the women indicated stressful life situations surrounding the occurrence. The nonmothers were more impacted by losses during this age period. Sibling relationships include mutual identity affirmation along with the sharing of a collective family identity (Weigert & Hastings, 1977); since almost half of the nonmothers had not established nuclear families, loss of a member from the family of origin could be more profound.

Several women had parents or spouses who died of cancer or other terminal chronic illnesses. The women often assumed major caretaking responsibilities for a family member during this time. These responsibilities weighed heavily on the women's own energy. Heloise Harvest, a mother, reported:

> My mother and father died within 9 months of each other. So for a while there I even had to give up working for the lawyers. I commuted practically back and forth [from San Francisco] to Dayton. . . . And I said, "I just can't take it any more. I'm just dead on my feet. My mother's got to go to the hospital."

Gladys Gilbert, a mother, had had a mixed relationship with her mother for many years. Her parents had "never related" to each other and had divorced after a difficult court trial. She had lived with her father between the ages of 9 and 15, then went to live with her mother, who had remarried. She did not see her father again; her mother seemed to be intermittently important in her life. Upon recounting transitions, she reported her mother's death only as it related to her financial status, "My mother died in '71 and left a few thousand. So I am secure and enjoying these years very much."

Louise Lane's mother had lived with her for 4 years before her death. Louise was working full-time in a position that required some travel. This mother reported significantly less disruption following her mother's illness and death:

> It certainly added in that you had to plan for when you were going to be gone . . . If I had not had a real supportive husband it would never have worked . . . At that point [when her mother died], I think we were about at the stages that we were doing lots of grant writing . . . I think I was too busy to have much of a vacuum.

Queenie Quincy, a nonmother, was vague about the death of her parents. Both of her parents died during the decade of her 50s:

> Father died in 1967 of cancer. Mother died 3 years later at the age of 90. Didn't care for them much.

Sally Salmon, a nonmother, lost a brother and her parents during her 50s. Her brother, a priest, died in Africa:

Well, it made us all very sad. But they sent pictures to my home, and I invited all my friends and neighbors in, and we saw just what went on . . . My parents were my life . . . [When they died] Well, I just felt that I was, it was, an awful thing that happened, and I just couldn't bear it, but I survived.

Eve Edwards, a nonmother, cared for her mother for 15 years before she died:

I had her as a responsibility. I was 53 when she died. And I had an apartment to take care of and laundry to do and groceries to buy and her sick. And for 15 years before she died, she didn't go any place, only to clinic to see Dr. Jones. . . . I had to give up the department club.

Carol Casey, a nonmother, lost her husband at age 55, did not remarry, and described the 10 years since his death:

Well, I mean, I like male companionship. I like being married. I like having someone to do for. I like to cook. I don't like eating alone. I eat out most of the time. I have people I can eat with . . . And, oh, I've kept up the house—the last couple of years I've gotten more arthritis and stuff, and it just gets a little harder, and I find I just want to run, sort of; I just don't like being alone . . . Finances have also become a problem. Well, I tell you the way the rates have been . . . See Jake's one pension, where he worked for 30 some years, stopped the day he died, the better one. Yeah, the old ones were set up that way. . . . My income keeps getting less until it makes it quite difficult.

Deaths and illnesses during women's 50s are particularly difficult. It is in this decade that women are between middle age and old age (Campbell 1983–84), when entry or reentry into the workforce is difficult, yet, until recently, pension policies resulted in significant income decreases for widowed or divorced women. Thus, the woman has to deal with several transitions—to the role of widow or divorcée, to approaching old age, and to decreased income and security.

The 60s: A Time of Loss.   In addition to being a time of retirement from work or career, the 60- to 69-year-old decade was the one in which the greatest percent of women reported transitions relating to death or to illness. Thirty percent of mothers and 27% of nonmothers reported illness-related transitions, and 34% of mothers and 37% of nonmothers reported death-related transitions during this decade. During their

60s, women experienced the deaths of spouses, parents, siblings, and children. As will be recounted later, these deaths did not have the overall negative effects during this regeneration/redirection period as similar losses had had during the early launching into adulthood, age-30 leveling, and age-40 liberating periods. For the women who had been burdened with caretaking responsibilities for many months or years, the death of a dependent person was frequently a relief. The death opened the door to a new life with greater freedom, both personally and financially. For a few women, the losses resulted in a more restricted view of self, in a great sense of loneliness, or a void that was difficult to fill. Many of the women, however, dealt with loneliness and loss by pursuing creative activities; this is discussed in detail in Chapter 9.

LOSSES: NORMATIVE OR NON-NORMATIVE?

Neugarten (1979) reported that nonnormative occurrences were more disruptive to the individual than the expected normative events. At certain age periods, one expects events to happen; for example, retirement is normative (in our society) between 62 and 65 years of age. The older (past 65) one's parents are, the greater the likelihood that they will die. Despite this concept of normativeness, it was difficult to determine when a loss was normative or if a loss could be normative. Few of the women were truly prepared for the death of a spouse or parent. Even though one would expect the women to outlive their spouses and parents, deaths of parents and spouses were, for the most part, difficult times for these women. A woman who was heavily invested in her career or marital family seemed less affected by the death of parents or siblings. Lieblich (1986) suggests that the dual roles career women occupy may help mitigate against crises in their lives. It certainly seemed to do so for Maude Morris, as we will describe later. Several of the nonmothers reported extreme distress upon the death of a parent, however.

It is well established that women outlive men, thus it would be expected that most of the married women eventually would be widowed. Several of the women were widowed during middle age, some more than once. With few exceptions, earlier widowhood was not reported as more difficult than widowhood in later life. This perhaps is an artifact of recall, in that more recent events stood out more clearly and the grief associated with them not completely resolved at the time of the interview, resulting in a more vivid recollection of the more normative experience of later widowhood. Constance Calvin was widowed three times,

the first at the age of 55. She described the deaths of her first two
husbands in a very matter of fact way:

> He died in 1955 after a 2 1/2-year bout with cancer. . . . After he died, [I
> met] a man . . . and he had had a very unhappy marriage and was di-
> vorced, and a year and a half after my husband died, I married him. And
> I was ecstatically happy. He was a wonderful man, and 8 months later he
> died of cancer. . . . I was devastated, needless to say.

Terry Tobias was also widowed at a fairly early age and remarried.
She described her husband's death:

> You can tell I loved him. He was sick for 2 years and, of course, when the
> doctors said they couldn't do anything. Anyway, we had our family confer-
> ences, which I would recommend for anyone who has somebody who is
> that ill and decided we'd do the best we could and help him out as much as
> we could, and I really think that helped the kids to realize that this was
> part their responsibility. It was their dad and they should, and I wanted
> them to know how serious it was, too. So they were real good about it, and
> they've turned out to be what I call good people, good citizens. . . . I
> met my husband now, 4 1/2 years after my husband died.

Susan Simms had been married and divorced, and then she remarried
at the age of 46. Her second husband had been dead 2 years at the time
of the interview. They had been married 22 years:

> I retired at 65. I had thought earlier I was going to retire at 62, and in the
> meantime, my husband's diagnosis [cancer] was established, and I realized
> to retire at 62 I would lose a fifth of my retirement, and they needed me,
> and I said, "I'll stay on" . . . and it gave a lot of stability to my life, and I
> needed that.
> [Her husband lived 7 years after the initial diagnosis.] I'd just have to
> say that I was just so numb when Dr. Brown said this was invasive, you
> know, that's a pretty mild way of saying that he didn't get it all . . . You
> know, it was just like saying it's a bad day today, but it will be a better
> day tomorrow. It was just a long time after that it really hit me. . . . But
> we were able to do a lot of good things, things that we'd wanted to do and
> enjoyed doing, up until December, and he died. So we were pretty
> lucky.

Noreen Nunnally was married for 37 years to a man 16 years older
than she. Noreen had always been a creative, artistic woman. She described life since her husband died:

Now Bob's gone . . . I don't feel like traveling until I can find somebody I could travel with . . . I haven't really been able to paint yet, but, I think, I'm just now beginning to think that what it must be is that I painted all these years with this happiness inside of me, and I don't have this happiness inside of me now, not one bit. I try, I go through all the motions, you know, and all, but it's not there. I just don't have that happy feeling inside of me. I'd love to have it back; I'm working, I'm working, trying to get it back, but I don't have it . . . It'll be 3 years in November. . . . I work real hard because there's no sense of caring, and maybe something would give and this big hurt of grief is the whole big negative trip. And I would so much like to not have the negative. It isn't that I don't love Bob; I love him dearly, but just the love; I don't want all this hurt, I don't want all this negative part of this.

Noreen Nunnally, perhaps, expressed the differences in responses to deaths between parents and husbands most eloquently:

When I lost my mother, for instance, it didn't really bother me too much. I could never take care of her. I'm just responsible for her and all. But it didn't really bother me all that much because I never was that close.

Noreen's relationship with her husband was very different; he was a friend, a companion, and a lover. Parkes (1971) notes that no one relinquishes a part of their world freely without some grief or protest. Noreen was also articulate about her initial impressions of the grief process:

And so I figured because I wasn't familiar with grief that you went through a certain length of time, and—wham—just like if you are sick physically, there you were, all well. That's what I was stupid enough to think. . . . And I discovered that really isn't the way it is. . . . well I lost this hurt right in here [chest], and so I thought, gee, I'm well now . . . Of course, I discovered . . . this big hurt of grief is a whole big negative trip. And I would so much like to not have the negative.

For those women whose spouses or parents were integral to their world, their deaths were experienced as much more difficult. Losses of relationships were felt strongly; these reflected the greatest identity loss. Identity loss has been defined as interactional loss of significant others in which the destruction "of a particular, meaningful, and positively affective self-other bond which has constituted a central personal identity for self" (p. 1171) occurs (Weigert & Hastings, 1977). For the woman who had not completely separated from her mother, loss of the mother may have represented a loss of part of self, and so it was even more difficult. Loss of the single remaining parent brings home the reality that the woman is a child no longer—she is an adult, a peer, a parent, but no longer a daughter.

ILLNESSES

The women reported a significant number of illnesses, both their own and those of family members. In most cases, illnesses of the spouse or parents had greater impact upon the overall life course of the woman. For example, Rose Rollins, a mother, related that when she was 16 her mother became seriously ill and she then assumed the role of the woman of the house. Clara Cohen's life was altered dramatically when her husband was diagnosed as being diabetic, then later when her daughter contracted polio, and finally when she herself, at age 47, was diagnosed as having multiple sclerosis. As with the other transitional events, the women responded in different ways to these experiences. Moos and Schaefer (1986) propose that background, personal, physical, social, and environmental factors all influence the impact that a crisis or transitional event has upon the individual. For some women, illness and loss events caused significant disruption to their lives; others took these events in stride. Particularly striking was one woman who recounted being trapped in a burning house with her two children:

> Well, when it was clear we could not get out the door, I broke the window and climbed out. Got all cut up, too. Just then someone got the door open, and my husband and the kids got out.

This woman's husband had also been severely injured in a farm vehicle accident, and one of her children had chronic health problems. She recounted all of this in a rather matter of fact way, as if to say, "Life goes on, and we make do."

Other women were greatly impacted by illnesses: Kathryn Kane left college because of a diphtheria epidemic. Later, when she was 31, her father had a stroke, and she returned home to care for him. At this time she also developed chronic kidney infections, which she associated with the stress of caring for her father. At 49 she had a ruptured appendix. Her father died when she was 63. Her husband died when she was 81. In recounting her life, illnesses were seen as the major transitional markers.

WOMEN AS CARETAKERS

Not surprisingly, caretaking was a role frequently assumed by the women. The mothers, obviously, had caretaking responsibilities for their children; however, more striking was the caretaking role of the nonmothers for their own parents, and the early age at which many of the women, particularly the mothers, had assumed caretaking responsibilities for siblings.

For the nonmothers, assumption of the caretaking role seemed to close out life choices for them. The financial and psychological burden entailed in supporting parents or caring for infirm parents seemed to keep them from engaging in the more normative (at that time) social activities that resulted in marriage and childbearing. Edna Ebert, one of the nonmothers, blamed her mother for her late marriage.

> Mother was not well; she developed diabetes . . . it was during 1918 that the doctor found she had diabetes. And at that time nobody had ever heard of insulin. . . . And she practically starved herself to death and that was the only way they had to control it. . . .
> [At 19, Edna got a job teaching in another town and moved out of the family home; this position lasted only 1 year, at which time she moved back home.] And it was shortly after that that mother went into a coma. Before that she would have no part of insulin. But when she went into a coma, they took her into the hospital and she had no choice. So my memories of my mother is that she died in 1930, and, uh, my memories of 1927 to 1930 of giving her insulin shots every day. So she, so there was no way she could do it herself. My father wouldn't do it so there was nobody, and since I was living at home—my brother had gotten married—and so I, I had the job. She was confined the last year or two; she was in bed. She must have been ill, or they wouldn't have had her in bed. . . . Actually, her lungs filled up with water. That's what she died from. Uh, I remember her arms were so swollen at the time from so much edema.
> [Edna's mother had influenced Edna's health habits.] Another thing I remember was my mother just couldn't stand smoking. She just thought it was the vilest thing for a woman to smoke. For women smoking—for men it was all right, you see. Uh, I must have cared an awful lot for her because as long as she lived I never smoked. And as soon as she died I started smoking.
> [Edna's mother also had extensive influence on her social life from her sickbed.] And I guess I was trying to make her as comfortable as I could because I went through three or four love affairs that she got very upset about during that time, but she didn't approve of the boys too much. She didn't think that I was ready yet to get married, and I wasn't and I didn't. . . .

I was quite upset about my mother's death. . . . I'd left her that morning, and I'd given her her breakfast and given her a shot and I left her . . . and the principal came, and then he told me that he had a call that my mother died.

But now I was really very upset, and I was going with a boy that my mother detested, just detested, and, uh, he was about a year or two younger, no, he was about my age, about a year younger maybe . . . Generally I'd make him leave around 9 o'clock because I knew it'd upset mother to have him there. And on the Sunday before she died, he ran away and married to some other gal. And, oh, she died 2 days later. And I swore that she lived just to keep me from marrying him. . . . Yeah, and it's because when she found out that he was married, she was hurt for me. She was very glad, and 2 days later she died. And I still maintain that she just fought and lived because she knew that I wouldn't marry him as long as she felt the way she did.

[Edna remembered her father being an alcoholic and caring for him after her mother died. In 1943, at the age of 37, she joined the Navy.] I left my dad by himself at the house . . . By that time he had gotten the liquor under control. It was my chance to get out.

[At 39, Edna met and married her husband; she neither regretted nor blamed her mother for her late marriage.] I just, that last love affair, I just couldn't see tying myself down, because I couldn't go traveling the way I wanted to. So I pretty well did all the 48 states before I got married.

Several women assumed the caretaking role for ill fathers, even though their mothers were still active in the household. Inez Inkles reported that she did not marry because of caring for her father:

I was going to be married, just at the time my father took sick, and then my mother took sick [8 years later], and things didn't work out . . . My family came first. I had made a promise to my father when I was very young. He was in the hospital for 9 months and 14 days with a ruptured appendix at that time, and he made me promise for years and years, that I would never put him in the hospital. So, when he got sick, I knew what I was up against, and I'd made that promise, and I kept it. That's the same with my mother. I couldn't put her in a rest home or anything; I came home and took care of her. She was critical for 5 years . . . It wasn't easy, but I'm glad I did it. I have no regrets at all.

Illness of a spouse sometimes meant more than just caring for that person; it could mean taking over a business. Beverly Bee, a nurse, related:

After a serious operation [on her husband], I took over [the advertising business], and he helped me, but I never cared about selling.

Thus, it became clear that for some women, the death of a parent or spouse after a difficult illness that had required her caretaking was a freeing experience. Teresa Townley reported that after the death of her third husband, she had a more free feeling:

Feeling that I can do what I want to do . . . like my life is my own now . . . Mine and his last few months were hell, because his son-in-law died, and his daughter was 57 when her husband died, and so she was wanting to come back home to live and I would not be her slave, and I said no. And so he thought he was going to make me take her in.

Bea Bullock reported that once her father died, the financial situation for the household improved greatly. Ursula Unger reported her first feeling of total independence at the age of 63, when her husband died, a feeling that was not always comfortable:

I really always thought I put him first, too, you know; if there were choices, I always did the things he wanted to do . . . And I think in retrospect, because I've had my career it's probably given me a little structure to my life now. But after he died [I felt] I can't stand my life the way it is; all I want to do is crawl up and die. But yet it's not what you do.

Nancy Newton identified the beginning of a change period for her when her mother died. At 43, Nancy started back to school. Iris Inning began a series of world traveling trips after her husband died. Daisy Dalton obtained her first driver's licence at age 60 when her husband became ill. Heloise Harvest opened a charge account at the age of 61 when her husband became ill: the first step, she felt, to a more independent self. Flossie Forrest reported that at age 46, when her mother died, "Life began."

For others, illnesses required significant changes that took away from the women's lives. Sarah Sanger stated that following her husband's bypass surgery, she "surrendered both professional identity and personal life in the subsequent move." Wilma Weeks reported that when her husband was diagnosed as having cancer, she was completely devastated and she quit work to care for him. At the age of 47, Clara Cohen was diagnosed as having multiple sclerosis and was promptly retired by her employer. When Joyce Jenkins' mother died when Joyce was 52, she felt a real space in her life. Ophelia Owens noted that after she had a stroke, suddenly no one asked her to do anything anymore, even though she was physically and mentally capable of continuing her activities.

CONCLUSIONS: IDENTITY CHANGE
THROUGH LOSS

Illnesses of both family members and of self caused major changes in these women's lives. Spousal illness resulted in family disruptions, such as moves, changes in wage-earning responsibility, and restrictions in activity. It was evident that for most of the women, illnesses were reported in more negative terms, probably because illnesses resulted in the women taking on additional caretaking responsibilities and led to their having to forsake activities they valued or to reconceptualize themselves.

Deaths, however, resulted in more mixed outcomes. For some, death meant release from the burden of caretaking, the opportunity to become a person in their own light, and the opportunity, time, and money to do other things. For others, deaths resulted in increased responsibilities, particularly in the earlier years of their lives. For some, deaths resulted in despair and loneliness.

Some women's lives were significantly affected by deaths of parents, siblings, or friends. In several instances, a loss heralded the beginning of a new life phase, for example, when death of a mother, father, or husband ended caretaking responsibilities.

While deaths or illnesses impacted each person individually, it was evident that some women were more influenced by these events than others. In addition, losses at earlier ages, particularly during the launching into adulthood period, ages 16 to 25, had a greater long-range impact on the direction the woman's life would take.

For several women, the death of either a parent or a spouse resulted in the women taking on a much more independent and, often, responsible role. One woman, whose mother died when she was 16, reported it was at this time that she made the transition to adulthood by taking on adult responsibilities. Several nonmothers lives were shaped at an early age by deaths in the family. One woman became the sole wage earner for her mother and siblings when her father died. She was 21.

Three women who lost boyfriends or fiancés in World War II decided not to marry or seek other relationships as they saw careers more rewarding, and safer, than relationships. For other women, death of the spouse or parent resulted in freedom from caretaking responsibilities to pursue creative and self-enhancing activities. One woman reported that the first time she experienced total independence was when her husband died; she was 63. Lillian Love entered practical nursing school at the age of 59 when her husband died.

From this study, it appears that illness and death can play a significant role in the course of a woman's life. The greatest impacts seem to be in the early years, that is before the age of 20, and again in the 60 to 69 age span, when more women are affected by identity loss.

Health professionals have significant opportunity to provide support and anticipatory guidance for women in these age ranges. The assumption that deaths are predominantly negative impacts on life is obviously erroneous, particularly in later life. Those who work with women during their pre- and postretirement years and during early widowhood are challenged to find social resources that enhance this developmental and creative potential. Illnesses, however, do seem more disruptive and have a longer and more negative impact. The need for support for women dealing with personal illness or illness of a family member or significant other is most apparent.

■ 9
The Emergence of Creativity in Later Life

SALLY H. RANKIN, Ph.D.

No thing great is created suddenly, any more than a bunch of grapes or a fig. If you tell me that you desire a fig, I answer you that there must be time. Let it first blossom, then bear fruit, then ripen.

Epictetus in *Discourses*,
book I, chapter 2°

Epictetus' description of the creative process is analogous to the emergence of creativity we identified in the lives of the study participants. Our interest in creativity in women's lives was a serendipitous reflection on the fact that many of the women in the study spoke of changes occurring in their lives during their sixth through eighth decades, especially during their early 60s. The nature of these changes was frequently an immersion in some type of creative activity that seemed to bring additional meaning to their lives. Creativity was usually nurtured and grew throughout the life span of the individual. If creativity emerged suddenly in older age, its genesis was usually a loss. "Creativity" is used here to describe a multitude of productive and satisfying activities and behaviors exhibited by the women in the study, either as a response to loss and loneliness or as a reawakening of previous artistic endeavors.

°*Source:* Bartlett's Familiar Quotations, E. M. Beck (ed.), p. 121, 1980.

Creativity has been defined by May (1975) as the process of bringing something new into being as the result of an intense meaningful encounter with the world. May recognizes that creativity occurs in the life of the artist or scientist as well as in the nature of the relationship of one person with another. Koestler's (1964) references to creativity speak of inventing new codes that deviate from old conventional rules. He tends to apply a more traditional meaning to creativity so that his work speaks to an understanding of creative genius as it arises from cognitive learning. Although none of the women in our study exhibited creative genius comparable to the great artistic and scientific creators, many did bring new work or meaningful relationships into being through encounter with their own worlds. It is to the emergence of this type of creativity in the lives of 80 remarkable women to which we speak.

✓   At least 86% of the participants told of some sort of creative activity that had occurred at some period in their lives. These creative endeavors included painting, music (organ, piano, violin, and choral activities), creative writing, drama, sewing, square dancing, volunteer activities, and, in some cases, extraordinary productivity and generativity in careers. Table 9.1 illustrates the frequency of creative activities and a few significant differences between mothers and nonmothers. Significantly more mothers reported creativity through music, and significantly fewer mothers reported no creative endeavor over their life course.

TABLE 9.1 Comparisons of Mothers' and Nonmothers' Creative Activities

	Mothers		Nonmothers	
Activity	n	%	n	%
Career creativity	11	22	9	30
Music	11	22	1	3[a]
Art	5	10	2	7
Writing	7	14	2	7
Volunteer activities				
Minimal	7	14	4	13
Maximal	13	26	4	13
Lack of creative endeavors				
None	3	6	8	27[a]
Minimal	1	2	3	10

[a]p < 0.05; Mann-Whitney U test.

This chapter examines creativity as a response to a deficit situation such as loss or loneliness and also as a thread that persisted through the lives of many of the women. Additionally, volunteer and career activities are considered as a meaningful outlet for creative impulses.

CREATIVITY AS A RESPONSE TO LOSS AND LONELINESS

Weiss (1973) has written of loneliness as a deficit condition that arises from either the absence of social bonds or the experience of emotional isolation. Social isolation is more likely to occur when people find themselves in new jobs or neighborhoods and no longer in the comfortable environments of their pasts with well-established social networks. This type of loneliness is probably easier to resolve than loneliness that results from emotional isolation, the loss of meaningful intimate relationships.

Both social and emotional isolation led to creativity in the study participants' lives. The link between loss and loneliness, and creativity is explicated in the works of Moustakas (1961, 1971) and portrayed in the lives of famous individuals such as Emily Dickinson. Moustakas asserts that loneliness is a universal experience, and that from isolation and loss arise positive and creative experiences and accomplishments. This approach to creativity is not unlike the compensatory theory of creativity— that is, creativity is a compensation for an individual's inadequacies. As May points out, the compensatory theory may help explain the motivation towards creativity but not the process of creating. May criticizes psychoanalytic theories about creativity for being reductionistic and representing creativity as expressive of poor mental health or neurosis. Although creative persons may be subject to psychiatric disorders, as is the rest of the population, May (1975, p. 39) argues against considering talent a disease and creativity a neurosis. Indeed, we are approaching creativity as a healthy response to the normative and nonnormative exigencies of human life.

Social Isolation and Creative Responses

Well-known examples of social isolation with which most health professionals working with the elderly are familiar include moves from the family home to a skilled nursing facility and the social disruption that results from such placements. The role of the activity director in such a facility is to decrease the social isolation through group activity and to

fill empty hours with meaningful enterprise. Examples of social isolation that occurred in the lives of study respondents included enforced
social isolation due to chronic illness, such as multiple sclerosis or
arthritis, or moves necessitated by husbands' employment. See Chapter
7 for more extensive discussions of the meaning of moves and Chapter 8
regarding the impact of illnesses and other losses to the participants.

Creative responses to social isolation among the women were demonstrated primarily in the sphere of volunteer activities. For example, one
minister's wife, Thelma Tiller, who moved frequently as a result of
her husband's career, led neighborhood bible-centered groups covering
such diverse topics as parenting and marital relationships. She was not
employed outside the home at this time in her life, and volunteerism was
an attempt to fill the void created by changes in locale.

Another participant recognized the social isolation she would encounter upon retirement and became involved in volunteer work at a
local hospital. This unmarried woman, Carol Casey, had lost both parents as a child from death and desertion, and characterized herself as
"always looking for a mother" so that her social isolation also included
components of emotional isolation. A third woman, who represented the
sociocultural climate of the 1950s and felt that it would be unaccept-
able to work when her children were young, became engrossed in her
volunteer work as a Brownie and Girl Scout leader. Her volunteer work
represented an attempt to develop social bonds that were otherwise
unavailable to her.

Emotional Isolation and Creative Responses

Emotional isolation frequently results from the loss of a loved one
through death, desertion, or other life transition. Interventions to decrease emotional isolation may be similar to those for social isolation, for
example, involvement in self-help groups. However, the formation of
new emotional bonds becomes more difficult as one ages and the social
network or "convoy" decreases in size (Kahn & Antonucci, 1980). Many
of our participants experienced significant losses beginning in childhood, and by the time of the interview, all had experienced deaths of
parents, husbands, children, or some other meaningful individual. Only
one woman did not relate to such loss as having a transitional impact on
her life.

The responses to emotional isolation frequently included solitary creative activities such as creative writing and oil painting. Although many
of the women who painted and wrote had been exposed to these artistic

endeavors as children or young adults, they generally had left these activities behind until some significant loss occurred. Avis Arbeit returned to oil painting when she was in her mid-60s as a response to the illness and death of her husband, brother, and a neighbor. She had been married at age 23 and said during the review of her life that if she had it to do again, she would have stuck with her art and married later in life. Her statement brings to mind the words of Anne Morrow Lindberg in *Gift from the Sea* (1955):

> I . . . understand why the saints were rarely married women. I am convinced it has nothing inherently to do, as I once supposed, with chastity or children. It has to do primarily with distractions. . . . Woman's normal occupations in general run counter to creative life, or contemplative life or saintly life (p. 29).

Women's "normal" occupations, that is caring for others in countless and time-consuming ways, did indeed stifle the production of creative works during the young adult and middle-age years. The amount of time that the women spent in caregiving activities was consistent for both mothers and nonmothers, although the recipients of care varied depending on the woman's marital and maternal status. The distractions of daily life consumed most of the free time of our participants, and once the bonds with significant others were loosened or severed, the women not only experienced loneliness and loss as an impetus for creative work, but they also had more time to devote to creative endeavors.

Volunteer work also became a creative response to emotional isolation, just as it was to social isolation. One 61-year-old woman, who began volunteer work at a senior citizen's center and as a foster grandparent after her mother's death, spoke with poignancy of being alone and what it meant to her:

> Well, I, of course, knew she was going to die. And that's the first time I'd ever stayed alone at night. I had never been alone in the house, alone all night until after she'd died. And I sat down and talked to myself and said, "Look you're no different than millions of other women. They live alone, so can you."

For this woman, involvement in volunteer activities was an attempt to cope creatively with the loneliness she encountered after the death of her mother.

In addition to losses experienced as a result of deaths, life transitions, such as the launching of children from the nuclear family home, caused shifts in women's lives that occasionally led to the emergence of creative activities. In a review of Deutsch's work, Thompson (1987) suggests that the drive for productivity in motherhood arises from the same source as intellectual and creative drives and that one can replace the other. Whether the emergence of creativity in the mothers' lives was a replacement of one drive with another or a response to the "empty nest" syndrome is unclear from our data. However, a number of mothers spoke of initiating volunteer work when their children left for college or married, becoming more actively involved in church work or working with foreign students in a large university setting.

Deutsch's explanation of the expression of creativity in motherhood may elucidate our finding that significantly more mothers (94%) than nonmothers (73%) exhibited some type of creative activity during the course of their lives. In other words, the drive to maintain some sort of meaningful creative endeavor in one's life may be given the impetus through motherhood, and for women who do not have such channels as careers or motherhood, the drive for creativity or productivity is never realized. These differences should be evaluated cautiously, since they may be an artifact of the nonrandom sample and the open-ended interview procedures. Nonmothers more often described attaining creativity through their careers.

Our findings are similar to those of others who have studied "successful" or "creative" aging. Hughes (1986), in a recent report on creative aging, maintains that certain life patterns were evident in the lives of 22 successful San Francisco Bay Area women who exhibited a successful approach to their own aging. These life patterns included maintaining meaningful activities, having close relationships with persons of all ages, exhibiting flexibility and adaptability, being nonconformist and taking risks, and sustaining a positive outlook on life even in the face of great adversity.

Although volunteerism is not generally considered creative activity, we have argued that for many of the women in the study, volunteer activity was an opportunity to create something new in their own lives. The impetus for the activity was indeed an intense encounter with the world, usually in the form of loss or loneliness that resulted in social or emotional isolation. Since women's development may be more closely tied to their relationships and affiliations with others, unlike men's development, which is frequently less relationship oriented, it seems possible that creativity in women's lives may be demonstrated as an altruistic response to the needs of other persons. For men, creativity may be exhibited more frequently in areas that suggest more solitary creation, such as science and the arts. Additionally, we have noted that other creative activities, such as writing and painting, served as a distraction from the loneliness and pain experienced as a result of losses. The next section of the chapter examines another means of understanding the creativity demonstrated by women in their seventh and eighth decades of life.

CREATIVITY AS REACTIVATION OF PREVIOUS PURSUITS AND WISDOM GAINED ACROSS THE LIFE SPAN

Whereas some women embarked upon significant volunteer activities during the later part of their lives and exhibited creativity in this realm, others returned to the music, art, and creative writing that had been shelved since adolescence or young adulthood. A third group, which was comprised mainly of women who had always been involved in music, continued in older age with the same creative pursuits that had always been an important part of their lives.

Most research indicates that discrepancies between young and old exist on laboratory test of creative thinking (Salthouse, 1982), the process part of creativity. Lehman's (1953) work is frequently cited as indicative of the creative productivity that he believes is more likely to occur in young adulthood (Stevens-Long, 1979), a product issue. Although there have been a number of challenges to both of these assertions, it seems important to examine them and also to scrutinize a commonly held assumption that women exhibit less creativity than men.

Differences in creative thinking between young and old as measured by laboratory tests involve discussion of the process aspect of creativity. Werner (1967) maintained that with higher individuation, persons are more creative and less egocentric. Data from our interviews do not elucidate the differences between young and old in terms of problem-solving or the ability to use flexible and divergent thinking; most of the women had, however, reached a high level of individuation. The data do, however, speak of the importance of family and parental encouragement, or discouragement, in the development of creative activities.

Parental Impetus for Creativity in Music and Art

Music and art in particular were given impetus by parents. For instance, Carrie Carmichael spoke of her involvement with music as stemming from her childhood days when the entire family enjoyed music together as a family activity. Later, she taught piano lessons, and she spoke at length of the pleasure she obtained from attending concerts in old age with her husband. Avis Arbeit attended art school beginning in 1921 at the encouragement of her father, who was also an artist, and returned to it after the death of her husband upon the suggestion of her daughter. Noreen Nunnally told of her happiness at taking art lessons in a convent at age 10 and her desire to become an artist thwarted in young adulthood by her mother who "pushed me into teaching." June Jorge spoke of her father's negativity towards her singing:

> I could sing pretty nice at one time they told me, but my father squashed that for me.

That these women were speaking of their early lives and the influence they perceived their parents had on their own creative development 50 to 60 years later speaks to the power of families in the creative process.

Creative Writing as a Product of Creativity in Later Life

The issue of creative product can be spoken to through our respondents' recounting of the output of later years. Creative writing in particular was an activity that many women turned to in their later years. In many cases, there was no evidence of the pursuit of this form of creativity in youth or young adulthood, which might indicate that creative writing either does not presuppose the earlier practice required for musicians or painters or that it is particularly well suited to the generative needs of aging women. One woman told of having a work of fiction published in her 80s. Gayle Goodman spoke about beginning creative writing in her 70s and the meaning that it had brought to her life: "What's exciting is that it's like a new career beginning." While their creative output did not approach that of such famous septua- and octogenarians as Harriet Duerr (1984), author of *Stones for Ibarra*, or Joan Erikson (Erikson et al., 1986), who co-wrote *Vital Involvement in Old Age* with her husband, Erik, in her 80s, their products do attest to the ability of the aged to create products that are equal in quality to those of younger individuals.

Creative writing frequently appeared to be an attempt to achieve the last stage of life span development that Erikson (1959) refers to as integrity. Creative writing classes were pursued initially by most of the participants out of a desire to write their own autobiographies, a sort of squaring one's self with one's family, an attempt to "leave something for my posterity," as Lillian Love stated it. In some cases, the respondents continued to write after the original autobiographical impulse had been fulfilled.

In terms of creativity and women, Arieti (1976) refers to the fact that in lists of creative persons, men far outnumber women. He points out that there are no biological reasons men should be any more creative than women and accounts for their diminished numbers with such reasons as structural-functionalist explanations of primitive society, historically less access to education, fewer occupational choices, and other sociocultural explanations. As more opportunities are made available to women, their numbers will certainly increase among those who are considered truly creative. Additionally, arguments can be made for the different avenues through which women express their creativity and which traditionally have not been considered representative of creativeness.

Creativity as Expressed in Career Activity

Since this cohort of women was even less likely to have the career paths open to them that are available to women in the late 1980s, outstanding career achievement seems an important benchmark of creativity. As one might expect, the nonmothers had greater opportunities to develop lifelong careers. The group of mothers in the study had fewer opportunities to pursue careers since there were few societal structures such as childcare agencies to encourage women with children to maintain careers. However, when evidence of creativity through employment was examined, there were no statistically significant differences between mothers and nonmothers for career creativity, although a larger percentage of nonmothers reported career creativity (30% to 22%).

Most of the women who worked steadily were either in the professions open to women at the time, nursing and teaching, or were employed in secretarial positions. Many of the women became leaders in the area of education. Some developed new curricula or initiated new programs, whereas others were involved at the national level in policy decisions regarding their profession. One elementary school teacher, Eve Edwards, established new teaching and visual arts methods in her school as a result of extra course work at a university in 1940. She recognized that she was in the forefront of elementary education and that she was part of the vanguard of creative teaching methods.

Although the loss of a relationship, particularly the loss of a spouse through divorce or death, was sometimes the impetus for the development of creativity in careers, the women who chose to respond to loss through career activity often exhibited surges of creativity. One woman, Ursula Unger, had been instrumental in the development of her husband's career and had nursed him through a long debilitating illness and death. She spoke of the importance of her own career after her husband's death:

> And I think for the first time since I've had a career, it's the most important thing to me.

She had exhibited creativity through many volunteer activities earlier, but never came to terms with her own abilities until her husband had died and she became more invested in her own career. She also illustrates the responsibility women feel in relationships to the exclusion of self-development, a different orientation that women have toward relationships than men, as was discussed in Chapter 6.

Another participant, Delilah Diamond, had experienced a rather sad and deprived childhood. Her marriage had essentially been one of convenience, and she had suffered disappointments as a result of decisions her children had made. Throughout her life most of her pleasures came from the successes she experienced in her career. She was an assertive, intelligent woman who made the most of all of her career opportunities and was able to speak with pleasure of the creativity she had brought to various jobs.

Creativity as Expressed Through Volunteer Activities

Participants from both the mother and nonmother groups demonstrated similar levels of volunteer activity. The mothers, however, tended to exhibit greater sustained volunteer involvement. For some of the mothers, volunteer work was an obvious attempt to fill the void left by giving up careers following the birth of children. These women made impressive contributions to the community through such creative endeavors as work with foreign university students and initiation of a Parents Without Partners chapter. Volunteer work took the place of paid employment for many of the mothers, whereas for the nonmothers, volunteer work was usually a response to the vacuum caused by retirement or death of a spouse or family member.

Although volunteer work is not generally considered a form of creativity, the differences in women's development as compared to men's mitigates for inclusion of volunteer activity as an important life structure for women. Gilligan (1980; 1982a) writes that the development of women is better understood in terms of attachment and separation. She believes that women's development is predicated on the relational bonds that they form. We assert that these relational bonds are the content of the life structure for women rather than work/career, which becomes the content of the life structure for men. Therefore, if volunteer activity is viewed as an attempt to develop identity in the context of relationship, we can point to a small group of study participants who became highly involved in creative volunteer activity partially out of their sense of responsibility to others. Indeed, their volunteer activity fulfills May's definition of creativity—that is, their volunteer work was the process of bringing something new into being as the result of an intense, meaningful encounter with the world.

SUMMARY AND IMPLICATIONS FOR INTERVENTION

The evidence of creativity seen in these women's lives suggests that creativity may have been developed in three different ways. First, creativity was a response to loss and loneliness in some of the women's lives. Second, creativity represented an important thread begun in childhood or adolescence and nurtured consistently across the life span. Third, it was an entirely new endeavor begun in older age.

By viewing creativity in its broadest sense and by applying Gilligan's approach to women's life span development, it has been possible to include such endeavors as career and volunteerism in the assessment of creativity in this sample of 80 women.

The finding that mothers had more expressions of creativity than nonmothers was an interesting one, although it must be interpreted conservatively. Perhaps Deutsch's work helps explain this difference with her suggestion that the drive for productivity in motherhood arises from the same source as intellectual and creative drives and that one drive can replace the other.

Implications for intervention include the recognition that creative writing was an important creative expression for many of the participants. Developmental neuroplasticity is currently being recognized as an important facet of human development throughout the life span (Featherman, 1983; Thomas, 1981). This fact, and the findings among our participants, suggest that creative writing may be a meaningful way for older persons to express themselves creatively. Additionally, since most of our participants had not carefully honed their writing skills over the years in the same way that others had developed musical and artistic talents, it may be that writing does not require practice in earlier years of life.

Music, and to a lesser extent painting and drawing, were sources of pleasure in later life to those women who had pursued them as children and young adults. Our data suggest that opportunities for continued creative expression in ways that are consistent with earlier life habits should be made available to older persons.

Lastly, most of the participants recognized the association between loss of a relationship and the commencement of some type of creative activity. This recognition did not diminish the satisfaction gained from the new endeavor. Perhaps health professionals and others working with persons experiencing loss should more openly recognize the association between loss and creativity and utilize it in an attempt at planned change rather than as diversionary activity.

In summary, this chapter has reviewed the possible sources and genesis of creativity in older age and has described its product in terms of the arts, writing, career, and volunteer activity. Additionally, implication for interventions with older persons, especially women, have been suggested.

■ 10
Conclusions: Reflections on Women's Development Over the Life Course

Although each woman's life history had unfolded uniquely according to her personality and familial traits, her social environment, and the period of history that she experienced, similarities were observed across groups. The life histories indicated a developmental process occurring over the entire life course as women adapted to their age-normative, history-graded, and nonnormative transitions. Stages in the developmental process, occurring by chronological age, were also observed.

An overview of answers to the major questions asked at the beginning of the study is presented to highlight our major findings. First, we discuss the major developmental stages in women's life cycles as evidenced by increased transitional activity at particular ages. The effect of the mothering role on women's development is discussed, followed by the factors and events that occurred with or preceded transitional periods in the women's life course, leading to characteristic profiles of the mother, married nonmother, and never-married nonmother. A discussion of the three groups of women's developmental outcome and influencing events concludes the chapter.

DEVELOPMENTAL STAGES OVER WOMEN'S LIFE CYCLE

To answer the question, Are there developmental eras in women's life cycles with comparatively uniform (by chronological age) transitional periods, parallel to those described for men, we examined the transitions of all of the study participants by 5-year periods. Although these transitional periods are discussed earlier in the book, we review them again here as background to a discussion of how women experience these transitional periods differently than do men, and how mothers and nonmothers differed. Overall, women in this study tended to experience developmental periods at later ages and in sequences that were much more irregular than those reported by Levinson et al. (1978) for men. There was, however, some consistency in parallel age periods for major developmental transitions, but with women focusing on different facets of their life structures than men. Five major developmental stages were observed by chronological age among the majority of the group of 80 women: launching into adulthood (ages 16 through 25), age-30 leveling (ages 26 through 30), age-40 liberating (ages 36 through 40), regeneration/redirection (ages 61 through 65), and age-80 creativity/destructiveness.

Launching into Adulthood

The launching into adulthood stage that represented the women's initial breaking away from their families was also the period of greatest transitional activity. Women's transitional life events during this stage included making plans for and physically separating from families of origin by leaving home to go to school, marry, or go to work. This initial physical separation or breaking away from their families was not usually accompanied by psychological separation or individuation from parents, especially from their mothers. In many situations, women transferred their dependence on parents to dependence on husbands. Some women assumed responsibility for taking care of parents and/or siblings and remained enmeshed in the home setting.

Although a few women followed the sequence of early adulthood tasks for men—establishing a life dream, finding a mentor to support the life dream, establishing an occupation, and finding a life mate and establishing a family—most followed a varied and erratic pattern, as was observed by others (Roberts & Newton, 1987). A few women's life dreams were formulated during school age—to be a teacher or a nurse—and they fulfilled this dream. Their role models were their current and later teachers.

The impact of losses—illnesses or deaths of parents, in particular— was greatest during the launching into adulthood period. Women who reported parental illnesses or deaths that necessitated their assumption of family responsibility of providing for siblings and/or the other parent had to relinquish their normative social interrelationships that usually lead to marriage during this time. Many never-married nonmothers were among this group.

The extent and impact of transitional events from age 16 to 25 indicates that the launching into adulthood period is a pivotal era in development. The continuity from adolescence to adulthood and overlap of major tasks of these periods was evident.

Although relationships were important to the women participating in this study, the majority of the events that they described as representing their transition to adulthood dealt with individual accomplishments: responsibility (25%), first job (28%), and graduation from high school or college (8%).

Goldscheider and Waite (1987) reported that women have been leaving the parental home at increasingly earlier ages over the past several decades; although they are leaving home earlier, they are postponing marriage. This earlier physical separation from parents may foster psychological separation and individuation, but whether some women will continue to transfer dependence from parents to husband, as Ursula Unger did, is a question for further study.

Age-30 Leveling Period

The transitional activity during the age-30 leveling stage was second only to that during the launching into adulthood stage. The finding of this period as a major developmental stage agrees with others' findings for women (Reinke, Holmes et al., 1985; Roberts & Newton, 1987) and for men (Levinson et al., 1978). Many women changed earlier established life structures, as was observed among men (Levinson et al., 1978). Marriage, separation, or divorce meant discontinuity in old roles as women faced major change with new roles in their lives.

Age-40 Liberating Period

For many women, the age-40 liberating period was the time of formulating a life dream. If they had rushed or were pushed into earlier choices such as marriage or had taken on a foreclosure identity, this was the time they focused on themselves. Earlier, their intense relationships with their husbands and children had had priority; as Sarah Sanger had said, "Everything I did centered around what he (husband) did." Thus, while the women's relationships were central, as Josselson (1987) had observed, during the early 20s and early 30s, relational terms were not as central as they sought a more gratifying life in their late 30s. Women were becoming one's own woman at a novice level in roles other than wife and mother at the age-40 transition, in contrast to men who opted to become more expert in their professional roles in Levinson et al's. (1978) study. Jones (1988), in defining changing seasons of a woman's work life, also named the late 30s and early 40s as "A time to be yourself."

The tenor of the age-40 liberating period that we observed may be changing due to the interaction of development with history-graded events, in particular the Women's Movement. There is an indication that the woman of this more recent historical period rejects the role of social secretary and the husband who requires it when it occurs at the expense of developing her own career (Kowalski, 1988). The Sarah Sangers, Felicia Fawnes, and Ursula Ungers who saw the wife's duty as including these responsibilities and going along with the husband "to make life fulfilling and keep morale up on the surface" at the expense of their own personal development may be growing fewer in number.

Regeneration/Redirection Period

Age 60 to 65 for men was described as the late adult transition by Levinson et al. (1978) and marks the end of middle adulthood and the beginning of late adulthood, representing significant development and a major turning point in the life cycle. This was the case with the women we studied. Women utilized this period following retirement from a first career or otherwise freed time in order to pursue creative activities, community work, and self-development pursuits, such as attending classes. Overall, they felt good about themselves and what they were accomplishing.

This was also a time when some women assumed responsibility for their aging parents. Their roles with the aging parents were reversed as they nurtured their parents. However, providing care for one's parents did not have the developmental impact it had on women who had to assume this role earlier during the launching into adulthood stage. Although this caregiving fatigued them and robbed them of recreational and creative pursuits, it did not limit their movement into major life roles. Death of a parent or husband was liberating to caretakers who had been severely restricted for years. Several women either initiated or resumed earlier creative endeavors following the loss of a loved one.

Age-80 Creativity/Destructiveness Period

The age from 76 to 80 represented a transition to an age of wisdom, as women who were challenged to adapt to the loss of their health, in addition to loss of friends and family members through death, faced life with equanimity. As a counterbalance to life's destructive forces, a surge of creativity was evident as women found pleasureable ways to fulfill their lives. An additional developmental challenge was preparing for the end of their own life course.

Although our findings overall concur with those of Levinson et al. (1978) that individuation from parents is a lifelong process, this did not seem to be the case for a minority of the women. By the seventh through ninth decades of life, long after the deaths of their parents, women who verbalized and seemed to have accepted their parents' shortcomings with understanding (as opposed to hostility) and others who seldom mentioned their parents seemingly had individuated from their parents. These few women gave little information about their parents without probing from the interviewer. Such women were comfortable with who they were and matter of factly recognized their own life's achievements.

DEVELOPMENT OF MOTHERS AND NONMOTHERS OVER THE LIFE COURSE

To answer the question, Does motherhood affect women's development over the life span, and, if so, how is the developmental trajectory affected, we compared mothers' and nonmothers' transitions by chronological age periods and examined the transitions for qualitative differences. Our findings were that development over the life span was not altered significantly by the experience of motherhood. The mothering role was not central to women's lives as they told their life stories; their own mothers emerged as a more powerful influence on their adult development.

The mothering role, however, added responsibilities and transitions related to their children so that mothers reported more transitions and a more variable sequencing of wife, career, and other roles. The experiential content of the women's life histories differed along with the timing of some events; for example, there were earlier marriages and more erratic movement in career trajectories among the mothers.

There were no significant differences between percentages of mothers and nonmothers reporting transitions at each of the 5-year age periods over adulthood, indicating that developmental events occurred at about the same rate for all women. However, mothers reported significantly more transitional events from 11 to 15 years than nonmothers, and twice as many mothers reported transitions from the age of 4 through 10 years.

Comparison of Transitional Events

Differences between mothers and nonmothers in the kind of transitions experienced during the developmental periods were more notable prior to age 50 than the numbers of transitions each group had experienced. From the early ages of 4 through 15, mothers' transitions were largely nonnormative traumatic events that seemed to deprive them of a carefree childhood more so than for the group of nonmothers. Mothers also differed from nonmothers during the early launching into adulthood period of 16 to 20 years of age; almost one-third married within this period, contrasted to only one nonmother. During the later launching into adulthood period of 21 to 25 years of age, all but two of the nonmothers (93%) had some type of paid employment, in contrast to 58% of the mothers. Thus, the nonmothers' achievement of the early adulthood tasks proceeded in a direction somewhat similar to that described for men (Levinson et al., 1978), whereas mothers' achievement of those tasks did not. Mothers described assumption of heavy family responsibility as the transition to adulthood more often than nonmothers (33% contrasted to 13%).

Nonmothers were more likely to marry during the age-30 leveling period; later marriages in part were related to their not having children. During their 30s, mothers focused on births of children, moves, family illnesses, and parental deaths. Thus, the mothering role had added complexity to the women's lives; there were more events to experience during this period. Since almost half (47%) of the nonmothers never married, these women also experienced fewer externally motivated relocations or moves.

During their 40s, moves, career change, marriages, graduate education, illnesses, and parental deaths were major transitions for nonmothers. Mothers also reported moves, career change, graduate education, widowhood, or divorce in addition to child-related transitions. Life events tended not to differ that greatly after 50 through their later years.

Developmental Periods

Although there were not significant differences between mothers' and nonmothers' number of transitions during adulthood by chronological age periods, there were differences in whether a majority (>50%) reported transitions at some of these ages. The majority of both mothers and nonmothers reported developmental transitions during the launching into adulthood and age-30 leveling periods. The majority of nonmothers (57%) also reported transitions during ages 31 to 35 years. Both internally and externally motivated transitions made up this period of change for nonmothers; however, parental illnesses and deaths, and marriages were among their important events. Further study is warranted to determine whether this age period also reflects a continuation of "A time to choose," (in employment roles) as suggested by Jones (1988).

The age-40 liberating period was more viable for mothers than for nonmothers (64% as contrasted to 47% reported transitions from 35 to 40 years) when the groups were examined separately. Nonmothers' perhaps did not feel the internal motivation to change their life structures as strongly as the mothers, who had married much earlier and given their own personal development little priority before this time.

The majority of both nonmothers and mothers reported transitions during the regeneration/redirection period; however an age-70 transitional period was also experienced by the majority of nonmothers (56% contrasted to 42% of mothers). This finding was in part due to later retirement for nonmothers. The age-80 transition was also experienced by the majority of nonmothers (67%), but not so for mothers (44%). Nonmothers were actively involved in community activities during this period.

The majority of the nonmothers experiencing age-70 and age-80 transitions is also reflected in a larger number of nonmothers having achieved integrity, the last developmental stage defined by Erikson (1959). Two-thirds of the mothers and over three-fourths (77%) of nonmothers had achieved integrity at the time of the interview. It was at this point in the analysis that we discovered the greater association of the wife role than the mother role with the achievement of integrity.

Impact of Wife Role Versus Mother Role

Upon examination of the achievement of the major task identified by Erikson (1959), integrity, as opposed to its counterpart, despair, an unexpected finding emerged. The percentage of women who had never married and who had achieved integrity (86%) was significantly larger than the percentage of all married women who had achieved integrity (67%); 66% of mothers and 69% of married nonmothers had achieved integrity.

The interview data indicated that some women had transferred dependence from their parents to their husbands during the launching into adulthood period when it is typical to break away from parents.

Mothers tended to marry earlier, and earlier marriages have been associated with foreclosed identities (Lutes, 1981); foreclosure is considered a response to doubt and anxiety in which the individual who is uncomfortable with uncertainty makes choices without the benefit of lengthy decision making. Josselson (1987) reported that married women (at ages 32 to 34) had less well defined selves and had in general done less exploration of the self. Deitz (1988) argued that the person who has not experienced at least 1 year of adult singleness has missed the chance to become a whole person and, in addition, has less of a chance to achieve happiness in love and is unprepared for the time when she or he will have to be alone.

The never-married nonmothers had developed self-reliance earlier in their life course, unlike the married women who relied on spouses to achieve their goals and satisfactions in life. Thus, in as far as the achievement of integrity is concerned, never-married persons have the advantage; development at this stage is more strongly associated with the wife role than with the mother role. However, whether a woman ever married was linked to her family constellation, birth order, and age at the time of the 1929 Depression. Being the oldest child or daughter or the only child and in their 20s during the Depression may have fostered achievement of integrity in later life (86% of the nonmothers who were aged 20 to 26 at the beginning of the Depression achieved integrity).

Husbands were more central to the mothers' lives, however, than to the married nonmothers. Parental relationships were as central to nonmothers as those with their husbands, if one accepts that frequency of references to important persons during an oral life history represents the centrality of that person.

In summary, there were differences in transitional events during earlier developmental periods between mothers and nonmothers. Mothers' earlier marriages increased the likelihood of motherhood, and nonmothers' later marriages or not marrying at all provided them with opportunities to pursue more serious career trajectories. A closer examination of events surrounding transitions indicated that externally motivated transitions impacted profoundly on the women's developmental trajectory.

COMMON FACTORS AND/OR EVENTS
SURROUNDING TRANSITIONS

To answer the question, What factors and events seem to occur with or precede transitional periods over a woman's life cycle, the life-span developmental framework proposed by Baltes et al. (1980) was particularly salient. The women's developmental trajectories occurred within a family, within a particular community, and within a particular historical time, all of which had interacted with her developing self as she experienced each event, to influence her developmental outcome.

The Woman's Psychobiological Self

First, the woman's stage of development, the developmental period of life that she was in at the time of a transitional event, appeared to have the greatest impact on long-term effects over her life course trajectory. The opportunities and the challenges that were experienced by women who were in the later launching into adulthood period (ages 21 to 25) and age-30 leveling period (ages 26 to 30), more so than at any other age, seemed to set the course for the majority of the women's lives. For a minority, events that occurred during school age and teenage years were critical.

Second, the women's responses to transitions were different, depending upon their overall perspective toward life; this differential response by either a family view, a worldview, or an amorphous view toward life was apart from family, social, or historical events. Although we did not begin our study or our analysis with classifications of identity status achievement in mind, the life view of the women—family, world, or amorphous—appeared to represent where the women were in their identity status: foreclosure, identity achievement, and moratorium or diffusion (Marcia, 1980; Josselson, 1987). We had identified the women by their view of life prior to reading Josselson's (1987) book, *Finding Herself: Pathways to Identity Development in Women.* Josselson's descriptions of women in their early 20s and early 30s who were experiencing one of the four identity statuses sounded very much like the women who we had identified in their seventh through ninth decades by their view of life. As was the case with Josselson's sample, it was not the content of or roles enacted in the women's lives that differed so greatly by the view they held of life, as it was the woman's underlying beliefs, approach to life, or personality characteristics.

Women who held a family view of life focused on family members and drew most of their relational experience from family; they could also be called "purveyors of heritage" (Josselson, 1987), with the majority of this group exhibiting behaviors of foreclosure identity status. Women with a family view had not undergone profound decision making; for many, their family situation left them with little or no choice. They went to college or married according to the financial situation or encouragement they received from their families. Mothers had been strong, revered women in these women's lives. These hardworking women had taken many nonnormative transitions in stride during their life time, had managed these crises with seemingly little anxiety, and emerged very pleased with the outcomes of their lives.

Women who held a worldview of life could also be called "pavers of the way" (Josselson, 1987) and overall were grouped in the identity achievement status. Many women with a worldview had achieved outstandingly in careers long before the feminist movement; many also had mentors to facilitate their acceleration in their careers. Others who had not achieved outstandingly in careers had demonstrated a sense of control over their lives, which they continued to examine and to reassess, made choices to achieve new goals as a result of self-examination, and took new directions that led to greater satisfaction with their lives. Fathers appeared to have played a particularly important role in these women's lives. These women in their later years had characteristics of the "active initiators" that Evers (1985) observed among an older sample of women.

Those women with an amorphous view of life were vague about transitions, indicated little or no insight into their development as individuals, lived life as it was dished out to them, had not made waves or protested when family responsibilities were thrust on them rather than other siblings, and did not have great expectations for themselves. Their behaviors appeared to be largely responses to environmental and social forces; they were reactive rather than proactive. Within this amorphous view of life group, there were two subgroups: women who had experienced much emotional lability over a life time of poor marriages, disappointment with children's outcomes, illnesses, and feelings of insecurity; and women who were noncommittal about their feelings as things "just happened," seemingly having a protective shell around them. The emotional sharing group who continued into later age with an amorphous view of life could perhaps be continuing in moratorium identity status; life was one crisis after another. Josselson (1987) noted that although moratoriums behave much like diffusions, moratoriums focus on feeling and "revel in their emotions" and as such are very sensitive women. The second amorphous view group did not disclose painful childhood memories or emotional deprivation as did the first group; in fact, they disclosed very little about their inner feelings or inner self. It is only conjecture that these women may have consciously avoided delving into any painful content; we did not sense that they were consciously or deliberately withholding information about their life experiences. This group appeared to represent the diffusion identity status. Claudia Call (Chapter 4), is an example of one who spoke of uprooting transitions matter of factly, as if she were separate from her history. Diffusions experience and make many changes and or moves in their lives without internalizing these events. Because of early separation from parents or other emotional trauma, Josselson (1987) observed that diffusions had actually differentiated prematurely before having made secure identifications with a parent as part of an identity to later accept or reject during adolescent individuation.

The Woman's Family

The woman's family of origin and the socioeconomic conditions in which the family was enmeshed were powerful influences on her adult development. Never-married nonmothers were either the only child, oldest child, or oldest daughter; all but three (79%) of these never-married women had assumed financial and/or physical care of their parents until the parents' deaths. It was curious that no mention was made of brothers assuming this care or even offering emotional support to the women providing this care, nor was there any resentment expressed by the women at having had to assume this responsibility. This practice of the only child, oldest child, or oldest daughter accepting responsibility for the parents seems to be a culturally accepted phenomenon, but one that also affects other life choices. The women very candidly stated that it was too much to expect a husband to take on responsibility for their parents, and opportunities for marriage were forfeited by their judgment of such unfairness. In some situations, marriage was forfeited at one of the parent's insistence that the man was not suitable for her.

Never-married women who were the only child, oldest child, or oldest daughter also experienced longer, uninterrupted career trajectories than married women, who often moved due to their husbands' careers. Birth-order research has suggested that firstborn children excel verbally and in leadership skills over later-born children. Further research is needed regarding the effects of early family socializations on adult development.

The family was often a source of the creativity that was a vital source of self-fulfillment during the women's seventh and eighth decades of life. Women recalled with pleasure and joy when a creative talent had been encouraged during childhood within the family, and with bitterness when a creative talent had been squelched.

The relationships that women had with their mothers were important in their continued self-assessments, indicating that most women do continue to identify with and perhaps do not ever individuate completely from their mothers over a lifetime. Women who had positive idealizations of their mothers or who had accepted the humanness of their mothers' shortcomings fared better in their interpersonal relationships with others and had a higher overall self-esteem than those women who had unresolved conflictual relationships with their mothers. Mothers and nonmothers did not differ significantly in their references to their own mothers; however, mothers referred to their husbands almost twice as often as to their mothers. Husbands who were nurturing and supportive of the woman's goals and pursuit of an identity apart from wife or mother could offset the self-denigration resulting from conflictual relationships with the mother. Phyllis Painter described her husband, whom she had married at age 25, as a "mother, father, and a husband"; he enabled Phyllis to make the break with her mother, who did not want her to marry.

Fathers played an important role in the women's development. Women described their fathers as teachers (especially of world events and politics), disciplinarians who instilled strong values, recreation providers, protectors who instilled the value of independence and security, and, importantly, as role models or prototypes for their future husbands. Father–daughter conflict centered around dependency needs of fathers who were reluctant to have their daughters marry.

The Community One Grows Up In

The differences found between women who were born and reared in rural and those in urban areas highlighted the impact of the community environment on launching into adulthood. Rural women less often went to college; only 16%, contrasted to 47% of urban women, had a college education. A recent report of a British researcher, Rosalind Miles, who studied 40 top women executives in the United States and Great Britain identified background characteristics of these women (Carden, 1987). All of these women were born in or near a city. In addition, there were common family characteristics: they had a strong grandmother, mothers who were nontraditional in shunning housework, a much-admired father who encouraged them, and fathers who had failed at business or who died young, and they themselves were the eldest child.

While churches and schools had been important to the study participants as children, religion in general had not played a central role during their adulthood; there were a few exceptions. Others have reported that religion is an important part of women's lives during adolescence and early adulthood (Josselson, 1987; Schenkel & Marcia, 1972). Churches and schools were described with nostalgia as centers of social activity during childhood. Church-sponsored picnics, parties, and other activities provided opportunity for families to interact with other community members.

The study participants were largely Caucasian (96%). The social stigma experienced by the one black woman and the woman from a different country at war with the United States indicate a need for further developmental research with oppressed groups to shed light on how self-esteem and identity achievement are affected long-term.

History-Graded Events

History-graded events emerged as much more powerful than had been anticipated. Historical events were intertwined with experienced losses, family need and responsibility, and the woman's personality and approach to life such that it was often difficult or next to impossible to separate these interrelationships.

Historical forces were associated with educational level attained, marital status, and age at birth of the first child. Women who were adolescents (aged 13 to 19) at the onset of the 1929 Depression had achieved the lowest educational level overall. They were also older at the birth of their first child (mean of 28.7 years, compared to women who were preadolescents or postadolescents, mean of 24.7 years). In addition, women who were adolescents at the onset of the Depression had fewer children.

Among the group of never-married women, 79% were in their 20s at the time of the Depression. Although many other factors were related to never marrying, the hard times brought on by the Depression cannot be ignored.

Women who were preadolescent at the onset of the Depression were less likely to have achieved integrity. These women were also the youngest group at the time of the interviews, and the achievement of integrity tended to occur in the 70s or older (Mercer, Nichols et al., 1988). However, deprivations during the school age stage of industry versus inferiority may have greater repercussions on later development; this certainly merits further study.

World War II had a greater impact on nonmothers than on mothers; 77% of nonmothers, contrasted to 44% of the mothers, spoke of the effects of this historical event. Only nonmothers reported having a fiancé killed during World War II. Mothers more often talked about geographical moves related to husbands' military transfers.

Summary of Developmental Outcome and Influencing Events

In summary, normative age-graded, history-graded, and nonnormative catastrophic events interacted with the woman's core self (in particular, her developmental stage), her family, and her community circumstances to affect her development over her life course. Some women in our study had lived their lives without reaching the identity achievement status. This did not mean that their lives had been unpleasureable or unfruitful; quite the contrary, women were in general pleased with their lives and the outcomes, and valued their experiences.

Only 16% of the women had not achieved integrity (accepted their life course as one with meaning and satisfaction) at the time of the interview, and these tended to be those with an amorphous view of life, who appeared as if they had remained in either moratorium or diffusion identity statuses. Early childhood events—preschool and school age nonnormative traumatic transitions, family need, and views of their mothers—appeared to set the stage for lifelong response patterns that foreshadowed identity achievement and adult development for those reporting transitions at an early age (nonmothers: 17% at ≤ age 10, 13% at 11 to 15 years; mothers: 34% at ≤ age 10, 36% at 11 to 15 years).

Identity change was more notable among some women than among others over their life courses; however, change occurred within the context of valued relationships with others—parents, husbands, other family members, role models, or friends. Change from moratorium to identity achievement was observed as late as the seventh decade of life. Loss of a longtime mate precipitated this developmental change, which occurred with professional help, in a few women; Josselson (1987) observed that loss of a relationship was growth-promoting for women because in losing the belief that someone would be there to provide emotional, tangible, and appraisal social support for them, women learn to take over those functions for themselves.

The family, environmental, and historical factors or influences in which the women's major life transitions were enmeshed are summarized as part of a profile of the modal mother, modal nonmother, and modal never-married nonmother.

Profile of the Modal Mother.   The modal mother married earlier than other women and was less likely to be living alone during old age. Her husband was the most important person to her over her life course. She was less often a firstborn or an only child and, in general, was from a family with more children. Her highest educational level was likely to be short-term vocational training or a baccalaureate degree. Her role model was most often a female—her mother, grandmother, aunt, or teacher—and she tended to have a family view toward life. She had a shorter childhood, from her own perspective, as she more often described the transition to adulthood as occurring prior to age 16. Her career trajectory was characterized by numerous interruptions due to childrearing and husband's moves. She was less likely than other women to have achieved integrity at the time of the interview.

Profile of the Modal Nonmother.   The modal nonmother most often was born and grew up in an urban area as a firstborn (63% contrasted to 38% of mothers) or an only child. She was more likely than mothers to have a graduate degree (40% contrasted to 14%). She was likely to be living alone during old age (73% contrasted to 42% of mothers). Nonmothers who married, married much later than mothers. Nonmothers more often reported having a male mentor than mothers. Nonmothers more often had a worldview of life. Nonmothers more often had achieved integrity than mothers (77% contrasted to 66%).

Profile of the Modal Never-Married Nonmother.   Never-married nonmothers were either the oldest child, only child, or oldest daughter. They were most often in their 20s at the beginning of the 1929 Depression (79%). They frequently assumed responsibility for caring for one or both parents during their 20s. The never-married nonmother was more likely than the married women to remain in the same job or career from her 20s until retirement. The never-married woman had most often achieved integrity (86% contrasted to 69% of married nonmothers and 66% of married mothers).

CONCLUSIONS

Eighty women, who were born from 1888 through 1925, provided some insight into women's adult development that is both new and refreshing. These women had careers despite cultural norms and biases, assumed

responsibility for parents when the time came—whether it was ii
20s or their 60s—maintained long-term ties with loved ones, and
came what seems to us to be overwhelming challenges without m
technology. Preparing for death was a developmental task we obse.
occurring within a context of peace and unhurried time during the
enth and later decades.

Transitional events representing losses contributed to the women's
identity development and, during their later adult years particularly, to
their pursuit of creative activities. Whether it was loss of friends due
to a relocation of residence, death of a parent or a beloved mate, or loss
of health, the women adapted to these transitional changes with equanimity. They found new relationships, new friends, and new activities to
bring meaning to their lives.

The exciting knowledge to us as women is that although aging means
physical degeneration, it does not mean psychosocial degeneration. The
creative work and contributions of these women in their seventh
through ninth decades of life illustrate that continuing learning and
development are a valid component of aging. It is a solace to know that
separation-individuation continues through life and that it is never too
late to resolve hang-ups from old relationships. Health care workers and
counselors in all fields who work with persons into their age-80 creativity versus destructiveness period have an opportunity to facilitate that
continued growth and to help maintain personal dignity when physical
deterioration impedes it.

Haan, N., & Day, D. (1974). A longitudinal study of change and sameness in personality development: Adolescence to later adulthood. *International Journal Aging and Human Development, 5,* 11–39.

Hancock, E. (1985). Age or experience? *Human Development, 28,* 274–280.

Hareven, T. (1986). Historical changes in the social construction of the life course. *Human Development, 29,* 171–180.

Harris, D. B. (1967). Problems in formulating a scientific concept of development. In D. B. Harris (Ed.), *The concept of development* (pp. 3–14). Minneapolis, Minnesota: University of Minnesota Press.

Harris, R. L. (1985). A retrospective study of women's psychosocial changes among women aged 30–60. *Human Development, 28,* 261–266.

Hollingshead, A. B. (1975). *Four-factor index of social status.* New Haven, Connecticut: Department of Sociology, Yale University.

Hughes, P. R. (1986, March 27). Study's good news for aging women. *San Francisco Chronicle,* p. 24.

Jackson, M. R. (1984). *Self-esteem and meaning: A life-historical investigation.* Albany, New York: State University of New York.

Jones, P. (1988, February). Changing seasons of a woman's work life. *Glamour,* pp. 216–220, 274–275.

Josselson, R. (1987). *Finding herself: Pathways to identity development in women.* San Francisco: Jossey-Bass.

Kahn, R. L., & Antonucci, T. C. (1980). Convoys over the life course: Attachment, roles and social support. *Life-Span Development and Behavior, 3,* 253–286.

Kakar, S. (Ed.) (1979). *Identity and adulthood.* Bombay: Oxford University Press.

Kapp, K. T., Hornstein, S., & Graham, V. T. (1963). Some psychologic factors in prolonged labor due to inefficient uterine action. *Comprehensive Psychiatry, 4,* 9–18.

Kegan, R. (1982). *The evolving self.* Cambridge, Massachusetts: Harvard University Press.

Kjervik, D. (1986). A conceptualization of women's stress. In D. K. Kjervik & I. M. Martinson (Eds.), *Women in health and illness: Life experiences and crises* (pp. 2–7). Philadelphia: W. B. Saunders Company.

Klineberg, S. L. (1984). Social change, world views, and cohort succession: The United States in the 1980s. In K. McCluskey & H. Reese (Eds.), *Life-span developmental psychology: Historical and generational effects* (pp. 129–142). Orlando: Academic Press.

Koestler, A. (1964). *The act of creation.* New York: Macmillan.

Kowalski, K. (1988). Karren Kowalski. In T. M. Schorr & A. Zimmerman, *Making choices, taking chances: Nurse leaders tell their story* (pp. 160–170). St. Louis, Missouri: C. V. Mosby.

LaBarre, M. B., Jessner, L., & Ussery, L. (1960). The significance of grandmothers in the psychopathology of children. *American Journal of Orthopsychiatry, 30,* 175–185.

Lebe, D. (1982). Individuation of women. *Psychoanalytic Review*, 69, 63–73.

Lehman, H. C. (1953). *Age and achievement*. Princeton, New Jersey: Princeton University Press.

Leifer, M. (1977). Psychological changes accompanying pregnancy and motherhood. *Genetic Psychology Monographs*, 95, 55–96.

Leininger, M. (1978). *Transcultural nursing: Concepts, theories, and practices*. New York: John Wiley & Sons.

Levinson, D. J. (1977). The mid-life transition: A period in adult psychosocial development. *Psychiatry*, 40, 99–112.

Levinson, D. J., Darrow, C. N., Klein, E. B., Levinson, M. H., & McKee, B. (1978). *The season's of a man's life*. New York: Alfred A. Knopf.

Lewis, H. B. (1958). Over-differentiation and under-individuation of the self. *Psychoanalysis and the Psychoanalytic Review*, 45(3), 3–24.

Lieblich, A. (1986). Successful career women at midlife: Crises and transitions. *International Journal of Aging and Human Development*, 23(4), 301–312.

Lindberg, A. M. (1955). *Gift from the sea*. New York: Pantheon.

Livson, F. B. (1976). Patterns of personality development in middle-aged women: A longitudinal study. *International Journal of Aging and Human Development*, 7(2), 107–115.

Lock, M. (1985). Models and practice in medicine. In R. A. Hahn & A. D. Gaines (Eds.), *Physicians of Western Medicine* (pp. 115–139).

Lowenthal, M. F., Thurnher, M., & Chiriboga, D. (1975). *Four stages of life*. San Francisco: Jossey-Bass.

Lutes, C. J. (1981). Early marriage and identity foreclosure. *Adolescence*, 16, 809–815.

Mahler, M. S. (1968). *On human symbiosis and the vicissitudes of individuation, Vol. 1*. New York: International Universities Press.

Mandelbaum, D. G. (1973). The study of life history: Gandhi. *Current Anthropology*, 14, 177–206.

Marcia, J. E. (1980). Identity in adolescence. In J. Adelson (Ed.), *Handbook of adolescent psychology* (pp. 159–187). New York: John Wiley & Sons.

Matthews, S. H. (1986). *Friendships through the life course*. Beverly Hills, California: Sage.

May, R. (1975). *The courage to create*. New York: Norton.

McBride, A. B. (1973). *The growth and development of mothers*. New York: Harper & Row.

McBride, A. B. (1983). Differences in parents' and their grown children's perceptions of parenting. *Developmental Psychology*, 19, 686–693.

McCluskey, K., & Reese, H. (1984). *Life-span developmental psychology: Historical and generational effects*. Orlando, Florida: Academic Press.

McKinlay, S. M., & Jeffreys, M. (1974). The menopausal syndrome. *British Journal of Preventive and Social Medicine*, 28, 108–115.

McLaughlin, S. D., Billy, J. O. G., Johnson, T. R., Melber, B. D., Winges, L. D., & Zimmerle, D. M. (October, 1985). *The cosmopolitan report on the changing life course of American women.* Seattle, Washington: Batelle Human Affairs Research Centers.

Mead, G. H. (1934). *Mind, self, & society.* Chicago: University of Chicago Press.

Medinger, F., & Varghese, R. (1981). Psychological growth and the impact of stress in middle age. *International Journal of Aging and Human Development, 13*(4), 247–263.

Mercer, R. T. (1986a). *First-time motherhood: Experiences from teens to forties.* New York: Springer.

Mercer, R. T. (1986b). The relationship of developmental variables to maternal behavior. *Research in Nursing and Health, 9,* 25–33.

Mercer, R. T. (1989). Theoretical perspectives on the family. In C. Gilliss, B. Highley, B. Roberts, & I. Martinson (Eds.), *Toward a science of family nursing* (pp. 9–36). Menlo Park, California: Addison-Wesley.

Mercer, R. T., & Ferketich, S. L. (1988). Stress and social support as predictors of anxiety and depression during pregnancy. *Advances Nursing Science, 10*(2), 26–39.

Mercer, R. T., Ferketich, S. L., DeJoseph, J., May, K. A., & Sollid, D. (1988). Effect of stress on family functioning during pregnancy. *Nursing Research, 37,* 268–275.

Mercer, R. T., Ferketich, S. L., May, K. A., DeJoseph, J., & Sollid, D. (1987). *Antepartum stress: Effect on family health and functioning.* Final Report of Project Supported by Grant No. R01 NR 01064, Nursing Center for Research, National Institutes of Health. San Francisco, California: Department of Family Health Care Nursing, University of California, San Francisco.

Mercer, R. T., Ferketich, S., May, K., DeJoseph, J., & Sollid, D. (1988). Further exploration of maternal and paternal fetal attachment. *Research in Nursing and Health, 11,* 83–95.

Mercer, R. T., Nichols, E. G., & Doyle, G. C. (1988). Transitions over the life cycle: A comparison of mothers and nonmothers. *Nursing Research, 37,* 144–151.

Moos, R. H. (1986). *Coping with life crises: An integrated approach.* New York: Plenum Press.

Moos, R. H., & Schaefer, J. A. (1986). Life transitions and crises: A conceptual overview. In R. H. Moos (Ed.), *Coping with life crises: An integrated approach* (pp. 3–28). New York: Plenum Press.

Moriarty, A. E., & Toussieng, P. W. (1976). *Adolescent coping.* New York: Grune & Stratton.

Moustakas, C. E. (1961). *Loneliness.* Englewood Cliffs, New Jersey: Prentice-Hall.

Moustakas, C. E. (1971). *Loneliness and love.* Englewood Cliffs, New Jersey: Prentice-Hall.

Neugarten, B. L. (1969). Continuities and discontinuities of psychological issues into adult life. *Human Development, 12,* 121–130.

Neugarten, B. L. (1970). Dynamics of transition of middle age to old age. *Journal of Geriatric Psychiatry, 4,* 71–87.

√ Neugarten, B. L. (1979). Time, age, and the life cycle. *American Journal Psychiatry, 136,* 887–894.

Neugarten, B. L., & Datan, N. (1973). In P. B. Baltes & K. W. Schaie (Eds.), *Life-span developmental psychology: Personality and socialization* (pp. 53–69). New York: Academic.

Newman, B. M. (1979). Coping and adaptation in adolescence. *Human Development, 22,* 255–262.

Niemela, P. (1980). Working through ambivalent feelings in woman's life transitions. *Acta Psychologica Fennica,* 99–107.

Oerter, R. (1986). Developmental task through the life span: A new approach to an old concept. In P. B. Baltes, D. L. Featherman, & R. M. Lerner (Eds.), *Life-span development and behavior, 7,* 233–269.

Olson, L. K. (1985). Older women: Longevity, dependency, and public policy. In V. Sapiro (Ed.), *Women, biology, and public policy* (pp. 157–175). Beverly Hills, California: Sage Publications.

Painter, C., & Valois, P. (1985). *Gifts of age.* San Francisco: Chronicle Books.

Parkes, C. M. (1971). Psycho-social transitions: A field for study. *Social Sciences & Medicine, 5,* 101–115.

Peck, R. C. (1968). Psychosocial developments in the second half of life. In B. Neugarten (Ed.), *Middle age and aging.* Chicago: University of Chicago Press.

Petersen, A. C. (1988). Adolescent development. *Annual Review of Psychology, 39,* 583–607.

Piaget, J. (1963). *The origins of intelligence in children.* New York: W. W. Norton.

Polster, S. (1983). Ego boundary as process: A systemic-contextual approach. *Psychiatry, 46,* 247–258.

Rankin, S. H., Mercer, R. T., Leonard, V., & Nichols, E. (1987). *Searching the archives of memory: Retrospective life themes as recounted by older women.* Unpublished paper presented at the National Council For Family Relations Annual Conference, Atlanta, Georgia.

√ Reinke, B. J. (1985). Psychosocial changes as a function of chronological age. *Human Development, 28,* 266–269.

√ Reinke, B. J., Ellicott, A. M., Harris, R. L., & Hancock, E. (1985). Timing of psychosocial changes in women's lives. *Human Development, 28,* 259–261.

√ Reinke, B. J., Holmes, D. S., & Harris, R. L. (1985). The timing of psychosocial changes in women's lives: The years 25–45. *Journal of Personality and Social Psychology, 48,* 1353–1364.

Riegel, K. F. (1975). Adult life crises: A dialectic interpretation of development. In N. Datan & L. H. Ginsberg (Eds.) *Life-span developmental psychology: Normative life crises* (pp. 99–128). New York: Academic Press.

Roberts, P., & Newton, P. M. (1987). Levinsonian studies of women's adult development. *Psychology and Aging, 2,* 154–163.

Roland, A., & Harris, B. (1979). *Career and motherhood.* New York: Human Sciences Press.

Rosenthal, D. A., Gurney, R. M., & Moore, S. M. (1981). From trust to intimacy: A new inventory for examining Erikson's stages of psychosocial development. *Journal of Youth and Adolescence, 10,* 525–537.

Rossi, A. S. (1980). Life-span theories and women's lives. *Signs: Journal of Women in Culture and Society, 6*(1), 4–32.

Rubin, L. B. (1979). *Women of a certain age: The midlife search for self.* New York: Harper.

Rubin, L. B. (1983). *Intimate strangers: Men and women together.* New York: Harper & Row.

Rubin, R. (1984). *Maternal identity and the maternal experience.* New York: Springer.

Ruddick, S. (1983). Maternal thinking. In J. Trebilcot (Ed.), *Mothering: Essays in Feminist Theory* (pp. 213–230). Rowman & Allanheld Publishers.

Ryff, C. D. (1982). Self-perceived personality change in adulthood and aging. *Journal of Personality and Social Psychology, 42,* 108–115.

Ryff, C. D. (1984). Personality development from the inside: The subjective experience of change in adulthood and aging. *Life-Span Development and Behavior, 6,* 243–279.

Ryff, C. D. (1985). The subjective experience of life-span transitions. In A. S. Rossi (Ed.) *Gender and the life course* (pp. 97–113). New York: Aldine.

Ryff, C. D., & Baltes, P. B. (1976). Value transition and adult development in women. *Developmental Psychology, 12,* 567–568.

Ryff, C. D., & Heincke, S. G. (1983). Subjective organization of personality in adulthood and aging. *Journal of Personality and Social Psychology, 44,* 807–816.

Ryff, C. D., & Migdal, S. (1984). Intimacy and generativity: Self-perceived transitions. *Signs: Journal of Women in Culture and Society, 9,* 470–481.

Salthouse, T. A. (1982). *Adult cognition: An experimental psychology of human aging.* New York: Springer-Verlag.

Sarason, I. G., & Sarason, B. R. (1985). Social support—insights from assessment and experimentation. In I. G. Sarason and B. R. Sarason (Eds.), *Social support: Theory, research, and applications* (pp. 39–50). Dordrecht, Holland: Martinus Nijhoff.

Scarf, M. (1980). *Unfinished business: Pressure points in the lives of women.* New York: Ballantine Books.

Schaie, W. (1984). Historical time and cohort effects. In K. McCluskey & H. Reese (Eds.), *Life-span developmental psychology: Historical and generational effects* (pp. 1–15). Orlando, Florida: Academic Press.

Scharlach, A. E. (1987). Role strain in mother-daughter relationships in later life. *The Gerontologist, 27,* 627–631.

Schectman, K. W. (1980). Motherhood as an adult developmental stage. *American Journal of Psychoanalysis, 40,* 273–282.

Schenkel, S., & Marcia, J. E. (1972). Attitudes toward premarital intercourse in determining ego identity status in college women. *Journal of Personality, 40,* 472–482.

Shereshefsky, P. M., Liebenberg, B., & Lockman, R. F. (1973). Maternal adaptation. In P. M. Shereshefsky & L. J. Yarrow (Eds.), *Psychological aspects of a first pregnancy and early postnatal adaptation* (pp. 165–180). New York: Raven Press.

Sherman, E. (1987). *Meaning in mid-life transitions.* Albany, New York: State University of New York.

Sholomakas, D., & Axelrod, R. (1986). The influence of mother-daughter relationships on women's sense of self and current role choices. *Psychology of Women Quarterly, 10,* 171–182.

Silverman, P. R. (1982). Transitions and models of intervention. *Annals of the American Academy of Political and Social Science, 464,* 174–187.

Spanier, G. B., Roos, P. A., & Shockey, J. (1985). Marital trajectories of American women: Variations in the life course. *Journal of Marriage and the Family, 47,* 993–1003.

Spence, D. L., & Lonner, D. T. (1978–79). Career set: A resource through transitions and crises. *International Journal Aging and Human Development, 9*(1), 51–65.

Steitz, J. (1981–82). The female life course: Life situations and perceptions of control. *International Journal of Aging and Human Development, 14*(3), 195–204.

Stevens-Long., J. (1979). *Adult life: Developmental processes.* Palo Alto, California: Mayfield.

Stewart, W. A. (1977). *A psychosocial study of the formation of the early adult life structure in women.* Unpublished doctoral dissertation, Columbia University, New York.

Suitor, J. J. (1987). Mother-daughter relations when married daughters return to school: Effects of status similarity. *Journal of Marriage and the Family, 49,* 435–444.

Terr, L. C. (1987). Childhood trauma and the creative product: A look at the early lives and later works of Poe, Wharton, Magritte, Hitchcock, and Bergman. *Psychoanalytic Study of the Child, 42,* 545–572.

Thomas, A. (1981). Current trends in developmental theory. *American Journal of Orthopsychiatry, 51,* 580–608.

Thomas, A., & Chess, S. (1980). *The dynamics of psychological development.* New York: Brunner/Mazel.

Thompson, L., & Walker, A. J. (1984). Mothers and daughters: Aid patterns and attachment. *Journal of Marriage and the Family, 46,* 313–322.

Thompson, N. L. (1987). Helene Deutsch: A life in theory. *Psychoanalytic Quarterly, 51,* 317–353.

Thurnher, M. (1983). Turning points and developmental change: Subjective and "objective" assessments. *American Journal Orthopsychiatry, 53,* 52–60.

Uddenberg, N. (1974). Reproductive adaptation in mother and daughter. *Acta Psychiatrica Scandinavica,* Supplementum 254.

Uddenberg, N., Fagerstrom, C., & Hakanson-Zaunders, M. (1976). Reproductive conflicts, mental symptoms during pregnancy and time in labour. *Journal of Psychosomatic Research, 20,* 575–581.

Uddenberg, N., & Nilsson, L. (1975). The longitudinal course of para-natal emotional disturbance. *Acta Psychiatrica Scandinavica, 52,* 160–169.

Uhlenberg, P. (1974). Cohort variations in family life cycle experiences of U. S. females. *Journal of Marriage and the Family, 36,* 284–292.

Valliant, G. E. (1977). *Adaptation to life.* Boston: Little, Brown & Co.

Vingehoets, A. (1985). *Psychosocial stress: An experimental approach.* Lisse: Swets & Zeitlinger.

Waechter, E. (1974). The developmental model. In M. E. Kalkman & A. J. Davis (Eds.), *New dimensions in mental health nursing* (pp. 31–57). New York: McGraw Hill.

Ware, S. (1982). *Holding their own: American women in the 1930s.* Boston: Twayne Publishers.

Watson, L. C. (1976). Understanding a life history as a subjective document: Hermeneutical and phenomenological perspectives. *Ethos, 4,* 95–131.

Weigert, A. J. & Hastings, R. (1977). Identity loss, family, and social change. *American Journal of Sociology, 82,* 1171–1185.

Weiss, R. S. (1973). *Loneliness: The experience of emotional and social isolation.* Cambridge, Massachusetts: MIT Press.

Weiss, R. S. (1974). The provisions of social relationships. In Z. Rubin (Ed.), *Doing unto others* (pp. 17–26). Englewood Cliffs, New Jersey: Prentice Hall.

Weisz, J. R. (1983). Can I control it? The pursuit of veridical answers across the life span. *Life-Span Development and Behavior, 5,* 233–300.

Wells, L. E., & Stryker, S. (1988). Stability and change in self over the life course. *Life-span development and behavior, 8,* 191–229.

Werner, H. (1967). The concept of development from a comparative and organismic point of view. In D. B. Harris (Ed.), *The concept of development* (pp. 125–148). Minneapolis, Minnesota: University of Minnesota Press.

Westbrook, M. T. (1976). Positive affect: A method of content analysis for verbal samples. *Journal of Consulting and Clinical Psychology, 44,* 715–719.

Westin, J. (1976). *Making do: How women survived the '30s.* Chicago: Follett Publishing Company.

Index

Please remember that this is a library book,
and that it belongs only temporarily to each
person who uses it. Be considerate. Do
not write in this, or any, library book.